The TREE & SHRUB EXPERT
Dr. D.G. Hessayon

1st Impression	300,000
2nd Impression	300,000
3rd Impression	200,000
4th Impression	200,000

Other Books in the Expert Series:

THE HOUSE PLANT EXPERT

THE ROSE EXPERT

THE LAWN EXPERT

THE FLOWER EXPERT

THE VEGETABLE EXPERT

THE INDOOR PLANT SPOTTER

BE YOUR OWN GARDENING EXPERT

BE YOUR OWN GARDEN DOCTOR

BE YOUR OWN VEGETABLE DOCTOR

Acknowledgements

The author wishes to acknowledge the painstaking work of Jane Jenks and Mary Hicks. Grateful acknowledgement is also made for the help or photographs received from Joan Hessayon, Angelina Hessayon, A-Z Botanical Collection Ltd, Bernard Alfieri, Heather Angel, Adrian Bloom, Pat Brindley, Bruce Coleman Ltd, Eric Crichton, Harry Smith Horticultural Photographic Collection and Michael Warren.

John Woodbridge provided both artistry and design work, and Norman Barber prepared most of the paintings for this book. Other artists who contributed were Deborah Achilleos, Bob Bampton, John Barber, Pat Harby, Stuart Lafford, David More, Gabrielle Smith and Yvon Still.

pbi
PUBLICATIONS

pbi PUBLICATIONS · BRITANNICA HOUSE · WALTHAM CROSS · HERTS · ENGLAND

Contents

Printed and bound in Great Britain by Jarrold & Sons Ltd., Norwich

ISBN 0 903505 17 7

© D G HESSAYON 1983

CHAPTER 1
TREES & SHRUBS IN THE GARDEN

Gardening styles may come and gardening styles may go, but ornamental trees and shrubs go on for ever. The only living thing which was common to the naturalistic British style of Capability Brown and the formal French style of Le Notre was the use of trees and large shrubs. But this is not a book about the grand gardens of yesterday. It is about the ordinary home gardens of today, ranging in size from tiny plots outside terraced houses to multi-acred estates surrounding stately homes. In both of these there is a place for shrubs, conifers and climbers, and the popularity of these plants has greatly increased in recent years.

There are several reasons for this growth of interest in woody plants. The advent of the garden centre is, of course, a major factor. Once we had to order our shrubs from a nursery – now we can see conifers, trees, climbers and so on all neatly displayed, in full leaf and perhaps in flower, and ready to take home for planting. Planting is no longer a task which must be completed in the cold months of the year – container-grown shrubs can be planted all year round.

Above all, perhaps, is a much wider understanding of the unique role of trees and shrubs in the garden. The lawns, paths and low-growing flowers form the ground-level pattern. Above them rise the woody plants, the trees, shrubs, conifers and climbers – the upright living framework of the garden. In summer they provide height, colour and fragrance – they give the garden its shape. In winter their role is equally or even more important. When the flower garden has died down, the bare branches of deciduous shrubs and the leaf-bedecked stems of the evergreens ensure that we are looking at a garden border and not a bare plot of ground.

Trees and shrubs have an additional virtue – they are much less trouble than annuals, vegetables, lawns and the herbaceous border. Once fully established there is little to be done – no constant feeding or spraying, no regular deadheading and staking, no annual planting ritual and no rushing out with the watering can every time the weather turns dry.

The labour-saving aspect of trees and shrubs is well-known – hardly any textbook fails to mention this virtue, but these plants are neither trouble-free nor child's play. You will need to apply some skill before you even lift a spade. Careful selection is vitally important because woody plants vary greatly in their environmental needs and the size they will eventually reach. Some types will flourish in chalky soil – others will quickly sicken and may die. A Hebe may reach less than 1 ft or more than 10 ft – a Pine tree may stay at less than 2 ft or tower 70 ft or more into the sky when mature – it all depends on the variety you have chosen. The golden rule is never buy a tree or shrub on impulse or because it looks so nice and is just about the right size in the garden centre. Much of this book is devoted to a series of A-Z guides – study them carefully before making your choice.

Container-grown specimens are not cheap to buy and once planted they should be regarded as permanent, as many do not take kindly to being moved. So plant them properly, and this does not mean digging a hole and just dropping them in. Chapter 6 provides a simple guide to the proper technique – above all, avoid planting expensive and choice specimens too closely together. Selection and planting call for some care, but the established plant needs little attention.

Shrubs and trees bring an air of maturity to the garden. They can provide beautiful flowers, heady fragrance, attractive leaves, eye-catching shapes and colourful bark. There is also a practical aspect – shrubs can reduce the effect of high winds, increase privacy, cut down the weed problem and screen out unsightly objects. They are truly a worthwhile investment, repaying over and over again the money and care bestowed on them.

Choosing the right type

It is so simple to buy a tree or shrub these days. You go along to the garden centre, pick out one which would look attractive in the spot you have in mind and then plant it... what could be easier?

It is certainly easy, but this all-too-common approach leads to a great deal of frustration and failure. That sweet little conifer, no taller than a trowel, may turn into a sprawling monster in your rockery after a few years. That beautiful Hibiscus in full flower may fail to produce a single new bloom when you take it home and plant it in your garden.

You want to buy some shrubs for your garden... ask yourself the following seven questions and the answers should give you a short list of plants which will succeed. Then go through the A-Z lists and pick out the ones which really appeal to you, for that is the most important consideration of all.

QUESTION 1: DO I WANT THE LEAVES TO STAY ON OVER WINTER?

Choose an *evergreen* if you want a plant which does not lose its leaves in autumn. Many trees and shrubs, a few climbers and nearly all conifers are evergreens, and at first glance they would seem to be the best choice– colour is provided when other plants are brown and bare.

But the ones which lose their leaves, the *deciduous* shrubs and trees, have an important role to play. Some of the most beautiful flowering types belong here, and there is the beauty of the changing scene as bare branches burst into leaf in spring and the floral display is followed by the rich hues of autumn foliage. *The usual advice is to have an approximately equal number of evergreen and deciduous shrubs in the garden.*

QUESTION 2: DO I WANT A SHRUB OR TREE?

SHRUB
A shrub is a perennial plant which bears several woody stems at ground level. A mature shrub may be only a few inches high or as tall as 20 ft, depending on the variety.
See pages 7–56

Several shrubs, such as Firethorn, Winter Jasmine and Rambler Roses, are not true climbers but they are commonly grown against walls and trellis-work.

The dividing line between trees and shrubs is not really clear-cut. Several shrubs, such as Holly, Flowering Dogwood and Hazel, may grow as small trees.

CLIMBER
A climber is a perennial plant which has the ability to attach itself to or twine around an upright structure. This climbing habit may not develop until the plant is established.
See pages 73–79

TREE
A tree is a perennial plant which bears only one woody stem at ground level. A mature tree may be only 2 ft high or as tall as 100 ft or more, depending on the variety.
See pages 57–72

CONIFER
A conifer is a perennial plant which bears cones. These cones are nearly always made up of woody scales, but there are exceptions (e.g., Yew). The leaves are usually evergreen but there are exceptions (e.g., Larch).
See pages 80–96

The most popular choice is a shrub, because within this vast group there are plants of all sizes and colours. You can find tiny rockery specimens or giants for the back of the border, and you can have flowers during every month of the year by planting quite a modest selection. They are chosen primarily to provide attractive foliage and/or flowers, and the shape is often of secondary importance.

Conifers are also popular, and they are chosen for their architectural shape rather than for their colour. Trees are bought in fewer numbers then either shrubs or conifers, as the average-sized garden can house very few. They are, however, of great importance and should not be overlooked. This group combines the colourful display of shrubs with the architectural value of conifers.

QUESTION 3: WHAT SHAPE AND SIZE DO I WANT?

Shape is an extremely important consideration when choosing trees and conifers. A columnar tree is a good choice where space is limited or where a specimen plant is required for a small lawn. When space permits both round-headed and open trees are picturesque and in all gardens conical, pyramidal and weeping trees make excellent focal points.

COLUMNAR (FASTIGIATE)   CONICAL   PYRAMIDAL   ROUND-HEADED   OPEN

WEEPING (PENDULOUS)   PROSTRATE   GLOBULAR (ROUND)   HORIZONTALLY-BRANCHED   LOW-BRANCHED

Size is even more important than shape. One of the commonest mistakes in gardening is to buy a plant which is far too vigorous for the space available – chopping back every year means that both natural beauty and floral display can be lost. In the A-Z guides for shrubs you will find a height given for each plant – this is the height the plant can be expected to reach in about 15 years under average conditions. For conifers you will find the expected 10 year height together with some indication of the ultimate height. Never forget that the size and shape of the plant in the garden centre gives little or no indication of its eventual size and shape in your garden.

QUESTION 4: WHAT WILL THE GROWING CONDITIONS BE LIKE?

Some shrubs and trees will grow almost anywhere but most of them have their own particular likes and dislikes. Always check in the A-Z guides before buying – the conditions in your garden may be just right (or entirely wrong) for the plant in question.

SOIL

Any reasonable garden soil is satisfactory for most varieties, although a few have a strong dislike for either heavy or sandy soil. Some do best in poor, dry ground whereas others will only thrive in fertile or humus-rich soil — in each case the A–Z guides will let you know if your soil is suitable.

Chalky soil can be a problem — there is an important group of lime-haters which includes Rhododendron, Azalea, Camellia, Pieris, Pernettya, Kalmia and Calluna. Another problem for many shrubs and trees is poor drainage — some varieties cannot stand even short periods of waterlogging. The A–Z guides will tell you when a free-draining soil is essential.

CLIMATE AND ASPECT

Most shrubs and trees and nearly all conifers are perfectly hardy throughout Britain, but there are some which can be badly damaged or even killed by heavy or prolonged frost. If you live in a cold, northern area you should avoid all plants described as not completely hardy in the A–Z guides.

Many plants can be damaged if exposed to biting north and east winds during winter and early spring. Don't choose a plant which requires protection unless it can be sited close to a wall or other shrubs which will serve as a windbreak. The A–Z guides will inform you if such protection is necessary. Sea winds close to the coast are a special problem — check the lists on pages 20 and 61 for plants which will flourish at the seaside.

QUESTION 5: DO I WANT TO PLANT IT NOW?

There are four types of planting material. Each one has its own particular advantages and disadvantages, but if you propose to plant the tree or shrub outside the normal planting season (see page 100) then you *must* buy a container-grown specimen.

Bare-rooted

The traditional way to buy deciduous trees and shrubs. Suitable for planting between October and March.
See page 100 for details.

Balled

The traditional way to buy evergreens, including conifers. Suitable for planting in September, October or April.
See page 100 for details.

Pre-packaged

The popular way to buy deciduous shrubs from shops and department stores. Suitable for planting between October and March.
See page 100 for details.

Container-grown

The most convenient way to buy both deciduous and evergreen trees and shrubs. Suitable for planting all year round.
See page 99 for details.

QUESTION 6: DO I WANT A POPULAR PLANT OR A RARITY?

There are about thirty shrubs which are distinctly common – you will see them in gardens everywhere. The list includes

Buddleia	Hypericum	Philadelphus	Snowberry
Escallonia	Japonica	Potentilla	Spiraea
Forsythia	Kerria	Privet	Sumach
Heather	Laurel	Pyracantha	Viburnum
Hebe	Lilac	Rhododendron	Weigela
Hydrangea	Mahonia	Ribes	Winter Jasmine

Do not reject these shrubs just because they are so popular – they are also inexpensive, colourful and have proved their ability to succeed under all sorts of conditions. Rarities, on the other hand, can be expensive, difficult to obtain and unsuited to your conditions. A good plan is to have a framework of popular shrubs, choosing from a larger list than just the top thirty. Then pick a number of rarities, after making sure from the A-Z guides that they are suitable, to add interest to the display provided by the better-known trees and shrubs.

QUESTION 7: WHAT JOB DO I WANT IT TO DO IN THE GARDEN?

This is a vital question – ignoring it is a common cause of disappointment. A screening plant to hide an unsightly object should be evergreen and quick-growing. An edging plant for a narrow pathway should be compact whereas a shrub for planting along the fence of a large garden should be tall and spreading. A specimen shrub or tree which will be planted on its own away from other woody plants should be attractive for a large part if not the whole of the year. It must also be in keeping with its surroundings – a 9 in. column-shaped conifer may look attractive now in the rockery, but if it is Chamaecyparis lawsoniana 'Columnaris' it will be 6 ft tall in about 10 years and will look completely out of place. Before buying read Chapter 9 carefully.

CHAPTER 2

SHRUBS

The largest section of this book is devoted to shrubs. This does not mean that the other groups are unimportant, but most trees are too large for the average garden, the range and use of climbers are limited and none of the conifers produces a floral display. The shrubs have none of these drawbacks – there are varieties for gardens of every size, there are types which exhibit every form of plant beauty and they will do every job you can expect from woody plants, bar one.

Shrubs will cover the ground, fill a bed or border, grow as attractive specimen plants or adorn the wall of a house, but they cannot be expected to tower into the sky as their maximum height is about 15 or 20 ft. For a house-high plant you will have to choose a tree or a conifer.

The most popular shrubs have green leaves and bear attractive flowers for a few weeks or even months, usually in spring but sometimes in summer or autumn. It would, of course, be nonsense to decry the importance of these popular plants, for in many cases they are the backbone of the garden. Rhododendron, Forsythia, Ribes, Mahonia, Lilac, Kerria, Hydrangea, Potentilla and so on are indispensable, but it is perhaps a shame that more gardeners do not widen their horizons.

Coloured foliage can be as important as a fine floral display – blooms last for a few weeks and then they are gone, but golden, purple, coppery or variegated foliage on an evergreen shrub provides colour all year round. Then there are shrubs with autumn foliage which can outshine almost any floral display – Fothergilla or Enkianthus can be a splendid fiery sight in October. Other shrubs produce their showiest foliage in spring – Pieris, Photinia and Sambucus racemosa 'Plumosa Aurea' are excellent examples.

Leaf colour, then, can light up a shrub border and there are shrubs which can add colour by producing either an abundant display of berries (Pernettya, Symphoricarpos, Skimmia, Pyracantha, Cotoneaster, etc.) or brightly-hued stems, such as Salix alba or Cornus alba. All this means that you should try to get colour into your shrubs by looking for showy leaves, berries and bark as well as bright flowers. The result will be a more interesting garden.

Another way to add interest is to grow a few rarities. Never try to turn your plot into a Botanical Garden devoted entirely to long-named specimens with which you can impress your friends, but it should still be more than a grown-up version of the bargain collection from a Sunday newspaper. There are many unusual shrubs listed in the following pages – be adventurous and buy one or two from your local garden centre. For the rarer ones you will have to visit, or send an order to, a specialist nursery.

Growing shrubs is one of the most interesting and rewarding aspects of gardening. You must choose sensibly, plant properly and then prune correctly. There are two extremely common errors to be avoided – planting too closely and pruning too haphazardly. Over-close planting will mean a constant battle to keep the branches cut back – read the section on Spacing (page 103) to avoid this trouble. Poor pruning is an equally frustrating problem – cutting off too much, too little, too early or too late can result in a poor display of flowers. Look up the correct time and method for each plant (pages 8-56) before getting out your secateurs.

In the following pages you will find pictures and descriptions of many of the shrubs grown in our gardens. Here you will find the full range of sizes, shapes, fragrances and colours to be found in this indispensable group of plants.

Key to the A–Z guide

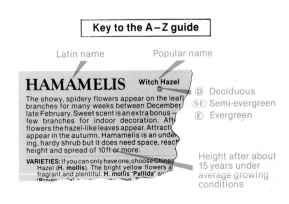

Latin name   Popular name

HAMAMELIS   Witch Hazel   D Deciduous
                               SE Semi-evergreen
The showy, spidery flowers appear on the leafl   E Evergreen
branches for many weeks between December
late February. Sweet scent is an extra bonus –
few branches for indoor decoration. Aft
flowers the hazel-like leaves appear. Attracti
appear in the autumn. Hamamelis is an unde
ing, hardy shrub but it does need space, reac
height and spread of 10 ft or more.   Height after about
                                              15 years under
VARIETIES: If you can only have one, choose Chines   average growing
Hazel (**H. mollis**). The bright yellow flowers a   conditions
fragrant and plentiful. **H. mollis 'Pallida'** an

ABELIA Abelia Ⓓ or ⓈⒺ

An uncommon plant which has an outstanding record for blooming over a long period — A. schumannii begins to flower in June and continues until October. Unfortunately its record for hardiness is not so outstanding — away from the south and west it needs the protection of other shrubs or a south wall. The reddish sepals remain after the petals have fallen.

VARIETIES: The pale pink flowers of **A. grandiflora** (6 ft) appear between July and September — the leaves are semi-evergreen. **A. schumannii** grows to a similar size, its lilac-pink tubular blooms clothing the bush for many months; unfortunately it can be cut down by severe frosts. The fragrant flowers of **A. chinensis** are white flushed with pink.

SITE & SOIL: Any free-draining garden soil will do — thrives best in full sun.

PRUNING: Cut away all dead and damaged wood in April.

PROPAGATION: Plant cuttings in a cold frame in summer.

A. grandiflora

ACER Japanese Maple Ⓓ

Most Acers are trees — you will find the Maples and Sycamores described on page 58. The Japanese Maples, however, are slow-growing and attractive shrubs which have a place in both modest and large gardens. They are grown for the colour and shape of their foliage, but these leaves need some protection from morning sun and cold winds.

VARIETIES: A. palmatum grows 12 ft or more in time. The leaves colour in autumn — for the brightest autumn hues choose **'Osakazuki'** and for season-long purple there is **'Atropurpureum'**. The popular choices are the compact (2–3 ft high) finely-divided leaf types — **A. palmatum 'Dissectum Atropurpureum'** provides an all-purple display. For· yellow leaves grow **A. japonicum 'Aureum'** (3 ft).

SITE & SOIL: Requires a neutral or acid soil. Grows best in partial shade.

PRUNING: Not necessary — cut out dead wood in spring.

PROPAGATION: Buy from a garden centre or nursery.

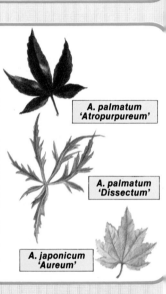

A. palmatum 'Atropurpureum'

A. palmatum 'Dissectum'

A. japonicum 'Aureum'

AMELANCHIER Snowy Mespilus Ⓓ

The Snowy Mespilus is for the larger garden, as it will reach 14 ft or more in time. You may never have seen one — it certainly is not a popular choice, but it is worth considering. Its charm is the frequent change in colour display — young coppery foliage, white flowers, red berries which turn black, and green leaves which turn yellow in autumn.

VARIETIES: Confusion reigns over the proper latin name for Snowy Mespilus — in the garden centre it may be labelled as **A. lamarckii, A. canadensis, A. laevis** or **A. grandiflora!** Never mind — whatever the label it will produce masses of small white flowers in April and edible berries in June. There is a pink-flowering form — **A. grandiflora 'Rubescens'**.

SITE & SOIL: Most soils are suitable, but avoid chalky sites. Thrives in sun and partial shade.

PRUNING: Not necessary — cut back in winter to keep growth in check.

PROPAGATION: Remove rooted suckers from the parent bush in autumn.

A. canadensis

ARALIA   Japanese Angelica
Ⓓ

A shrub which is definitely not for the small garden. It must be planted as a specimen plant with enough room to display its foliage. Each leaf is 3 or 4 ft long, neatly divided up into a complex pattern of leaflets. The thorny branches reach 13 ft or more, and the large shrub suckers very freely. In mild areas it can reach tree-like proportions.

VARIETIES: A. elata is the only species you are likely to find. Large heads of small white flowers are produced in early autumn. Two variegated forms are available — in spring the leaves of **'Aureovariegata'** are edged and blotched with yellow; **'Variegata'** with creamy white. Later in the season the variegation of both turns silvery white.

SITE & SOIL: Light, well-drained soil is preferred. Thrives in sun or partial shade.

PRUNING: Not necessary — prune in spring to keep in check.

PROPAGATION: Remove rooted suckers from the parent bush.

A. elata 'Aureovariegata'

Aralia elata 'Variegata'

ARBUTUS   Strawberry Tree
Ⓔ

An interesting evergreen which is worth growing if you like something out of the ordinary. The variety you are most likely to find is A. unedo, and this bears pendent flowers and bright orange, strawberry-like fruits at the same time in late autumn. The leaves are dark and glossy, and the shrub is slow-growing.

VARIETIES: A. unedo will reach about 8 ft in time, but for years it will remain a mound of evergreen leaves. The fruits which follow the white flowers are flavourless. The flowers of **A. unedo 'Rubra'** are flushed with pink. **A. andrachnoides** flowers in winter, but this variety is grown for its red bark rather than its floral or fruit display.

SITE & SOIL: Any reasonable garden soil, including chalk. Full sun is best.

PRUNING: Not necessary. Cut back weak, straggly branches in spring.

PROPAGATION: Difficult — sow seed under glass or plant cuttings in a propagator in summer.

A. unedo 'Rubra'

Arbutus unedo

ARUNDINARIA   Bamboo
Ⓔ

There is no problem in recognising Bamboo — arching, hollow canes bear grass-like leaves, providing an exotic touch to the garden. The difficulty arises at the garden centre, where each of the popular varieties may be listed under several different names, and each one a tongue-twister. All are easy to grow in a wide variety of soils.

VARIETIES: The dwarf varieties have colourful leaves — there is **A. viridistriata (Pleioblastus viridistriatus)** with yellow-striped leaves and **A. variegata (A. fortunei)** with cream-striped leaves. Both grow 3 – 4 ft tall — for a 20 ft giant, grow **A. fastuosa**. In the 10 – 12 ft range are **A. nitida** (purple stems) and **A. murieliae** (yellow stems).

SITE & SOIL: Any reasonable garden soil will do. Partial shade is best.

PRUNING: Not necessary except just after planting — cut back half-way.

PROPAGATION: Divide clumps or remove rooted suckers in autumn or spring.

A. nitida

Arundinaria variegata

AUCUBA
Aucuba
Ⓔ

A laurel-like shrub which is widely planted where little else will grow — in grimy industrial areas and in the dense shade under broad-leaved trees. The popular varieties are the variegated ones (Spotted Laurels) and they need some sun to show off the yellow splashes on the leaves. Plants are male or female — red berries appear on female bushes if a male is nearby.

VARIETIES: The basic species is **A. japonica**, a rounded 7 ft × 7 ft shrub which bears all-green leaves. All the varieties have glossy and oval leaves — the narrow-leaved form is the female **'Salicifolia'**. The best of the yellow-spotted varieties is the male **'Crotonifolia'** — more widely grown, however, is the female **'Variegata'**.

SITE & SOIL: Will succeed in any garden soil and in any situation — sun or deep shade.

PRUNING: Not necessary, but will stand drastic pruning in May if required.

PROPAGATION: Plant cuttings in a cold frame in summer.

Aucuba japonica

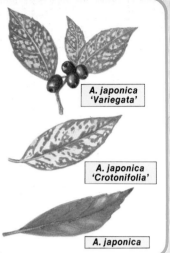

A. japonica 'Variegata'

A. japonica 'Crotonifolia'

A. japonica

BERBERIS
Barberry
Ⓓ or Ⓔ

Even modest garden centres usually offer a wide and bewildering choice of Berberis varieties, and you should always check the expected final height before buying one. There are both dwarfs and giants, and you can find a Berberis for the rock garden as well as the shrub border, for hedging, covering banks or screening, and for growing on its own as a showy specimen bush. They are all spiny and the range of flower colours is limited — pale yellow to orange. All are easy to grow and require little or no pruning. Always buy container-grown plants.

VARIETIES: The evergreen varieties are grown for their decorative, deep green leaves — many have attractive flowers. The two most popular ones are **B. darwinii** (8 ft, shiny foliage like miniature holly leaves, deep yellow flowers in April and purple berries in autumn) and **B. stenophylla** (9 ft, arching sprays of yellow flowers in April and May). Other evergreens are **B. verruculosa** (3 ft, very glossy leaves, black berries), **B. candidula** for ground cover (2 ft, dense mounds bearing yellow flowers in May) and **B. julianae** for screening (9 ft, leaves turning red in autumn). The deciduous varieties are grown for their colourful leaves and bright berries. **B. thunbergii** (5 ft × 5 ft) is the basic type, with bright red autumn leaves and berries. **B. thunbergii atropurpurea** (6 ft) and its dwarf **'Nana'** (2 ft) have dark bronze leaves which turn red in autumn. **B. thunbergii 'Aurea'** (5 ft) has yellow leaves. Even more colourful is **B. ottawensis 'Purpurea'** (6 ft) with rich, purple leaves.

SITE & SOIL: Any reasonable garden soil will do, in sun or partial shade.

PRUNING: Not necessary — remove damaged or unwanted branches from deciduous varieties in February and from evergreens immediately after flowering.

PROPAGATION: Layer branches or plant cuttings in a cold frame in summer.

Berberis darwinii

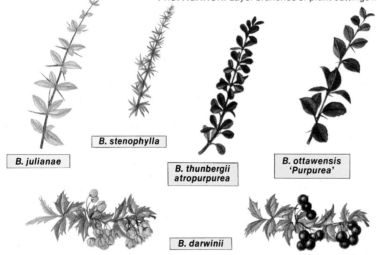

B. julianae

B. stenophylla

B. thunbergii atropurpurea

B. ottawensis 'Purpurea'

B. darwinii

Berberis thunbergii atropurpurea

Buddleia davidii 'Harlequin'

BUDDLEIA Butterfly Bush
D or SE

A favourite shrub, as a walk down almost any street in late summer will show. The popular varieties are tough and easy to grow, but in most gardens their true glory is dimmed by neglect. Failure to prune B. davidii properly results in a gaunt bush with flowers perched on top of tall, bare branches. Buddleias have tapering leaves which are usually distinctly downy below, and they are quick-growing. All have pretty flower clusters, but one (B. alternifolia) can be considered an attractive bush when not in flower.

VARIETIES: B. davidii is by far the most popular species. The broad bush grows 8 ft or more if left unpruned, and from July to September it bears tiny, honey-scented flowers in cone-shaped spikes. They are highly attractive to butterflies — hence the common name. Colours are white, mauve and purple — pick from **'Black Knight'** (dark purple), **'Empire Blue'** (violet-blue), **'White Cloud'** (white) or **'Royal Red'** (purple-red). There is a variegated form — **'Harlequin'** (purple). **B. alternifolia** is quite different — a large shrub (9 ft × 9 ft) with arching stems wreathed in clusters of lilac flowers in June; the name 'Fountain Buddleia' is clearly descriptive. So is 'Orange Ball Tree' for **B. globosa** — this tall, straggly shrub produces globular heads of small, orange flowers in May. It is virtually evergreen.

SITE & SOIL: Any reasonable garden soil will do, provided it is well-drained. B. davidii thrives in chalky soil. All Buddleias prefer a sunny situation.

PRUNING: B. davidii requires hard pruning — in March cut back last year's growth to within 2 in. of the old wood. B. globosa should be trimmed to shape after flowering. With B. alternifolia cut back branches bearing faded blooms immediately after flowering.

PROPAGATION: Easy — sow seed in spring or plant cuttings outdoors in autumn.

B. globosa

B. davidii 'White Cloud'

B. davidii 'Royal Red'

B. davidii 'Empire Blue'

B. alternifolia

Buddleia alternifolia

Fragrant Shrubs

Many shrubs bear sweet-smelling flowers — Honeysuckle, Mock Orange, Daphne, Viburnum and Witch Hazel are all well known for their perfume. Fragrance is not restricted to the flowers — some shrubs have aromatic foliage.

❀ Fragrant flowers

🍃 Aromatic leaves

Abelia chinensis ❀
Berberis stenophylla ❀
Buddleia alternifolia ❀
Buddleia davidii ❀
Buddleia globosa ❀
Carpenteria californica ❀
Caryopteris clandonensis 🍃
Chimonanthus praecox ❀
Choisya ternata ❀ 🍃
Clerodendrum trichotomum ❀
Clethra alnifolia ❀

Corylopsis species ❀
Cytisus battandieri ❀
Daphne species ❀
Elaeagnus commutata ❀
Elaeagnus ebbingei ❀
Escallonia macrantha 🍃
Hamamelis species ❀
Laurus nobilis 🍃
Lavandula species ❀ 🍃
Lonicera fragrantissima ❀
Magnolia grandiflora ❀
Magnolia stellata ❀
Mahonia species ❀
Myrtus communis ❀ 🍃
Osmanthus species ❀

Perovskia atriplicifolia 🍃
Philadelphus species ❀
Phlomis fruticosa 🍃
Pittosporum tobira ❀
Rhododendron — deciduous Azaleas ❀
Ribes odoratum ❀
Romneya hybrida ❀
Rosa species ❀
Rosmarinus officinalis 🍃
Rubus tridel 'Benenden' ❀
Santolina species 🍃
Skimmia japonica 🍃
Syringa species ❀
Viburnum bodnantense ❀
Viburnum fragrans ❀

BUXUS

Box
Ⓔ

An excellent choice if you want a dense, evergreen screen which can be regularly clipped. Buxus produces an abundance of small, glossy leaves and it stands up well to drastic pruning. A favourite for hedging, screening and topiary work. It is also an excellent tub plant, clipped as a cone or pyramid — never let the soil dry out.

VARIETIES: The Common Box (**B. sempervirens**) is the most popular one, and will exceed 10 ft if left untrimmed. There are more compact and colourful varieties — **B. sempervirens 'Marginata'** (yellow-edged leaves) and **B. sempervirens 'Aureovariegata'** (yellow-blotched leaves) are examples. For path edging a few inches high, use **B. sempervirens 'Suffruticosa'**.

SITE & SOIL: Any reasonable garden soil in sun or partial shade will do. Exposed sites are not a problem.

PRUNING: Not essential. Remove unwanted growth or trim to shape in summer.

PROPAGATION: Plant 4 in. cuttings in a cold frame in summer.

B. sempervirens

B. sempervirens 'Marginata'

B. sempervirens 'Aureovariegata'

CALLICARPA

Beauty Berry
Ⓓ

The beauty of this bush is seen in the autumn. The leaves will have turned red or violet, and when they fall the polished purple berries are revealed on the bare stems. The colourful clusters persist until Christmas. Plant in groups rather than singly to make sure that berries will be formed. The flowers are insignificant.

VARIETIES: The most popular type is **C. bodinieri giraldii**. It will reach about 6 ft high, with lilac flowers in July and pale purple berries in September or October — some nurseries offer **C. bodinieri 'Profusion'**. A smaller and more delicate Callicarpa is **C. japonica**, growing 3 ft tall and bearing pink flowers and violet berries.

SITE & SOIL: Well-drained, reasonably fertile soil is required, and the site should be sheltered and sunny.

PRUNING: Not essential. Remove unwanted or damaged branches in early spring.

PROPAGATION: Layer shoots in autumn or plant cuttings in a cold frame in summer.

C. bodinieri giraldii

CALLUNA

Heather
Ⓔ

The Common Heather of our northern and western moors has given rise to hundreds of named varieties which grow 9-24 in. high and bloom in late summer. A large number have coloured foliage — golden, silvery, bronze and red with flowers in white, pink or purple. Unlike Ericas, none of them will tolerate lime — all like hungry soil and sunshine.

VARIETIES: There is only one species (**C. vulgaris**) but there are many varieties. One of the most popular is **'H. E. Beale'** with long spikes of pink, double flowers. **'Alba Plena'** has white, double flowers. For coloured leaves choose **'Gold Haze'** (bright yellow), **'Silver Queen'** (silvery grey) or **'Blazeaway'** (red in winter).

SITE & SOIL: Well-drained, acid soil is necessary; full sun is preferred. Add peat at planting time.

PRUNING: In March lightly clip over the plants to remove dead flowers. Prune back straggly shoots.

PROPAGATION: Layer shoots in spring or plant 1 in. cuttings in a cold frame in summer.

C. vulgaris 'Gold Haze'

C. vulgaris 'H. E. Beale'

CAMELLIA Camellia Ⓔ

Camellias should be much more popular, but they have an unfair reputation for being difficult and delicate. In fact, they are no more difficult than Rhododendrons and most varieties on offer are hardy. Unfortunately, cold winds and frost can damage the flower buds so they should generally be grown in the shelter of other shrubs or close to a wall. Camellia is an ideal plant for growing in tubs, and some experts claim that it is the best of all garden shrubs — glossy foliage all year round, large and showy blooms from early March until May, no pruning problems and an attractive, bushy growth habit reaching 6-8 ft.

VARIETIES: Most Camellias are varieties of **C. japonica**. There are scores to choose from — popular favourites are **'Adolphe Audusson'** (red, semi-double), **'Elegans'** (peach pink, anemone-flowered) and **'Apollo'** (red, blotched white, semi-double). A fine white is **'Alba Simplex'** (single) and a good pink is **'Lady Clare'** (semi-double). Striped blooms are available — choose **'Lady Vansittart'** (white, striped pink) or **'Contessa Lavinia Maggi'** (red, striped pink). The hybrids of **C. williamsii** are a step forward — the shrubs are hardier, freer flowering and the dead blooms drop off naturally. The most popular one is **'Donation'** (pink, semi-double). Others recommended are **'J. C. Williams'** (pale pink, single) and **'Anticipation'** (red, peony-flowered). Worth considering is **C. 'Leonard Messel'** (bright pink, semi-double).

SITE & SOIL: Avoid chalky soil; incorporate peat at planting time. Mulch around the bushes with peat each spring. Light shade is best, but will thrive in full sun.

PRUNING: Not essential. Cut back thin, damaged and unwanted branches in May.

PROPAGATION: Layer shoots in autumn or plant 3 in. cuttings in a cold frame in summer.

Camellia japonica 'Elegans'

C. japonica 'Adolphe Audusson'

C. japonica 'Alba Simplex'

C. japonica 'Lady Clare'

C. williamsii 'Donation'

C. williamsii 'J. C. Williams'

C. 'Leonard Messel'

Camellia williamsii

CARPENTERIA Carpenteria Ⓔ

Here is an eye-catching shrub which the neighbours won't have. Large and fragrant white flowers appear amid the narrow and shiny evergreen leaves in June and July. It requires little attention and does not need rich soil, but it is rather tender and should therefore be planted in the shelter of a south wall.

VARIETIES: There is only one species — **C. californica.** It will grow about 10 ft high and should produce beautiful flowers with a central boss of golden stamens. Unfortunately, nursery stock is variable — if possible buy a container-grown specimen when it is in flower and make sure that you choose **C. californica 'Ladham's Variety'**.

SITE & SOIL: Full sun and some shelter are essential. Any reasonable garden soil will do if it drains freely.

PRUNING: Little pruning is necessary — simply cut back over-long and old branches in spring.

PROPAGATION: Layer shoots or plant cuttings in a cold frame in summer.

Carpenteria californica

C. californica

CARYOPTERIS
Blue Spiraea
Ⓓ

An excellent rounded shrub for the front of the border. Plant several in a group and enjoy the clusters of small, fluffy blue flowers in August and September. It will thrive in chalky soils and is reliable in all areas, but the stems are often killed in a severe winter. This is not a problem — new shoots readily appear in the spring.

VARIETIES: **C. clandonensis** is the one you will find — bright blue flowers and grey aromatic leaves on a 3 ft x 3 ft shrub. There are several named varieties — **C. clandonensis 'Arthur Simmonds'** is the favourite one, but pick **C. clandonensis 'Heavenly Blue'** if you want a darker colour. Avoid **C. mongolica** — it's too unreliable.

SITE & SOIL: Any reasonable garden soil will do, provided it is well-drained. Full sun is required.

PRUNING: In March cut the stems back to about 2 in. above ground level.

PROPAGATION: Easy — plant 3 in. cuttings in a cold frame in summer.

C. clandonensis

CEANOTHUS
Californian Lilac
Ⓓ or Ⓔ

One of the most attractive of all blue-flowering shrubs, but a source of disappointment in cold, exposed gardens. There are many varieties to choose from, but none is safe in a severe winter. Each Ceanothus belongs to one or other of two groups — the evergreen group has small leaves, tight thimble-like clusters of tiny flowers and they should always be grown against a south- or west-facing wall. The deciduous group is rather hardier, with larger leaves and looser clusters of flowers. Always plant Ceanothus in the spring.

VARIETIES: Choose an evergreen variety which is noted for its hardiness, such as **C. 'Autumnal Blue'** (rich blue flowers in late summer and autumn, 6 ft). There is also **C. 'Burkwoodii'** (deep blue, 6 ft) and **C. impressus** (deep blue flowers in spring, 5 ft). For a low, spreading effect choose **C. thyrsiflorus repens** (mid-blue flowers in spring, 3 ft). The deciduous varieties bloom in late summer and autumn — popular choices are **C. 'Gloire de Versailles'** (powder blue, 7 ft) and **C. 'Topaz'** (mid-blue, 6 ft). There are also one or two pink ones, such as **C. 'Marie Simon'**.

SITE & SOIL: Choose a well-drained, warm site in full sun. Never plant in an exposed spot.

PRUNING: Little or no pruning is required for evergreen varieties. Pruning is needed for deciduous varieties — in March cut back flowered shoots to within 3 in. of the previous year's growth.

PROPAGATION: Plant cuttings in a cold frame in summer.

C. 'Gloire de Versailles'

C. 'Burkwoodii'

Ceratostigma willmottianum

CERATOSTIGMA Hardy Plumbago
Ⓓ

A pretty, low-growing shrub suitable for the herbaceous border or the shrub border. In a cold winter the stems may be killed by frost, but hard pruning in April ensures the appearance of new stems which bear clusters of bright blue, phlox-like flowers in summer and early autumn. The foliage turns red in autumn.

VARIETIES: Even large garden centres offer only a single species — **C. willmottianum**. It grows about 2 ft high, but may reach 3 ft when planted against a wall. The flower clusters appear from July until October, and this shrub is a good choice for a sunny spot in dry, chalky soil.

SITE & SOIL: Any soil with reasonably good drainage. Full sun and some wind protection are required.

PRUNING: Once the bush is established, cut back the stems almost to ground level each April.

PROPAGATION: Lift and divide the bush in spring or plant cuttings in a cold frame in summer.

C. willmottianum

Chaenomeles superba 'Knap Hill Scarlet'

CHAENOMELES Japonica
Ⓓ

The latin name of this garden favourite is Chaenomeles, but it is better known as Japonica, Japanese Quince or Cydonia. The reason for its popularity is obvious — it thrives in all soils, in sun or shade, and its spring flowers are followed by golden fruits in the autumn. Grow it in the border, against a wall or as a hedge.

VARIETIES: The Common Japonica is **C. speciosa**, bearing red flowers from March to May. There are several named varieties which grow 4 – 6 ft high — choose **C. speciosa 'Nivalis'** (white) or **C. speciosa 'Simonii'** (semi-double, blood red). Equally attractive are varieties of **C. superba** — the best is **'Knap Hill Scarlet'**.

SITE & SOIL: Any reasonable garden soil will do. Best in full sun, but will also thrive in shade.

PRUNING: Not necessary for bushes; thin some of the branches of wall-trained plants in summer.

PROPAGATION: Layer shoots or plant cuttings in a cold frame in summer. Alternatively remove rooted suckers.

C. speciosa

C. speciosa 'Nivalis'

Chimonanthus praecox 'Luteus'

CHIMONANTHUS Winter Sweet
Ⓓ

The small, pale flowers borne in winter on the leafless stems of this willow-like shrub are not particularly eye-catching. Their fragrance, however, is special — cut a few shoots for indoor decoration and enjoy the spicy aroma. Train the bush against a sunny wall and be patient — it may take several years before the first blooms appear.

VARIETIES: The best-known type is **C. praecox** (**C. fragrans**). The pale yellow, purple-centred flowers appear between December and March on a bush which grows about 9 ft high. The variety **C. praecox 'Grandiflorus'** has deeper yellow, red-centred flowers; **C. praecox 'Luteus'** is easily distinguished by its all-yellow, larger flowers.

SITE & SOIL: Any reasonable soil will do, provided it is well-drained. Choose a sunny spot.

PRUNING: Not essential. Remove unwanted or damaged branches immediately after flowering.

PROPAGATION: Sow seed under glass in spring or layer shoots in summer. Cuttings are very difficult.

C. praecox

C. praecox 'Luteus'

CHOISYA Mexican Orange Blossom
ⓔ

Choisya is one of the candidates for the title of Ideal Garden Shrub. The neat, rounded bush is well-clothed with shiny, evergreen leaves and its white, starry flowers appear as a main flush in May and then occasionally throughout the summer. It tolerates some shade and needs no pruning.

VARIETIES: There is only one variety — **C. ternata**. This shrub will reach 6 ft or more, but it can be kept in check by cutting back in spring — new shoots are readily produced. Both the blooms and crushed leaves are fragrant. The drawback of Choisya is that it is mildly sensitive to frost — plant against a wall in northern districts.

SITE & SOIL: Any reasonable garden soil is suitable. Plant in full sun or light shade.

PRUNING: Not necessary — in spring cut back unwanted and frost-damaged branches.

PROPAGATION: Easy — plant 3 in. cuttings in a cold frame in summer.

Choisya ternata

C. ternata

CISTUS Rock Rose
ⓔ

The flowers of the Rock Rose are short-lived, the papery petals opening in the morning and falling before nightfall. But new buds appear regularly during the flowering season, and the shrub is constantly in bloom during June and July. This is not a plant for shade or heavy soil, although it thrives in other problem sites such as chalky soils, sands and seaside gardens. Always use pot-grown specimens at planting time. The great enemy is frost — no variety is completely hardy. Take summer cuttings to replace the winter casualties. Some exude a sweet-smelling gum and all bear attractive flowers in various hues.

VARIETIES: The most popular variety is **C. 'Silver Pink'** (2–3 ft, pale pink flowers), although it is not the hardiest nor the most attractive. The trio with the best reputation for hardiness are **C. laurifolius** (6 ft, white flowers), **C. cyprius** (6 ft, white flowers with maroon-blotched centres) and the much more compact **C. corbariensis** (3 ft, white flowers, crimson buds). The smallest is the wide-spreading **C. lusitanicus 'Decumbens'** (1½ ft, white flowers with maroon-blotched centres). The most spectacular is the large-flowered **C. purpureus** (5 ft, rosy crimson flowers with maroon centres). Some of the most beautiful Rock Roses are unfortunately tender — an example is the large-flowered Gum Cistus (**C. ladanifer**).

SITE & SOIL: Well-drained soil in full sun is essential. Avoid frost pockets; protect from N and E winds.

PRUNING: Not necessary — in spring both unwanted and frost-damaged growth should be removed, but avoid cutting into old wood.

PROPAGATION: Sow seed in spring or plant cuttings in a cold frame in summer.

C. laurifolius

C. purpureus

C. cyprius

C. ladanifer

C. 'Silver Pink'

C. lusitanicus 'Decumbens'

Cistus ladanifer

Cistus 'Silver Pink'

CLERODENDRUM

Clerodendrum
Ⓓ

'Clerodendrum' or 'Clerodendron' — it all depends which catalogue you read. No other shrub has such a contrast in smells — the flowers which appear in August and September emit a pleasant fragrance, but the large leaves when bruised emit a horrible smell. Two species, C. trichotomum and the much less popular C. bungei, are grown.

VARIETIES: C. trichotomum (Glory Tree) can grow to a height of 12 ft or more. Each white starry flower is followed by a turquoise blue berry which is borne in a crimson calyx. The more tender **C. bungei** (snowball-like reddish purple flower-heads) is cut down by frost, but new shoots appear from the base in spring.

SITE & SOIL: A sunny and sheltered spot is necessary. The soil should be well-drained — add peat at planting time.

PRUNING: Not necessary — cut back unwanted and frost-damaged branches in spring.

PROPAGATION: Sow seed in spring or remove rooted suckers from the parent bush.

C. trichotomum

Clerodendrum trichotomum

CLETHRA

Summersweet
Ⓓ

In August the small, white flowers appear, clustered together in a slender spike which may be 5 in. long. These 'bottle-brush' flower-heads have a strong fragrance which can be enjoyed at some distance from the bush. Clethra, despite its rarity, is not difficult to grow but it does need a lime-free soil which has been enriched with peat.

VARIETIES: C. alnifolia bears creamy white flower-heads in profusion for 4 – 6 weeks in August and September. The variety **C. alnifolia 'Paniculata'** is considered a superior form, and will reach about 7 ft. They will both grow successfully in salt-laden air and wet soil. A pink-flowered variety (**C. alnifolia 'Rosea'**) is available.

SITE & SOIL: The soil must be acid — a moist situation in light shade is the ideal site.

PRUNING: Not necessary — cut back damaged or unwanted branches in February or March.

PROPAGATION: Sow seed in spring or plant cuttings in a cold frame in summer.

C. alnifolia

Clethra alnifolia 'Paniculata'

Shrubs suitable for Heavy Shade

Aucuba japonica
Buxus sempervirens
Camellia species
Elaeagnus ebbingei
Elaeagnus pungens
Euonymus radicans
Fatsia japonica
Hypericum calycinum
Ligustrum species
Lonicera nitida
Mahonia aquifolium
Osmanthus heterophyllus
Pachysandra terminalis
Prunus laurocerasus
Prunus lusitanica
Rubus species
Skimmia japonica
Symphoricarpos species
Viburnum davidii
Vinca species

Shrubs suitable for Clay Soils

Aucuba japonica
Berberis species
Chaenomeles species
Choisya ternata
Cornus species
Corylus species
Cotoneaster species
Forsythia species
Hypericum species
Mahonia species
Philadelphus species
Potentilla species
Pyracantha species
Ribes sanguineum
Skimmia japonica
Spiraea species
Symphoricarpos species
Viburnum species
Vinca species
Weigela species

COLUTEA Bladder Senna
Ⓓ

Bladder Senna used to be a popular plant in the shrubbery, renowned for its rapid growth and ability to grow in poor soil. The pea-like flowers are small and not particularly numerous but they do appear from June until October. The main feature is the appearance of the inflated seed pods ... and generations of children have loved to pop them!

VARIETIES: The only Colutea you are likely to find listed is the Common Bladder Senna (**C. arborescens**). It grows very quickly, reaching 8 ft or more, and is useful for screening. The flowers are yellow and the seed pods 2–3 in. long. Other varieties are **C. media** (coppery flowers) and **C. orientalis** (grey leaves, coppery flowers).

SITE & SOIL: Thrives in sun and poor sandy soil, but will grow in loam or heavy soil.

PRUNING: Inclined to become leggy — each March shorten back the shoots to half their length.

PROPAGATION: Easy — sow seed in spring or plant cuttings in a cold frame in summer.

Colutea arborescens

C. arborescens

CORNUS Dogwood
Ⓓ

There are no general rules for the Dogwoods because there are two distinct groups, each with quite different features and requirements. The first group is made up of the coloured bark Dogwoods, bearing eye-catching stems which are so useful for providing winter colour. Some bear variegated leaves and all are easy to grow — the only rule to remember is that they must be hard pruned each spring. The other group consists of the varieties grown for their flowers and autumn-coloured leaves. With the exception of C. mas, these tall shrubs are distinctly uncommon.

VARIETIES: If you want a red-barked variety choose **C. alba**. The new stems produced each spring will form a 5 ft high thicket which spreads each year. Choose **C. alba 'Sibirica'** for the brightest stems, **C. alba 'Elegantissima'** for white-edged leaves and **C. alba 'Spaethii'** for the brightest leaves of all. Not all of the coloured bark group bear red stems — the yellow-stemmed **C. stolonifera 'Flaviramea'** is extremely effective in winter when grown next to C. alba. In the flowering group there is the popular but not particularly attractive Cornelian Cherry (**C. mas**) which reaches about 10 ft, producing masses of small yellow flowers in March, followed by red berries and colourful autumn foliage. For large flowers and bright autumn colours choose either **C. kousa chinensis** (8 ft, white flowers) or **C. florida rubra** (8 ft, rosy red flowers).

SITE & SOIL: Most reasonable garden soils will do — some of the flowering types require a chalk-free garden. Will grow in sun or partial shade.

PRUNING: The coloured bark types must be cut back to a few inches above ground level in March. The flowering types require no pruning — remove unwanted wood in spring.

PROPAGATION: Easy for the coloured bark types — plant cuttings in a sheltered spot outdoors in autumn.

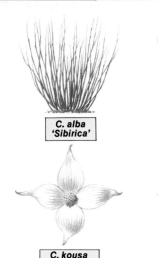
Cornus alba 'Sibirica'

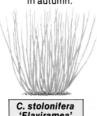
C. alba 'Sibirica'

C. stolonifera 'Flaviramea'

C. alba 'Elegantissima'

C. alba 'Spaethii'

C. kousa chinensis

C. florida rubra

C. mas

Cornus mas

CORYLOPSIS   Winter Hazel
Ⓓ

Like its relative the Witch Hazel, this shrub bears yellow flowers before the leaves appear. It has a special charm of its own — the fragrant blooms which appear in March or April are borne in pendent catkins and the hazel-like leaves often have attractive autumn tints. The flowers may be damaged by frost — plant in a sheltered site.

VARIETIES: The usual height is about 6 ft and several species are available, including **C. spicata, C. pauciflora** and **C. platypetala**. The best is **C. willmottiae**, growing to 10 ft or more with erect branches and 3 in. long tassels of flowers. The young foliage is purple and the cowslip-like scent of the blooms is strong.

SITE & SOIL: Any reasonable garden soil is suitable, in sun or partial shade. Avoid frost pockets.

PRUNING: Not necessary — remove unwanted or damaged branches after flowering.

PROPAGATION: Layering is the best method. Alternatively, plant cuttings in a cold frame in summer.

Corylopsis pauciflora

C. spicata

CORYLUS   Hazel
Ⓓ

The Common Hazel of the hedgerows has several unusual relatives which are recommended for garden use. Both yellow- and purple-leaved varieties are available, bearing attractive catkins in early spring. The most popular garden variety, however, has been chosen for its unusual branches rather than the beauty of its foliage.

VARIETIES: C. avellana 'Contorta' (Corkscrew Hazel) has oddly twisted stems which bear yellow catkins in February. It slowly grows to 10 ft — a curiosity rather than a thing of beauty. **C. avellana 'Aurea'** is an attractive yellow-leaved shrub, especially when grown next to **C. maxima 'Purpurea'** (Purple-leaved Filbert) which produces purple catkins, nuts and leaves.

SITE & SOIL: Sun or partial shade, and any well-drained soil. Excellent in wind-swept sites.

PRUNING: Cut out old, exhausted branches in March.

PROPAGATION: Layer shoots or remove rooted suckers from the parent bush.

Corylus avellana 'Contorta'

C. avellana 'Contorta'

C. maxima 'Purpurea'

COTINUS   Smoke Bush
Ⓓ

Cotinus coggygria is the modern name for the old favourite Rhus cotinus. It is perhaps best grown on its own as a large and showy specimen shrub, although it is frequently seen in mixed borders. The rounded leaves turn golden in autumn, after the large, wispy flower-heads have appeared — the feathery flower-stalks provide the attraction.

VARIETIES: C. coggygria grows about 10 ft high, the pinkish flower-heads appearing in June and turning grey with age. The effect is supposed to be smoke-like, hence the popular name. **C. coggygria 'Royal Purple'** bears wine-coloured leaves which turn red in autumn. **C. coggygria 'Notcutt's Variety'** reaches about 5 ft, its pink and purple flower-heads rising above the red leaves.

SITE & SOIL: Any reasonable garden soil will do, but light loam is best. Full sun is preferred.

PRUNING: Remove unwanted branches in spring.

PROPAGATION: Remove rooted suckers from the parent bush. Taking cuttings is difficult.

C. coggygria

Cotinus coggygria

COTONEASTER

Cotoneaster
Ⓓ or Ⓢ Ⓔ or Ⓔ

Cotoneasters come in all shapes and sizes, ranging from prostrate ground covers to 20 ft trees. The leaves, which can be as small as a finger-nail or grow several inches long, may fall in the autumn or remain on the plant throughout the year. Despite all these variations there is a general feature which makes them valuable shrubs in any garden — an abundance of showy berries and rich foliage colours in autumn. Pink buds open into small white flowers in May or June, and they may be plentiful enough to be highly decorative. All the Cotoneasters are hardy and tolerant of poor conditions — they will grow almost anywhere and need no attention apart from cutting back if they start to get out of hand.

VARIETIES: The favourite type is the Fishbone Cotoneaster **(C. horizontalis)**. It is a frequent sight in gardens, hugging the bricks of the house wall or spreading as a low bush, 2–3 ft high, between taller shrubs. The branches have a distinctive herring-bone pattern and both berries and autumn leaves are bright red. Another deciduous ground cover, **C. adpressus** is even more prostrate, and one of the best of the taller deciduous shrubs is **C. divaricatus** (6 ft x 6 ft). **C. bullatus** grows to a similar height, and is recognised by its large, dark green corrugated leaves.

The evergreens offer many splendid choices. One of the finest ground covers in the whole of the plant kingdom is **C. dammeri**. At the other end of the scale are **C. salicifolius** (15 ft, long narrow leaves) and **C. 'Hybridus Pendulus'** which can be grown as a weeping tree. For hedging choose the semi-evergreen **C. simonsii**. For a lovely low-growing shrub choose **C. conspicuus 'Decorus'**.

Cotoneaster berries are nearly always red and fairly small. For the largest berries, pick the strong-growing **C. 'Cornubia'**. As a change from red berries there is **C. 'Rothschildianus'** (yellow) or **C. franchetii** (deep orange).

SITE & SOIL: Any garden soil. Best in full sun, but will also thrive in partial shade.

PRUNING: Not necessary. Remove unwanted or damaged branches in spring.

PROPAGATION: Sow seed or plant cuttings in a cold frame in summer.

Cotoneaster horizontalis

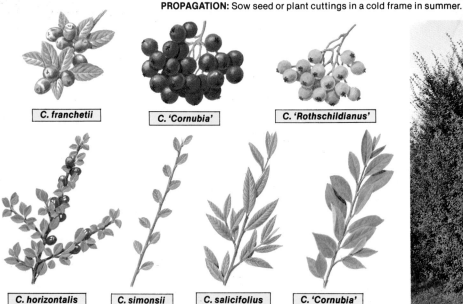

C. franchetii

C. 'Cornubia'

C. 'Rothschildianus'

C. horizontalis

C. simonsii

C. salicifolius

C. 'Cornubia'

Cotoneaster simonsii

CYTISUS

Broom

Ⓓ or Ⓢ⒠ or Ⓔ

Many shrubs are grown for their foliage, but Cytisus is grown for its flowers which are numerous enough to clothe completely the whippy stems and tiny leaves. The usual flowering season is May, and nearly all are deciduous. Always buy pot- or container-grown plants and remember to prune them every year. Old wood will not sprout new stems, and so once a bush has become leggy it should be dug out and replaced. The pea-like flowers are often yellow, but a wide variety of colours are available and there are some attractive bi-colours. Cytisus will flourish in poor, starved soil, but it may die after a few years for no apparent reason.

VARIETIES: Our native Broom is **C. scoparius**, growing about 7 ft tall and carrying its yellow blooms in May and June. There are many excellent hybrids, including **C. 'Burkwoodii'** (crimson-red with yellow edge), **C. scoparius 'Andreanus'** (yellow and crimson) and **C. 'Killiney Red'** (rich red). A shrub which grows to a similar height but with arching stems is **C. praecox**. It is the earliest of all to flower, and its rich yellow variety (**C. praecox 'Allgold'**) is popular. White-flowered brooms (e.g., **C. albus**) are available. Smaller types of Cytisus exist — there is **C. kewensis**, a pale yellow spreading bush which reaches only 18 in., and even smaller is the sprawling **C. purpureus** (1 ft, lilac flowers) and **C. decumbens** (4 in., yellow flowers). At the other end of the scale is the 15 ft Moroccan Broom (**C. battandieri**) with spikes of yellow, pineapple-scented blooms in July.

SITE & SOIL: Full sun is required. Does best in poor, sandy soil.

PRUNING: After flowering cut back the stems which have borne blooms to about half their length. Never cut into the old wood.

PROPAGATION: Sow seed. For hybrids, plant cuttings in a cold frame in summer.

Cytisus 'Burkwoodii'

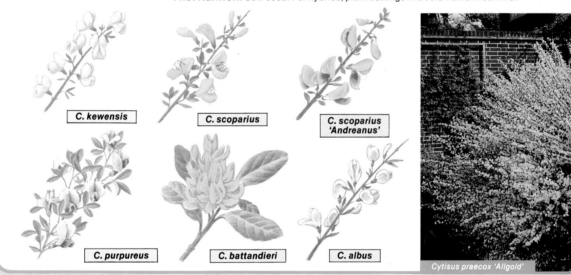

C. kewensis

C. scoparius

C. scoparius 'Andreanus'

C. purpureus

C. battandieri

C. albus

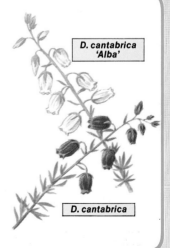

Cytisus praecox 'Allgold'

DABOECIA

Irish Heath

Ⓔ

A small group of heathers which have most of the typical family characteristics — bushy growth habit, reaching about 2 ft high, with small leaves and terminal spikes of pendent flowers. However, the blooms are not borne all round the flower-stalk and they are larger than ordinary heather blooms. The flowering period lasts from June until October.

VARIETIES: A tender variety (**D. azorica**) is offered by a few specialist nurseries but the only species you are likely to find is the hardy **D. cantabrica**. The leaves are dark green (silvery below) and the flowers are pale purple. Other types available include **D. cantabrica 'Alba'** (white) and **D. cantabrica 'Atropurpurea'** (deep purple).

SITE & SOIL: Well-drained, acid soil is necessary; full sun is preferred. Add peat at planting time.

PRUNING: Trim plants lightly as soon as the flowers have faded. Prune back straggly shoots.

PROPAGATION: Plant 1 – 2 in. cuttings in a cold frame in summer. Seed can be sown in spring.

D. cantabrica 'Alba'

D. cantabrica

Daboecia cantabrica

DANAE
Alexandrian Laurel
Ⓔ

A small shrub which is grown for two special properties. It thrives in the dense shade under trees and in
soggy soil where little else would succeed, and it
provides excellent foliage material for indoor
flower arrangements in winter. The so-called leaves
are actually flattened stems. Bright orange-red
berries are borne in autumn.

VARIETIES: There is just one species — **D. racemosa**. It
grows about 3 ft tall, its arching stems bearing narrow,
glossy leaves. This close relative of Butcher's Broom (it
sometimes appears in catalogues as **Ruscus racemosus**) spreads in the shrub border as its creeping
rootstock grows outwards. An uncommon plant, but it is
listed by the larger tree and shrub nurseries.

SITE & SOIL: Partial or deep shade is essential — so is
moist soil. Avoid an open, sandy situation.

PRUNING: Remove unwanted branches in spring.

PROPAGATION: Easy — divide the plant or remove a small
rooted section in spring or autumn.

D. racemosa

DAPHNE
Daphne
Ⓓ or ⓈⒺ or Ⓔ

D. burkwoodii

The ever-popular D. mezereum is a common sight in
February or March when its stiff, upright stems are
clothed with purplish-red flowers. There are others
to choose from, all producing fragrant flowers like
the common-or-garden one, but usually more fussy
over their requirements. They transplant badly —
buy container-grown specimens.

VARIETIES: The deciduous **D. mezereum** is sold everywhere — a white variety (**D. mezereum 'Alba'**) is also
available. The evergreen **D. odora 'Variegata'** (purplish
flowers, yellow-splashed leaves) blooms even earlier.
May-flowering varieties are **D. burkwoodii** (3 ft, pink)
and the dwarf **D. cneorum** (1 ft, rose-pink).

SITE & SOIL: Sun or partial shade. Main soil requirement is
humus — add peat at planting time.

PRUNING: Not required — hard pruning should be avoided.
Remove damaged wood after flowering.

PROPAGATION: Sow seed for D. mezereum, plant cuttings
in a cold frame in summer for others.

D. mezereum

DECAISNEA
Blue Bean
Ⓓ

Here is one to surprise the neighbours. Tall and
slender stems bear large, divided leaves about 2 ft
long, and in summer drooping clusters of greenish,
bell-like flowers are produced. In autumn the
sausage-shaped blue pods appear. Despite its
exotic appearance, Decaisnea is hardy and quite
easy to grow.

VARIETIES: D. fargesii is the only species grown. Its upright
stems are stiff and packed quite closely together,
growing about 10 ft high. The fat pods are 3 – 4 in. long,
hanging from the bush during October and November.
Decaisnea is not killed by low temperatures in winter,
but the stems may be damaged by late spring frosts.
Remove damaged stems when pruning.

SITE & SOIL: Plant in moist, well-drained soil. It will thrive in
sun or partial shade.

PRUNING: Remove old and damaged stems in spring after
danger of frost has passed.

PROPAGATION: Sow seed in a greenhouse in spring.

D. fargesii

DESFONTAINEA

Desfontainea
Ⓔ

Many of the shrubs in this book will grow anywhere and offer little challenge to the adventurous gardener. Desfontainea is different — it is difficult to please, requiring a sheltered position in a locality where the air is mild and moist. Worth a try if you live in a western coastal district — the reward is a splendid display of flowers and holly-like leaves.

VARIETIES: A single variety is available — **D. spinosa**. It looks like a typical holly bush, reaching 6–10 ft high, until June when the flowers appear. These are tubular and brightly coloured with red and yellow petals. The floral display continues until October. Apply a mulch in spring and water in dry weather.

SITE & SOIL: Plant against a sheltering wall in partial shade. Moist, free-draining soil is best.

PRUNING: Not necessary — remove dead and unwanted branches in spring.

PROPAGATION: Plant cuttings in summer or sow seed in a warm greenhouse in spring.

D. spinosa

Desfontainea spinosa

DEUTZIA

Deutzia
Ⓓ

If Deutzia is given sufficient room the small flowers will cover the whole bush in June. It is a good plant for the smaller garden, as most varieties grow no more than 4–6 ft high. The flowers may be single or double, with colours ranging from white to pale purple. It is easy to grow, but it does need pruning every year. A few are sensitive to frost.

VARIETIES: The tall-growing **D. scabra 'Plena'** (double white flowers, rosy purple outside) is popular — so is **D. rosea**, a more graceful, smaller bush with pale pink flowers. **D. magnifica** bears double flowers, and the largest blooms are borne by the hybrids, such as **D. 'Mont Rose'** (rose-pink flowers), **D. 'Contraste'** (lilac-purple flowers) and **D. 'Perle Rose'** (rose flowers).

SITE & SOIL: Not fussy — any well-drained soil will do. Grow in full sun or partial shade.

PRUNING: After flowering, prune back shoots which have flowered. Cut out old, unproductive wood.

PROPAGATION: Plant cuttings outdoors in autumn.

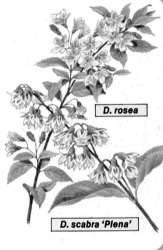

D. rosea

D. scabra 'Plena'

Deutzia rosea

DIPELTA

Dipelta
Ⓓ

An uncommon relative of the common-or-garden Weigela — it is taller-growing and considered by some to be more attractive. Dipelta is hardy and easy to grow, capable of reaching 12 ft or more. The stems bear long, pointed leaves and in late spring the colourful and fragrant flowers appear.

VARIETIES: Only one species is likely to be found growing in gardens, the large shrub **D. floribunda**. The flexible branches bear masses of flowers, singly or in small clusters, during May and June. The yellow-throated pink blooms are sweetly scented. An additional feature is the attractive peeling bark. Dipelta is not stocked by the average garden centre — try a specialist nursery.

SITE & SOIL: Plant in moist, loamy soil — Dipelta grows well in chalky areas. Thrives in sun or partial shade.

PRUNING: In June prune back the shoots which have flowered. Cut out unwanted branches at the same time.

PROPAGATION: Plant cuttings in a sheltered spot outdoors in autumn.

D. floribunda

Dipelta floribunda

ELAEAGNUS Oleaster
ⓓ or ⓔ

The white flowers are fragrant but generally insignificant — Elaeagnus is grown for its foliage. The young leaves and shoots have a metallic sheen, and these easy-to-grow shrubs are useful for hedging exposed sites. The branches are beloved by flower arrangers, and the variegated forms brighten up the winter garden.

E. ebbingei

E. pungens 'Maculata'

VARIETIES: **E. pungens 'Maculata'** is by far the most popular, its evergreen leaves splashed with bright yellow. **E. ebbingei** grows about the same height (8–10 ft) and bears down-covered evergreen leaves. The deciduous Silver Berry (**E. commutata**) is grown for its silvery leaves and berries.

SITE & SOIL: Not fussy — any reasonable garden soil will do. Plant in full sun or partial shade.

PRUNING: Not necessary — cut back unwanted branches in spring. Trim hedges in early and late summer.

PROPAGATION: Remove rooted suckers from the parent bush, or plant cuttings in a cold frame in summer.

s suitable for Industrial Areas

Forsythia species
Garrya elliptica
Genista species
Hibiscus syriacus
Hydrangea species
Hypericum species
Ilex species
Kerria japonica
Ligustrum species
Lonicera pileata
Magnolia species
Mahonia species
Pernettya mucronata
Philadelphus species
Potentilla species
Prunus laurocerasus

Pyracantha species
Rhododendron species
Rhus typhina
Ribes sanguineum
Rubus tridel 'Benenden'
Salix species
Skimmia japonica
Spartium species
Spiraea species
Symphoricarpos species
Syringa species
Tamarix tetrandra
Ulex species
Viburnum species
Vinca species
Weigela species

ENKIANTHUS Pagoda Bush
ⓓ

According to some experts, the brilliant yellows and flaming reds of the autumn foliage are not outshone by any other shrub. If your garden produces an impressive display of Rhododendrons and Azaleas, you will succeed with Enkianthus. The erect-growing bush will produce its long-lasting display of flowers in May. Mulch with peat each year.

Autumn leaves

Spring flowers

E. campanulatus

VARIETIES: The only one you are likely to find is **E. campanulatus**. It grows 6–9 ft high, and the pendent bell-shaped flowers are cream-coloured with red veins and edges. The red-coloured branches are borne in distinct whorls. At a specialist nursery you might find **E. cernuus rubens** (red flowers) or **E. perulatus** (white flowers).

SITE & SOIL: Lime-free, moist soil is essential — add peat at planting time. Light shade is preferred.

PRUNING: Not required — merely remove dead or unwanted branches after flowering.

PROPAGATION: Layer shoots or plant 3 in. cuttings in a cold frame in summer.

Erica carnea

ERICA Heather
Ⓔ

The word *heather* conjures up a picture of a compact plant, needle-leaved and bell-flowered, which hates lime and grows about 9 in. tall. However, the largest group, the Ericas, range from a height of a few inches to 10 ft or more, and can be used in the rockery, as ground cover or as a specimen shrub. Some can be grown in chalky soil, and by choosing carefully you can have a heather bed which is in bloom all year round. The basic rules are to choose suitable types, plant firmly and each year mulch around the plants with peat in late spring.

VARIETIES: Be guided by the final expected height of the plant and not by its beauty in the pot when making your purchase. If you want a specimen bush, choose a Tree Heath. There is **E. arborea** (8 – 12 ft, in bloom March – April) and two lime-tolerant smaller ones — **E. terminalis** (6 – 8 ft, in bloom July – September) and **E. mediterranea** (3 – 5 ft, in bloom March – May). For a 1½ – 2 ft high shrub, pick either the Cornish Heath **E. vagans** (in bloom July – October) or **E. darleyensis** (in bloom November – April).
The most popular heathers are low-growing ground covers. Many excellent named varieties, ranging from pure white to deep red, belong to the Winter Heather **E. carnea** (in bloom January – April). The Bell Heather **E. cinerea** (in bloom June – September) also has many varieties, ranging from white to near-black. The Cross-leaved Heath **E. tetralix** (in bloom June – October) has grey foliage.

SITE & SOIL: Well-drained soil is necessary; full sun is preferred. Add peat at planting time.

PRUNING: Trim plants lightly as soon as the flowers have faded. Prune back straggly shoots but do not cut into old wood. Overgrown Tree Heaths should be hard pruned in April.

PROPAGATION: Layer shoots or plant 1 – 2 in. cuttings in a cold frame in summer.

E. carnea   E. vagans   E. darleyensis

E. tetralix   E. cinerea   E. arborea

Erica arborea

Escallonia 'Apple Blossom'

ESCALLONIA Escallonia
Ⓔ

Both the shiny leaves and the tubular flowers are small, but their abundance makes this shrub a favourite everywhere. It can be seen as a hedge in many coastal areas as well as in the shrub border, bearing clusters of white, pink and red flowers from June to early autumn. Average height is 6 ft and it is evergreen in most parts of Britain.

VARIETIES: E. macrantha is the large and vigorous one used for seaside hedging, and **E. 'Langleyensis'** is tall and arching, bearing rose-pink flowers. Most gardeners plant named hybrids and there are many to choose from — **E. 'Apple Blossom'** (pink and white flowers), **E. 'C. F. Ball'** (red flowers), **E. 'Crimson Spire'** (crimson flowers) and **E. 'Glory of Donard'** (pink flowers).

SITE & SOIL: Any reasonable garden soil, in sun or partial shade. In the north, plant against a wall.

PRUNING: In autumn prune back shoots which have flowered. Trim hedges at the same time.

PROPAGATION: Plant cuttings in a cold frame in summer.

E. 'Langleyensis'

E. 'Apple Blossom'

EUCRYPHIA

Eucryphia
(D) or (E)

A distinctly uncommon shrub which rewards its owner by producing a display of attractive white flowers between July and September, but which is not easy to grow. Begin with a container-grown plant and make sure that you can provide a fertile, well-drained site which is protected from strong winds. Grow ground cover plants around the base of the newly-planted shrub.

VARIETIES: Tall and graceful shrubs which eventually become trees. There are two to choose from — **E. glutinosa** (15 ft tall with autumn tints of the foliage as a bonus) and the evergreen **E. nymansensis** (taller, more tolerant of chalky soil and later flowering).

SITE & SOIL: Not suitable for exposed northern gardens. Deep, lime-free loam in full sun is best.

PRUNING: Not necessary — all you have to do is remove dead and damaged shoots in April.

PROPAGATION: Not easy — cuttings are difficult to root and layering is the most reliable method.

Eucryphia nymansensis

E. glutinosa

EUONYMUS

Euonymus
(D) or (E)

There are two distinct groups — the ones which lose their leaves in winter and the ones which remain evergreen. The first group, the Spindleberries, are large shrubs or trees which are grown for their attractive fruits and colourful autumn foliage. They are useful plants, especially on chalky soils, but it is the evergreen group which is so popular. In this latter group are the variegated ground-covering varieties of E. radicans and the upright bushy forms of E. japonicus. A must for any shrub border, but they are a breeding ground for blackfly and the fruits are poisonous.

VARIETIES: Among the deciduous types of Euonymus, the Common Spindle (**E. europaeus**) is the basic form. Growing 20 ft or more, its oval leaves turn pink or red in autumn and the lobed fruits split open to reveal their orange seeds. Even brighter is the variety **E. europaeus 'Red Cascade'** and the novelty member of the group is **E. alatus** with its corky-winged stems. The evergreen varieties are grown for the beauty of their foliage, and amongst the most useful are the low-growing ground covers which can cling against a wall like ivy. You will find them in the catalogues as **E. radicans** or **E. fortunei radicans**. The favourite variety is **E. radicans 'Silver Queen'**. If you want something taller, especially for hedging in coastal areas, choose **E. japonicus**. Its variegated forms, **'Ovatus Aureus'** and **'Aureopictus'** are particularly colourful.

SITE & SOIL: Any garden soil will do. Sun or partial shade, but deciduous and variegated types prefer full sun.

PRUNING: Little or no pruning is required, but you can cut them back hard, if required, in May. Trim hedges of E. japonicus in May and again in early autumn.

PROPAGATION: Easy. Layer shoots or plant cuttings in a cold frame in summer.

Euonymus europaeus

DECIDUOUS VARIETIES

EVERGREEN VARIETIES

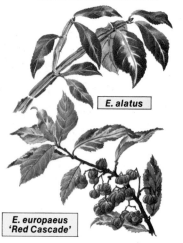

E. alatus

E. europaeus 'Red Cascade'

E. japonicus

E. japonicus 'Aureopictus'

E. japonicus 'Ovatus Aureus'

E. radicans 'Silver Queen'

Euonymus radicans 'Silver Queen'

Exochorda macrantha 'The Bride'

EXOCHORDA   Pearl Bush
Ⓓ

A beautiful bush when in flower, the branches festooned with short spikes of white blooms. The 1½-2 in. flowers look like large pear blossoms, but the display in May is short-lived, lasting for only about a week. Exochorda needs plenty of space and plenty of sun, and you should plant only container-grown specimens. Annual pruning is necessary.

VARIETIES: The most popular type, **E. racemosa**, is the one to choose provided your soil is not chalky. It is a wide-spreading bush, reaching a height of about 9 ft, with snow-white flowers. **E. giraldii** is a taller, more upright shrub. **E. macrantha 'The Bride'** forms a compact mound of weeping branches.

SITE & SOIL: An open sunny situation is required, with fertile and well-drained soil.

PRUNING: Immediately after flowering cut back shoots which bear faded blooms. Remove weak branches.

PROPAGATION: Plant cuttings in a propagator in summer or dig up and plant suckers bearing roots.

E. racemosa

Fabiana imbricata violacea

FABIANA   Fabiana
Ⓔ

A rarity which could fool even the most experienced gardener. It looks like a Tree Heather, with tiny leaves and rows of small flowers in June. It is actually a member of the potato family, with flowers which are tubes and not heather bells. Try it if you like unusual shrubs, but you will need to provide a warm and sheltered site.

VARIETIES: **F. imbricata** is the type you are most likely to find. It is an upright shrub, reaching 6 ft or more, with white summer flowers. A rather similar but more spreading variety is available with lavender flowers (**F. imbricata violacea**). For the rockery pick the dwarf, mauve-flowering **F. imbricata 'Prostrata'**.

SITE & SOIL: Plenty of sun is needed with shelter from cold winds and hard frost. Sandy soil is preferred.

PRUNING: Not necessary. Cut back unwanted stems in July after flowering.

PROPAGATION: Plant 3 in. cuttings in a propagator in summer.

F. imbricata violacea

F. imbricata

Fatsia japonica

FATSIA   Fatsia
Ⓔ

Fatsia appears in all the house plant books but not in all the shrub guides. With this in mind, and looking at the large exotic leaves, you could be excused for regarding it as a tender plant, but in fact it is quite hardy in most parts of Britain. It grows to 10 ft, with candelabra-like flowers in October.

VARIETIES: There is a single species — **F. japonica**, sometimes called Aralia or the Castor Oil Plant. The deeply-lobed, shining leaves are more than 1 ft across, borne on long leaf-stalks. It is particularly successful as a seaside shrub or as a specimen bush in town gardens. A variety with white-edged leaves (**F. japonica 'Variegata'**) is available.

SITE & SOIL: Prefers a partially shaded, sheltered spot. Will grow in any reasonable garden soil.

PRUNING: Not necessary — cut back in the spring only if it is getting too large.

PROPAGATION: Plant cuttings in a cold frame in summer. Alternatively sow seed in spring.

F. japonica

FORSYTHIA Golden Bells
ⓓ

Gardens are brightened each March and April by the masses of yellow flowers on the leafless branches. Many varieties are available, ranging from palest yellow to glowing orange. There are Forsythias to cover walls and bare ground or to grow as hedges and specimen shrubs. They are extremely easy to grow but there are two enemies — birds which strip off the flower buds (thread black cotton between the branches) and there are gardeners who hack down the branches each summer "to keep the bushes in check". The result is lots of growth and very few flowers.

VARIETIES: F. intermedia 'Spectabilis' is seen everywhere, growing about 8 ft high with a profusion of bright yellow flowers. The petals are narrow and slightly twisted. **F. 'Lynwood'** has much broader petals and **F. 'Beatrix Farrand'** bears blooms up to 2 in. across.

Not all varieties grow as tall, upright shrubs — some are rambling bushes belonging to the species **F. suspensa**. One of them (**F. suspensa fortunei**) has stout, arching stems but the popular **F. suspensa sieboldii** has lax branches which trail along the ground if not trained against a wall.

Less well known are the compact varieties. **F. ovata** only reaches 4–5 ft; even shorter is **F. 'Arnold Dwarf'** which will cover a large area but be warned — it bears few flowers.

SITE & SOIL: Any garden soil will do. Best in full sun, but will also thrive in partial shade.

PRUNING: Avoid excessive pruning. Immediately after flowering cut back only those shoots which bear faded blooms. Every few years shorten some of the most mature branches.

PROPAGATION: Easy. Layer shoots or plant cuttings outdoors in autumn.

Forsythia suspensa

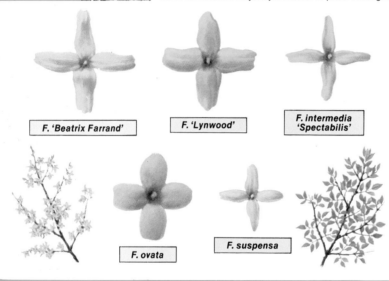
F. 'Beatrix Farrand'
F. 'Lynwood'
F. intermedia 'Spectabilis'
F. ovata
F. suspensa

Forsythia intermedia 'Spectabilis'

FOTHERGILLA Fothergilla
ⓓ

This shrub would not win any prizes in a popularity contest, and you may have to search to find one. The white bottle-brush flowers appear in April before the foliage, but they are unusual rather than showy. The summer display of large, hazel-like leaves is not in any way spectacular, but it comes into its own in autumn with brilliant yellow and red foliage.

VARIETIES: All the Fothergillas are slow-growing, and the smallest one is **F. gardenii**. This 3 ft shrub is not robust and it is better to choose one of the others. **F. major** will eventually reach a height of 6 ft, with leaves which turn golden in autumn. **F. monticola** is a similar shrub, but its autumn foliage is red.

SITE & SOIL: There must be no lime or chalk in the soil. Apart from that it is not fussy, succeeding in sun or partial shade.

PRUNING: Not essential — cut out old stems in winter.

PROPAGATION: Rooting cuttings is difficult — layering stems in autumn is more reliable.

Fothergilla monticola

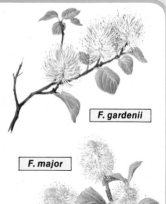
F. gardenii
F. major

FUCHSIA
Fuchsia
D

From July right up till October the colourful, bell-like flowers hang from the branches. In many areas the stems are killed by frost, but if you have chosen a recommended garden variety then new shoots should sprout from the base in the following spring. Plant rather deeply — cover the crown with peat. In the S.W. it can be grown as a hedge.

VARIETIES: The hardiest and most popular variety is **F. magellanica 'Riccartonii'** — it grows 6 ft high in frost-free areas. **F. magellanica gracilis** is a slender bush bearing slender flowers, and **F. magellanica 'Versicolor'** has variegated leaves. There are many hybrid Fuchsias, such as **'Mrs Popple', 'Madame Cornelissen'** and the dwarf **'Tom Thumb'**.

SITE & SOIL: Any ordinary soil, provided it retains moisture and is well fed. Full sun or partial shade.

PRUNING: In March cut back to 1 in. above the ground.

PROPAGATION: Easy — plant 2 in. cuttings in a cold frame in summer.

Fuchsia magellanica

F. magellanica gracilis

F. magellanica 'Riccartonii'

F. 'Madame Cornelissen'

GARRYA
Silk Tassel Bush
E

Garrya is best known for the long and slender catkins which drape the bushes in January and February, but even without these silken tassels it is a valuable shrub for the garden. Fast-growing, it reaches about 9 ft and flourishes in sun or shade. The foliage is glossy and evergreen. Transplants badly — always use container-grown plants.

VARIETIES: Specialist nurseries may offer more, but you are likely to only find one — **G. elliptica**. The oval leaves have a wavy edge and the catkins are silvery green at first, later pale yellow. Male plants have the longest tassels, reaching 6 — 10 in. Buy the variety **'James Roof'** if you can find it — the tassels are 14 in. long.

SITE & SOIL: Not fussy — will grow on chalk or poor, sandy soil. In cold, northern gardens grow against a wall.

PRUNING: Not essential. Trim back dead or over-long branches in April or May.

PROPAGATION: Easy. Layer shoots or plant 3 in. cuttings in a cold frame in summer.

Garrya elliptica

G. elliptica

GENISTA
Broom
D

This group of Brooms generally have wiry stems, tiny leaves and a mass of yellow, pea-like flowers in June. There are no general rules about height — it may be 12 ft or 12 in. high, depending on the variety. All bloom freely if given plenty of sun and no food — fertile soil reduces flowering.

VARIETIES: The most popular is **G. lydia**, a spreading shrub reaching about 2 ft. Its arching stems are covered with golden yellow flowers in May and June. Another excellent ground cover is **G. hispanica** (Spanish Gorse) which has very spiny branches. The giant is the 12 ft **G. aetnensis** (Mount Etna Broom). Spectacular when in bloom in July, but it is not very hardy.

SITE & SOIL: Full sun is required. Nearly all soil types will do, but best in poor, sandy ground.

PRUNING: After flowering, cut back stems which have borne blooms but do not prune into old wood.

PROPAGATION: Sow seed. Summer cuttings root with some difficulty in a propagator.

Genista lydia

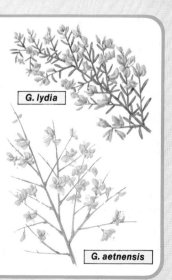
G. lydia

G. aetnensis

HAMAMELIS Witch Hazel
Ⓓ

The showy, spidery flowers appear on the leafless branches for many weeks between December and late February. Sweet scent is an extra bonus — cut a few branches for indoor decoration. After the flowers the hazel-like leaves appear. Attractive tints appear in the autumn. Hamamelis is an undemanding, hardy shrub but it does need space, reaching a height and spread of 10 ft or more.

H. mollis 'Pallida'

VARIETIES: If you can only have one, choose Chinese Witch Hazel (**H. mollis**). The bright yellow flowers are large, fragrant and plentiful. **H. mollis 'Pallida'** and **H. mollis 'Brevipetala'** are recommended. The Japanese Witch Hazel (**H. japonica**) has less fragrance, fewer flowers and blooms later. **H. virginiana** is a poor choice — the early blooms are small and hidden by the autumn leaves.

SITE & SOIL: Suffers when soil is alkaline or badly drained. Choose a sunny or lightly shaded spot.

PRUNING: Not essential. Remove unwanted or damaged branches after flowering. Pull out suckers.

PROPAGATION: Not easy — only practical method is layering. Nursery-raised plants are grafted.

H. mollis 'Brevipetala'

Hamamelis japonica

HEBE Veronica
Ⓔ

These evergreen shrubs come in all sizes, but the two most popular ones (H. 'Autumn Glory' and H. brachysiphon) represent the typical Hebe growth habit — neat, compact bushes with shiny oval leaves and spikes of small blue or white flowers. They are both quite hardy, but unfortunately many Hebes are not — the larger the leaf, the more tender the variety is likely to be. Tenderness apart, Hebe is easy to grow even in smoky or salt-laden air, and many types flower all summer and autumn long.

VARIETIES: There are scores to choose from — make sure the one you pick is the right size for the spot you have in mind. Some are suitable for the rockery or as ground cover — good 1 ft-high varieties include **H. 'Carl Teschner'** (violet-blue flowers, June-July), **H. pinguifolia 'Pagei'** (white flowers, May) and the cypress-like **H. armstrongii** and **H. ochracea**. The medium-tall group offers many choices, such as **H. 'Autumn Glory'** (violet-blue flowers, June-November), **H. 'Midsummer Beauty'** (lavender flowers, July-November) and **H. brachysiphon** (white flowers, June-July). The giant of the family is **H. salicifolia**, a summer-flowering shrub which reaches 10 ft or more.

SITE & SOIL: Choose a sunny or lightly shaded spot. Any garden soil with reasonable drainage will do, but it is unwise to plant the less hardy varieties in northern gardens away from the coast.

PRUNING: Not essential. Cut back straggly shoots in May. Remove frost-damaged branches.

PROPAGATION: Easy — plant 3 in. cuttings in a cold frame in summer.

Hebe 'Autumn Glory'

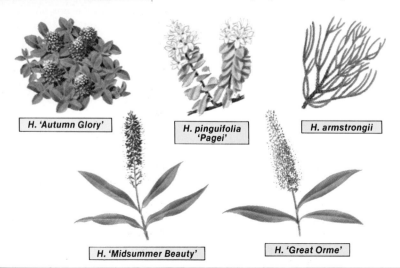

H. 'Autumn Glory'

H. pinguifolia 'Pagei'

H. armstrongii

H. 'Midsummer Beauty'

H. 'Great Orme'

Hebe salicifolia

HELIANTHEMUM   Sun Rose, Rock Rose
(E)

Each bright flower lasts for only a day, but they are borne in profusion from May to July. These wiry-stemmed, spreading shrubs reach a height of only 6-9 in., making them an excellent choice for the rockery or a dry bank. They are straggly and bare when wrongly treated — follow the rules below for site selection and pruning to ensure success.

VARIETIES: The named Helianthemums are all varieties or hybrids of the wild species **H. nummularium**. The flowers of these named garden types are about 1 in. across and are available in many colours. Popular types include **'Ben Nevis'** (buttercup yellow, deeper centre), **'Ben Hope'** (carmine), **'Fire Dragon'** (orange-red) and **'The Bride'** (white).

SITE & SOIL: Full sun is necessary. Requires free-draining and unfertilized soil — suffers in rich, clayey ground.

PRUNING: Very important. Remove dead flower-heads and in late July cut back all straggly stems.

PROPAGATION: Easy — plant 2 in. cuttings in a cold frame in summer.

Helianthemum nummularium

H. nummularium 'Ben Hope'

H. nummularium 'Fire Dragon'

HIBISCUS   Tree Hollyhock
(D)

One of the best late-flowering shrubs, but not for every garden — it needs full sun, well-drained soil and some protection from cold winds. Under these conditions it provides an abundance of large, saucer-shaped flowers from July to October. Bushes reach 6 – 8 ft but there is little growth in the first year. Leaves do not appear until late spring.

VARIETIES: Hibiscus is available in many colours and in both single and double varieties. If you can have only one, choose **H. syriacus 'Blue Bird'** (violet-blue with dark eye, 3 in. across). Other fine varieties are **H. syriacus 'Hamabo'** (white with crimson eye), **H. syriacus 'Woodbridge'** (rose-pink with dark eye) and **H. syriacus 'Duc de Brabant'** (double, magenta).

SITE & SOIL: Full sun and some shelter are essential. Any reasonable garden soil will do if it drains freely.

PRUNING: Little pruning is necessary — simply cut back over-long and old branches in spring.

PROPAGATION: Easiest method is layering. Nursery-raised plants of named varieties are grafted.

Hibiscus syriacus

H. syriacus 'Blue Bird'

H. syriacus 'Woodbridge'

Shrubs suitable for Chalky Soil

Arbutus	Forsythia	Prunus lusitanica
Arundinaria	Fuchsia	Pyracantha
Aucuba	Garrya	Rhus
Berberis	Hebe	Ribes
Buddleia	Hypericum	Romneya
Buxus	Ilex	Rosmarinus
Callicarpa	Kerria	Sambucus
Ceanothus	Kolkwitzia	Santolina
Choisya	Lavandula	Senecio
Cistus	Ligustrum	Spartium
Colutea	Mahonia	Symphoricarpos
Cornus mas	Olearia	Syringa
Cotoneaster	Paeonia	Tamarix
Deutzia	Philadelphus	Vinca
Elaeagnus	Photinia	Weigela
Escallonia	Pittosporum	Yucca
Euonymus	Potentilla	

Hippophae rhamnoides

HIPPOPHAE

Sea Buckthorn
ⓓ

A hedge of Sea Buckthorn provides an excellent windbreak in seaside gardens. It is resistant to drought and immune to salty air, and its dense, spiny growth is tolerant of both hard winters and hard pruning. It is worth considering as a barrier hedge inland, but do not grow as a single bush — both male and female plants are needed for berries.

VARIETIES: Just one variety is grown — **H. rhamnoides**. A strong-growing shrub, reaching 10–20 ft, bearing willow-like silvery leaves and sharp thorns. The flowers in March and April are inconspicuous, but they are followed by masses of orange berries which are left untouched by birds. They remain on the bush from September until February.

SITE & SOIL: Will succeed in any reasonably well-drained soil. An open site is best, in sun or partial shade.

PRUNING: Not essential. Trim hedges in summer.

PROPAGATION: Easy — sow seed from berries in autumn. Alternatively, layer shoots or plant rooted suckers.

H. rhamnoides

Hydrangea macrophylla

HYDRANGEA

Hydrangea
ⓓ

It is not surprising that Hydrangeas are universally popular. The large flower-heads are borne in late summer when the shrub border is so often short of flowers, and the heads may be numerous enough to almost cover the bush. Most popular are the Mopheads, with large, ball-like blooms. The Lacecaps are quite different — each flat flower-head has an outer ring of large flowers surrounding a central group of much smaller ones. Hydrangeas are not difficult but you must satisfy their needs — good soil, plenty of water and some protection against heavy frosts.

VARIETIES: Most types are derived from **H. macrophylla**, with flowers borne from July to September on bushes which are usually about 5 ft x 5 ft. The Mopheads (or Hortensias) are available in white, pink, red and blue. Blue flowers only appear under acid conditions — in order to "blue" Hydrangeas in alkaline soil it is necessary to apply blueing powder every 7–14 days.
The Lacecaps are more graceful than the Mopheads — popular varieties include **H. 'Blue Wave'**, **H. 'Mariesii'** and **H. 'Lanarth White'**.
Not all garden Hydrangeas belong to H. macrophylla. There is **H. paniculata 'Grandiflora'**, a tall shrub bearing white cone-shaped spikes in August and September. **H. villosa** is regarded as one of the loveliest of all August-flowering shrubs, and the 3 ft high **H. serrata 'Bluebird'** is a good choice for the smaller garden.

SITE & SOIL: Well-drained, rich soil is best — add peat at planting time. Prefers light shade.

PRUNING: Remove the dead flower-heads of Mophead varieties in March, not in autumn. At the same time remove any weak branches. Only H. paniculata 'Grandiflora' requires hard pruning.

PROPAGATION: Easy — plant 4 in. cuttings in a cold frame in summer.

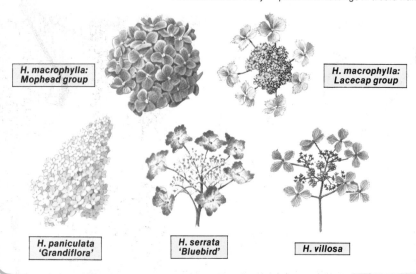

H. macrophylla: Mophead group

H. macrophylla: Lacecap group

H. paniculata 'Grandiflora'

H. serrata 'Bluebird'

H. villosa

Hydrangea paniculata 'Grandiflora'

Flowers for Every Season

JANUARY–APRIL
(for MAY–AUGUST see page 37)
(for SEPTEMBER–DECEMBER see page 44)

By careful selection it is quite easy to ensure that even a modest shrub border will be in bloom during every month of the year. For each month there is a list of shrubs which can be expected to be in full flower — remember that some of these plants may come into bloom earlier and can continue to bloom for many weeks afterwards.

JANUARY
Chimonanthus praecox
Erica carnea
Erica darleyensis
Garrya elliptica
Hamamelis mollis

Jasminum nudiflorum
Lonicera fragrantissima
Viburnum bodnantense
Viburnum fragrans
Viburnum tinus

FEBRUARY
Corylus avellana
Daphne mezereum
Daphne odora
Erica carnea

Erica darleyensis
Hamamelis japonica
Mahonia 'Charity'
Mahonia japonica

MARCH
Camellia japonica
Chaenomeles speciosa
Cornus mas
Corylopsis species
Erica arborea
Erica mediterranea

Forsythia species
Magnolia stellata
Mahonia aquifolium
Prunus incisa
Ribes sanguineum
Salix species

APRIL
Amelanchier canadensis
Berberis darwinii
Berberis stenophylla
Camellia japonica
Fothergilla species
Kerria japonica
Magnolia soulangiana
Osmanthus delavayi

Pieris japonica
Prunus species
Rosmarinus officinalis
Skimmia species
Spiraea arguta
Spiraea thunbergii
Ulex europaeus
Viburnum — spring-flowering species

Hypericum calycinum

HYPERICUM   St John's Wort
Ⓢ or Ⓔ

The Hypericum you are most likely to see is Rose of Sharon or H. calycinum. This low-growing shrub spreads rapidly, suppressing weeds and providing a colourful floral display from June to September. It will flourish under trees and on dry banks, and its large, buttercup-like flowers are a familiar sight. It is a useful work-horse in the garden, but it is sometimes despised as an over-popular invasive "weed". For people who would like something more unusual there are a number of varieties to choose from, ranging from rockery Hypericums to bushes which reach 6 ft or more.

VARIETIES: H. calycinum grows 1–1½ ft high and bears bright yellow flowers — it will grow anywhere except in waterlogged soil. There are smaller Hypericums for the rockery — **H. polyphyllum** is the baby of the family, growing only 6 in. tall.
If you want a Hypericum which grows about the same height as Rose of Sharon but is less invasive, choose **H. moserianum 'Tricolor'**. The flowers are small, but the leaves are an eye-catching blend of green, cream and pink. For a shrub in the 3–4 ft range, **H. inodorum 'Elstead'** is worth considering, as attractive egg-shaped fruits follow the floral display.
The tall Hypericums are perhaps the best of all. If you can have only one, choose **H. 'Hidcote'**, a fine 6 ft shrub bearing an abundance of large golden flowers from July to October. Even finer is **H. 'Rowallane'**, but it is a tender plant which needs a sheltered, warm spot.

SITE & SOIL: Will grow in any garden soil. Most of them will flourish in shade.

PRUNING: Cut back H. calycinum almost to ground level in March. Taller varieties require less drastic treatment — remove the top third of the branches each spring.

PROPAGATION: Easy — plant 3 in. cuttings in a cold frame in summer.

H. calycinum

H. 'Hidcote'

H. polyphyllum

H. inodorum 'Elstead'

H. moserianum 'Tricolor'

Hypericum 'Hidcote'

Ilex aquifolium

ILEX Holly
Ⓔ

Common Holly (I. aquifolium) needs no description. The spiny, deep green leaves and bright red berries are known to everyone, but there are also many garden varieties which differ from the basic type in both leaf and berry colour. As a rule the Hollies are slow-growing, taking many years to reach tree-like proportions, and they are not fussy about soil type or situation. All will grow in shade, but the variegated forms need a sunny spot. Buy a small plant — large plants transplant badly. Nearly all Hollies are either male or female, so plant a group for berry production.

VARIETIES: The right type to pick depends on the role it will have to play in the garden. If you want a single specimen which will bear berries, you must choose a self-fertile type such as **I. altaclarensis 'J.C. van Tol'** or the columnar-shaped **I. aquifolium 'Pyramidalis'**. If, on the other hand, you plan to grow a group of Hollies then the choice is much wider. For a green and gold effect pick the badly-named male variety **I. aquifolium 'Golden Queen'**, or the equally badly-named female variety **I. altaclarensis 'Golden King'**. For silver-margined leaves choose **I. aquifolium 'Argentea Marginata'**. Holly makes an excellent barrier hedge — **I. aquifolium 'Madame Briot'** is a strongly-spined variety. There are several out-of-the-ordinary Hollies — examples are **I. aquifolium 'Ferox'** (spines on the leaf surface), **I. aquifolium 'Bacciflava'** (yellow berries) and **I. crenata 'Mariesii'** (dwarf; tiny round leaves and black berries).

SITE & SOIL: Not fussy, but add some peat when planting. Will grow in sun or shade.

PRUNING: Trim hedges in spring, specimen shrubs in summer. Can be drastically cut back if necessary without harm. Remove all-green branches from variegated varieties.

PROPAGATION: Slow-rooting. Layer branches or plant 3 in. cuttings in a cold frame in autumn.

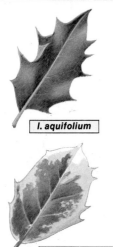
I. aquifolium

I. aquifolium 'Argentea Marginata'

I. aquifolium

I. altaclarensis 'Golden King'

I. aquifolium 'Ferox'

I. aquifolium 'Bacciflava'

Ilex aquifolium 'Golden Queen'

Indigofera gerardiana

INDIGOFERA Indigo
Ⓓ

You will not find Indigo in any popular selection of shrubs, and it does have one distinct disadvantage — the leaves do not appear until late May or June. But if you have a sheltered sunny spot to fill and the soil is sandy and free-draining, it is worth considering. Graceful spikes of pale purple flowers appear continuously from July until October.

VARIETIES: I. gerardiana (I. heterantha) is the only one you are likely to find. It grows about 4 ft tall in the open — more if planted against a south-facing wall. The pea-like flowers are rosy purple. This variety is not completely hardy — the stems are damaged by hard frosts but new growth appears readily from the base. A taller, rarer variety is **I. potaninii**.

SITE & SOIL: There are two important requirements — full sun and free-draining soil. Feeding is not necessary.

PRUNING: Trim in April. Old plants and frost-damaged branches should be cut back close to the base.

PROPAGATION: Plant cuttings in a cold frame in summer.

I. gerardiana

Jasminum nudiflorum

JASMINUM   Jasmine
Ⓓ

Winter Jasmine (J. nudiflorum) is a must for every shrub border — nothing else will provide such a bold splash of colour from November to late February. It is not a true climber — its lax branches can be left to trail over unsightly banks or they can be trained up a wall or trellis. The stems will reach 10 ft or more.

VARIETIES: Tubular, bright yellow flowers open on the leafless green stems of **J. nudiflorum**. It is an undemanding plant, growing in any ordinary soil and flourishing quite happily against a north-facing wall. Summer-flowering shrubby Jasmines do occur, but you will have to search hard to find one.

SITE & SOIL: Jasmine will thrive in any garden soil. Do not plant against an east-facing wall.

PRUNING: In March cut back all side shoots which have flowered. Thin out some of the old branches.

PROPAGATION: Easy. Layer shoots or plant 3 in. cuttings in a cold frame in summer.

J. nudiflorum

Kalmia latifolia

KALMIA   Kalmia
Ⓔ

There is just one popular variety — the Mountain Laurel or Calico Bush (K. latifolia) which grows wild in N. America. When not in flower you could mistake it for a rhododendron, but in flower it is quite distinctive. The cluster of buds looks like a group of chinese lanterns, which then open into attractive saucer-shaped flowers.

VARIETIES: **K. latifolia** grows about 8 ft high, bearing clusters of delicate pink flowers in June. It is completely hardy in Britain, but it cannot stand dry soil. Apply a mulch around the stems in late spring. A smaller, less common variety is **K. angustifolia** (Sheep Laurel) which produces small, rosy-red flowers in June.

SITE & SOIL: An acid soil is essential — add peat at planting time. Thrives in partial shade.

PRUNING: Not required — merely remove the dead blooms after flowering.

PROPAGATION: Layer shoots or plant cuttings in a cold frame in summer.

K. latifolia

Kerria japonica 'Pleniflora'

KERRIA   Jew's Mallow
Ⓓ

A very popular, trouble-free shrub which can be relied upon to produce an abundance of yellow flowers in April and May, and occasionally at other times of the year. Most people choose the double form (K. japonica 'Pleniflora') and train the long stems against a wall or trellis. Less gaunt is the shorter-growing K. japonica.

VARIETIES: The most graceful variety is **K. japonica**, its arching stems growing about 6 ft high and its 2 in. single flowers resembling large buttercups. **K. japonica 'Pleniflora'** produces double blooms which look like golden pompons, and its stems can reach 8 ft or more. The dwarf Kerria is **K. japonica 'Variegata'** — a pretty variety with white-edged leaves.

SITE & SOIL: Any garden soil in sun or partial shade. If possible avoid an open or wind-swept site.

PRUNING: In June prune the shoots which have flowered.

PROPAGATION: Remove rooted pieces from the parent bush, or plant cuttings in a cold frame in summer.

K. japonica

K. japonica 'Pleniflora'

KOLKWITZIA
Beauty Bush
Ⓓ

Kolkwitzia is an easy-to-grow shrub which thrives in all types of soil, and each May and June the arching stems are festooned with pretty, bell-shaped flowers. An excellent plant for the shrub border, but it has never achieved the popularity of the rather similar Weigela. Size may be the problem — its spread can exceed 8 ft if not regularly pruned.

VARIETIES: There is a single species — **K. amabilis**, introduced from China at the turn of the century. It grows 6-8 ft high and bears foxglove-like flowers — pink with yellow markings at the throat. Choose the improved variety (**K. amabilis 'Pink Cloud'**) which was raised at the Royal Horticultural Society Gardens at Wisley.

SITE & SOIL: Any reasonable garden soil will do — thrives in chalky soil. Choose a sunny spot.

PRUNING: After flowering cut back branches which bear faded blooms. Remove dead and weak stems.

PROPAGATION: Remove rooted pieces from the parent bush or plant cuttings in a cold frame in summer.

K. amabilis

LAURUS
Bay Laurel
Ⓔ

The laurel around the heads of Greek heroes was Laurus, but the laurel around the garden is more likely to be Aucuba or Prunus lusitanica. The reason for this lack of widespread popularity is its susceptibility to winter damage — leaves are often scorched by frost and cold winds when planted outside. It is much used as a tub plant.

VARIETIES: L. nobilis grows to 20 ft or more if left unpruned. The stems can withstand drastic trimming and the glossy foliage (bay leaves) are used in the kitchen. Yellowish flowers appear in spring and are followed by black berries on female plants. Tub-grown specimens are often attacked by scale — spray with permethrin.

SITE & SOIL: Any reasonable soil in a spot well-sheltered from cold winds will do. Thrives in sun or shade.

PRUNING: Remove damaged stems and leaves in spring — trim to produce decorative shapes in summer.

PROPAGATION: Layer shoots or plant cuttings in a cold frame in summer.

L. nobilis

LAVANDULA
Lavender
Ⓔ

A favourite in English gardens for centuries. The bushy stems and grey-green leaves provide an edging or low hedge for countless paths and borders, and the aromatic flowers and foliage are used for making pot-pourri. The flowers which appear between July and September are not always lavender — there are white, pink and blue varieties.

VARIETIES: Plants labelled **L. spica** are Old English Lavender (3 ft, grey-blue flowers) — choose the variety **'Hidcote'** (1½ ft, deep violet flowers in dense spikes). **'Munstead'** has green leaves — **'Loddon Pink'** has pink flowers. **L. vera** is Dutch Lavender — pale blue and robust, 3-4 ft high.

SITE & SOIL: Any soil (preferably limy) provided it is well-drained. Best in full sun but will grow in partial shade.

PRUNING: Remove stalks when flowers fade, then trim back plants in April. Do not cut into old wood.

PROPAGATION: Plant cuttings in a cold frame in summer or outdoors in autumn.

L. spica 'Hidcote'

Lespedeza thunbergii

LESPEDEZA
Bush Clover
Ⓓ

You will have to go to a nursery with a large selection of shrubs to find this one, and even then you will only find the weeping form. However, if you have sandy soil and you need an autumn-flowering specimen bush for planting in the lawn, Lespedeza is a good choice. The arching branches are borne down by large flowering trusses from September to November.

VARIETIES: The weeping form is **L. thunbergii,** growing about 6 ft tall and 10 ft wide. The flowers in the trusses are rosy purple and pea-like and the stems bow down to the ground in the flowering season. These branches die down in winter — new ones shoot up in the spring. **L. bicolor** is rather similar but it has a semi-erect growth habit, reaching about 10 ft.

SITE & SOIL: Any reasonable garden soil which is not heavy. Choose a site in full sun.

PRUNING: Cut away all dead stems in March.

PROPAGATION: Divide plants in autumn.

L. thunbergii

Leycesteria formosa

LEYCESTERIA
Pheasant Berry
Ⓓ

When not in flower this shrub has an unusual and rather gaunt appearance — tall bamboo-like stems covered with a waxy coating. These hollow stems may be killed by severe frosts, but new shoots grow up readily from the base in spring. The small flowers which appear in July and August are followed by purple berries much loved by birds.

VARIETIES: L. formosa was a feature of Victorian shrubberies. It is rarely seen in gardens nowadays although it is often planted in pheasant covets. Leycesteria is quick-growing, new shoots reaching 6 ft in a single season. The unusual flower-heads are long tassels composed of a series of wine-coloured bracts within which the flowers and later the berries appear.

SITE & SOIL: Very accommodating — any reasonable garden soil will do and it thrives in sun or shade.

PRUNING: In March cut back all old and damaged shoots to a few inches above ground level.

PROPAGATION: Easy — sow seed under glass in spring.

L. formosa

Flowers for Every Season

MAY – AUGUST
(for JANUARY – APRIL see page 33)   (for SEPTEMBER – DECEMBER see page 44)

By careful selection it is quite easy to ensure that even a modest shrub border will be in bloom during every month of the year. For each month there is a list of shrubs which can be expected to be in full flower — remember that some of these plants may come into bloom earlier and can continue to bloom for many weeks afterwards.

MAY
Ceanothus impressus
Choisya ternata
Cornus florida
Cotoneaster species
Cytisus species
Exochorda racemosa
Genista species
Helianthemum nummularium
Kolkwitzia amabilis
Paeonia species
Pernettya species
Pittosporum tobira
Pyracantha species
Rhododendron species
Rubus tridel
Tamarix tetrandra

JUNE
Abelia schumannii
Buddleia alternifolia
Buddleia globosa
Cistus species
Cotinus coggygria
Deutzia species
Erica cinerea
Erica tetralix
Escallonia species
Fabiana imbricata
Genista species
Hebe species
Kalmia latifolia
Lonicera tatarica
Philadelphus species
Senecio greyi
Syringa species
Weigela species

JULY
Buddleia davidii
Callicarpa species
Calluna vulgaris
Carpenteria californica
Daboecia cantabrica
Erica terminalis
Erica vagans
Eucryphia species
Indigofera species
Lavandula species
Lupinus arboreus
Olearia species
Potentilla species
Santolina species
Spiraea — summer-flowering species
Symphoricarpos species

AUGUST
Caryopteris clandonensis
Ceanothus 'Autumnal Blue'
Ceanothus 'Burkwoodii'
Ceanothus 'Gloire de Versailles'
Ceratostigma willmottianum
Clerodendrum trichotomum
Fuchsia species
Hibiscus syriacus
Hydrangea species
Leycesteria formosa
Magnolia grandiflora
Myrtus communis
Perovskia atriplicifolia
Rhus typhina
Romneya species
Spartium junceum
Tamarix pentandra
Vinca species

LIGUSTRUM
Privet
(SE) or (E)

The privet hedge has performed legion service in British gardens. For generations countless urban plots have been clothed in green by them — resistant both to dense shade and smoky air. Nowadays it is often regarded with contempt by many — dull leaves which are semi-evergreen on bushes which produce an insignificant display of pungent-smelling white flowers in June or July, followed by black berries in autumn. This view is not correct — there are a number of colourful varieties for use as hedging or border plants.

VARIETIES: Some privet hedges are composed of **L. vulgare**, a native shrub which will reach 10 ft if left untrimmed. There are a few interesting varieties of this wild species, such as **L. vulgare 'Aureum'** (yellow leaves) and **L. vulgare 'Xanthocarpum'** (yellow berries). It is, however, much better to use a variety of **L. ovalifolium** for hedging — the leaves are larger and it branches more freely. The best to choose is **L. ovalifolium 'Aureum'**, the Golden Privet. It retains its leaves except in a severe winter. Another colourful variety is **L. ovalifolium 'Argenteum'**, with cream-edged leaves. There are privets for the shrub border, such as the Japanese Privet (**L. japonicum**). Camellia-like leaves cover the 6 ft shrub, and large sprays of white flowers appear from July onwards. A larger shrub, equally attractive in flower, is **L. lucidum**.

SITE & SOIL: Extremely adaptable — any garden soil will do and it thrives in sun or shade.

PRUNING: Trim hedges to shape in May and again in August. With specimen bushes pruning is not essential — cut away damaged or unwanted branches in spring.

PROPAGATION: Easy — plant cuttings in a cold frame in summer or outdoors in autumn.

Ligustrum vulgare

L. vulgare

L. vulgare 'Aureum'

L. japonicum

L. ovalifolium

L. ovalifolium 'Aureum'

L. ovalifolium 'Argenteum'

Ligustrum ovalifolium 'Aureum'

LONICERA
Honeysuckle
(D) or (SE) or (E)

Honeysuckles are usually thought of as climbing plants with sweetly-scented flowers, but there are also shrubby varieties. Their most popular use is for hedging, but there are also types which can be planted for ground cover or as specimen shrubs.

VARIETIES: Most frequently seen is the evergreen **L. nitida**, extensively grown as a hedge. Such hedges need frequent clipping and stout supports — the best variety to choose is **'Fertilis'**, the most colourful is the yellow-leaved **'Baggesen's Gold'**. The dwarf, semi-evergreen **L. pileata** is used for ground cover; the deciduous **L. tatarica** (10 ft, pink flowers in June) and **L. fragrantissima** (7 ft, creamy flowers in January) are for the border.

SITE & SOIL: Add peat and fertilizer to the soil before planting. Choose a sunny spot.

PRUNING: Clip hedges in May and August. With flowering shrubs cut back shoots with faded blooms.

PROPAGATION: Layer shoots or plant cuttings outdoors in autumn.

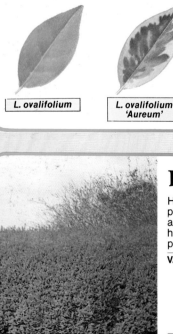

Lonicera nitida

L. tatarica

L. pileata

LUPINUS   Tree Lupin
Ⓔ

Lupins are a familiar sight but the Tree Lupin is a rarity. This soft-stemmed shrub reaches about 5 ft high, bearing colourful flowering spikes which are shorter than those produced by its more popular relative. It grows quickly and thrives best in sandy or stony soil. Dead-head faded blooms and do not expect it to live for more than a few years.

VARIETIES: L. arboreus is an evergreen branching shrub, its fragrant, pale yellow flowers opening in June and July. The advantage of growing the original species is that it can be easily propagated from seed, but there are several attractive named varieties — **'Snow Queen'** (white), **'Golden Spire'** (deep yellow) and **'Mauve Queen'** (pale purple).

SITE & SOIL: Choose a sheltered, sunny spot. It needs a free-draining site — do not plant in heavy or rich soil.

PRUNING: Shorten the stems in March or April.

PROPAGATION: Raise L. arboreus from seed — plant cuttings of named varieties in a cold frame in summer.

Lupinus arboreus

L. arboreus

MAGNOLIA   Magnolia
Ⓓ or Ⓔ

Everybody admires Magnolias but not everybody grows them — these shrubs and trees are thought by many to be difficult. This is not really true, but you do have to take care at planting time. April is the best month, and you should pick a spot which is sheltered from cold winds. Add plenty of peat to the soil and don't plant too deeply. Water the new bush copiously if there is a drought and never dig or plant close to the stem. Each spring apply a layer of peat or well-rotted compost around the shrub.

VARIETIES: The most impressive Magnolia is really a tree — **M. grandiflora**. Although slow-growing it will reach 20 ft or more in time, although it is more usually grown as an evergreen wall shrub. It bears fragrant, creamy white blossoms, sometimes as large as dinner-plates, between July and September. Choose the variety **M. grandiflora 'Exmouth'**. The most popular Magnolia is **M. soulangiana**, a spreading bush which can reach 10 ft high. The flowers appear in April before the leaves — goblet-shaped, white within and purple-tinged at the base. **'Lennei'** and **'Alexandrina'** are excellent varieties — for something different choose **'Rubra'** (rosy red) or **'Alba Superba'** (white). Where space is limited, the Star Magnolia (**M. stellata**) is the one to pick. It grows to only 4 or 5 ft, but each March or April it is covered with fragrant, creamy white flowers.

SITE & SOIL: Many Magnolias do not like chalk, but any reasonable garden soil will do if it is thoroughly cultivated and enriched with humus. Pick a site which is in full sun or light shade.

PRUNING: Not necessary. Remove dead wood after flowering. Unwanted branches can be cut off at the same time, but don't overdo it.

PROPAGATION: Layer branches in early summer. Taking cuttings in summer is difficult — a heated propagator is necessary.

Magnolia soulangiana

M. soulangiana

M. soulangiana 'Rubra'

M. grandiflora

M. soulangiana 'Alba Superba'

M. stellata

Magnolia stellata

MAHONIA

Mahonia
(E)

This evergreen shrub suffers from only one major drawback — it seems to occur in everybody's garden. Its year-round beauty and usefulness has made this inevitable — attractive foliage with holly-like leaflets, fragrant yellow flowers early in the year and a crop of blue-black berries later in the season. The popular types grow in shade and are often used as ground cover under trees. There are also more unusual varieties — bold plants which make excellent specimen bushes. In the catalogues you may find the Mahonias listed as Berberis.

VARIETIES: The low-growing, spreading form of Mahonia you will find at the garden shop or nursery is **M. aquifolium** (Oregon Grape). It is used as ground cover or as a low hedge, its leaves turning bronze or purple in winter. The flowers are borne in dense clusters in March and April. The other popular Mahonia, **M. japonica**, is taller and more erect, reaching 6 ft or more. The flowering spikes are highly decorative, radiating from the stem like the spokes of a wheel. They appear from December onwards, the yellow flowers possessing a strong lily-of-the-valley fragrance. A rather similar species is **M. bealei**, with erect flowering spikes giving a shuttlecock effect. **M. 'Undulata'** makes a good specimen bush, but perhaps best of all is **M. 'Charity'** — shapely and erect, 6 ft tall, with long spikes of flowers from Christmas to early spring.

SITE & SOIL: Any reasonable garden soil will do, including chalk. Thrives in shady situations — will grow under trees.

PRUNING: Not necessary. Cut back unwanted growth in April.

PROPAGATION: Remove and plant up rooted suckers of M. aquifolium. For other varieties plant cuttings in a cold frame in summer.

Mahonia aquifolium

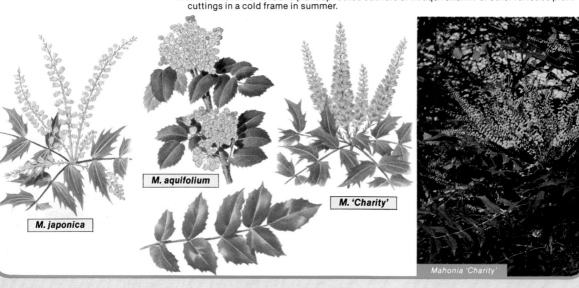

M. aquifolium

M. japonica

M. 'Charity'

Mahonia 'Charity'

MYRTUS

Myrtle
(E)

The Common Myrtle (M. communis) has been grown in Britain for over 400 years, but you will have to search round the garden centres to find one. The problem is lack of hardiness — it is only reliable in the milder parts of the country. It is a sweet-smelling bush, the fragrance arising from both the flowers and from the leaves when they are crushed.

VARIETIES: **M. communis** is the hardiest species and the only one you are likely to find. It grows about 10 ft tall, bearing an abundant display of small, white flowers in July and August. Black berries appear later. The leaves are dark green and glossy. The compact **M. communis tarentina** (3 ft) has narrower leaves and white berries.

SITE & SOIL: Any reasonable garden soil will do if it is well-drained. The site must be sheltered and sunny.

PRUNING: Not necessary. Cut back unwanted growth in late spring.

PROPAGATION: Sow seed under glass in spring. Summer cuttings root with difficulty — bottom heat is needed.

Myrtus communis

M. communis

NEILLIA   Neillia

An uncommon relative of the common-or-garden Spiraea. It is a graceful shrub which steadily spreads to form a thicket. Its slender stems carry distinctive foliage — 3-lobed leaves with toothed edges and prominent veins. In May and June the tubular flowers appear in long sprays. Neillia is very accommodating and easy to grow.

VARIETIES: N. longiracemosa (other name **N. thibetica**) originally came from China and is the only species grown in our gardens. The downy stems can reach 6 ft or more, and in summer they bear the flowering sprays at their tips. Each spray is several inches long, bowed down by the 20 to 30 rosy pink flowers it carries.

SITE & SOIL: Any reasonable garden soil will do. It thrives in both sun and partial shade.

PRUNING: After flowering cut back old branches which have borne flowers. Shorten young shoots.

PROPAGATION: Remove rooted pieces from the parent bush, or plant cuttings in a cold frame in summer.

N. longiracemosa

Neillia longiracemosa

OLEARIA   Daisy Bush

The clusters of daisy-like flowers may cover the whole bush, but only if you have been able to meet its specific requirements. It loves full sun and hates frost, and it seems to relish the strong winds and salt-laden air which occur in seaside gardens. The taller types of this New Zealand shrub can be used for hedging in coastal districts. The underside of the leaves is silvery or grey.

VARIETIES: The only type of Daisy Bush you are likely to find at your garden centre is **O. haastii**, and this is the only one that can be considered hardy. It grows 6 ft tall and flowers in July and August. Smaller in height and earlier flowering is **O. scilloniensis** (4 ft, May) and the giant is the holly-leaved **O. macrodonta** (8 ft, June).

SITE & SOIL: Any reasonable, well-drained soil will do. Grows in partial shade but full sun is best.

PRUNING: Dead-head the faded blooms with shears after flowering. Remove dead branches in April.

PROPAGATION: Plant cuttings in a cold frame in summer.

O. scilloniensis

Olearia haastii

OSMANTHUS   Osmanthus

Osmanthus may never be the star of your shrub border but it provides an excellent foil for planting between the more showy specimens. The bush is neat and well-rounded, the leaves are plentiful, dark and evergreen, and the white flowers have the beautiful fragrance of jasmine. It needs protection from east and north winds.

VARIETIES: O. delavayi is the most popular species, growing about 6 ft tall and flowering in April. The tubular flowers are small but plentiful. **O. burkwoodii**, also known as **Osmarea burkwoodii**, is rather similar but the leaves are glossy. Quite different is **O. heterophyllus** — this shrub can be mistaken for holly and the flowers appear in September.

SITE & SOIL: Any reasonable garden soil will do provided it is well-drained. Thrives in both sun and partial shade.

PRUNING: Remove dead branches in spring or summer.

PROPAGATION: Layer branches in autumn or plant cuttings in a cold frame in summer.

O. burkwoodii

O. heterophyllus

Osmanthus delavayi

PACHYSANDRA

Pachysandra
(E)

Most textbooks on shrubs fail to mention Pachysandra and your local garden centre will probably not stock it, yet it is an excellent ground cover. The wide-spreading evergreen growth reaches no more than a few inches high, and it is able to thrive in the dense shade under trees. Unfortunately, the flowers which appear in early spring are small and insignificant. A good choice, but not for chalky soil.

VARIETIES: Specialist nurseries can offer you **P. procumbens** but the only one you are likely to find is the Japanese Spurge (**P. terminalis**). The diamond-shaped leaves are borne in clusters at the top of the short stems which grow no more than 8 in. high. More attractive is **P. terminalis 'Variegata'** with its cream-edged leaves.

SITE & SOIL: Succeeds best in moist soil. Does not like sun — partial or full shade is essential.

PRUNING: Not required. Trim stems in summer if growth becomes too invasive.

PROPAGATION: Divide clumps in autumn or plant cuttings in a cold frame in summer.

P. terminalis 'Variegata'

PAEONIA

Tree Peony
(D)

Peonies are much more familiar in the herbaceous border than in the shrubbery, but there are several spectacular Tree Peonies. The foliage may be highly ornamental but the flowers are really eye-catching — large bowls or balls of papery petals in May. Pick a single or semi-double variety — the blooms of double varieties may need individual staking.

VARIETIES: Tree Peonies are rather slow-growing, eventually reaching 5 or 6 ft. For large white, pink or red flowers, 6 in. or more in diameter, choose one of the **P. suffruticosa** hybrids — the Moutan Peonies. For a similar flower in yellow or orange pick a **P. lemoinei** hybrid. The species have rather smaller flowers — the red **P. delavayi** and yellow **P. lutea ludlowii** are popular.

SITE & SOIL: The soil should be fertile and well-cultivated. Choose a sunny and sheltered site.

PRUNING: Remove dead and damaged branches in April.

PROPAGATION: The species can be raised from seed sown in the spring — propagate others by layering branches in early spring.

P. suffruticosa

P. delavayi

PERNETTYA

Prickly Heath
(E)

One of the finest of all berrying shrubs, with large, porcelain-like fruits throughout the winter. It grows about waist-high and spreads steadily to form an extensive thicket. The small, glossy leaves are stiff and prickly, and the creamy white flowers which appear in May are followed by white, pink, red or purple berries if a male plant is grown nearby.

VARIETIES: The species grown in Britain is **P. mucronata**. It rarely exceeds 3 ft in height and the wiry stems bear masses of small, bell-like blooms. The berried stems are excellent for indoor decoration. If Pernettya is not in your garden — buy some. There are several varieties with different coloured berries — **'Alba'** (white), **'Bell's Seedling'** (dark red) and **'Sea Shell'** (pink).

SITE & SOIL: Acid soil is essential — add peat at planting time. Grows in sun or partial shade.

PRUNING: Trim back in summer if growth gets out of hand.

PROPAGATION: Sow seed in spring or remove rooted pieces from the parent bush in autumn.

P. mucronata

P. mucronata 'Alba'

PEROVSKIA Russian Sage
ⓓ

From a distance this shrub looks like an oversized lavender bush. The blue flowers are borne in long spikes, rising above the stiff, erect stems and grey leaves. On closer inspection it is quite different — the leaves are toothed or finely cut and the crushed foliage has the fragrance of sage. A plant for the shrub or herbaceous border.

VARIETIES: Only one variety is popular — **P. atriplicifolia**. The stems grow about 4 ft tall and the small, lavender blue flowers appear in August and September. Choose the variety **P. atriplicifolia 'Blue Spire'** — the flower spikes are larger and a beautiful shade of deep blue. Its leaves are lobed and deeply cut.

SITE & SOIL: Any reasonable garden soil will do if it is well-drained. A sunny spot is essential.

PRUNING: In spring cut back the stems to about 9 in. above the ground.

PROPAGATION: Sow seed under glass in spring or plant cuttings in a cold frame in summer.

P. atriplicifolia

Perovskia atriplicifolia

PHILADELPHUS Mock Orange
ⓓ

Mock Orange is a basic component of most shrub collections but it is often wrongly called Syringa. The white flowers appear in profusion in June and July, and the orange-blossom fragrance can be detected some distance away on a warm summer evening. The average height is about 6 ft, but there are both dwarf and much taller varieties available. One of the great virtues of this shrub is its ability to grow almost anywhere — in poor soil, industrial smoke and salt-laden air. For a good display, however, give it a sunny spot and learn how to prune it properly.

VARIETIES: The best and most popular of the taller varieties is **P. 'Virginal'**. If left lightly pruned this upright bush will reach 10 ft or more, bearing large clusters of pendent double flowers in summer. Equally tall but rather more spreading is the old favourite **P. coronarius** with flat single flowers which are renowned for their scent. In the medium-sized range there are several excellent varieties. You can choose from the yellow-leaved **P. coronarius 'Aureus'** and the hybrids with flowers flushed purple at the base — **P. 'Beauclerk'** and **P. 'Belle Etoile'**. One of the smaller Mock Oranges is the purple-blotched variety **P. 'Sybille'** but the daintiest of all is **P. microphyllus** which grows no more than 2 or 3 ft high. The leaves are very small and the flowers very fragrant — ideal for the back of the rockery.

SITE & SOIL: Any reasonable garden soil will do; it can be acid or chalky. Pick a sunny or lightly shaded site.

PRUNING: Immediately after flowering cut out some of the old stems which have bloomed. Make sure that the bush is not overcrowded — remove a few old branches if necessary.

PROPAGATION: Easy — plant cuttings in a cold frame in summer or outdoors in autumn.

Philadelphus 'Virginal'

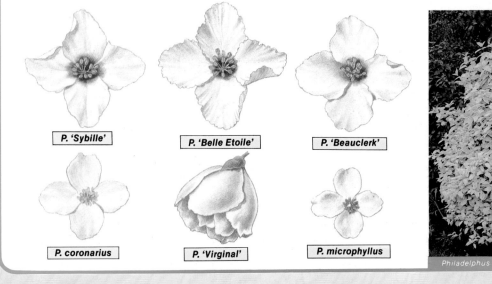

P. 'Sybille'

P. 'Belle Etoile'

P. 'Beauclerk'

P. coronarius

P. 'Virginal'

P. microphyllus

Philadelphus coronarius 'Aureus'

PHLOMIS

Jerusalem Sage
Ⓔ

Phlomis is an uncommon evergreen which is grown for its distinctive foliage as well as its flowers. The grey-green leaves are covered with fur and in June the hooded flowers appear, a ring of attractive yellow blooms around the stem. Frost can be a problem — plant Phlomis in a sheltered sunny spot away from cold northerly winds.

VARIETIES: P. fruticosa is the hardiest species and the only one you are likely to find. It is small, rarely reaching 3 ft, but it is wide-spreading. The deep yellow flowers are borne at the ends of the branches and the grey foliage provides an attractive contrast to the shiny green leaves which abound in the average border.

SITE & SOIL: Any well-drained soil will do, but choose a spot which is protected from cold winds.

PRUNING: Cut back unwanted and frost-damaged branches in spring.

PROPAGATION: Sow seed under glass in spring or plant cuttings in a cold frame in summer.

P. fruticosa

PHOTINIA

Photinia
Ⓔ

A surprising shrub, because you will find it in many garden centres but in only a few textbooks. The reason is that until quite recently Photinia had little to offer and then Photinia fraseri appeared in 1955. This hybrid bears new growth in spring which is fiery red, like Pieris, but with the added advantage that it grows well in neutral and chalky soils. Frost damage can be a problem.

VARIETIES: The best variety to choose is **P. fraseri 'Red Robin'**. The young foliage is bright red in spring, changing to deep green as it matures. In time this shrub reaches 8 ft — an even taller-growing variety is **P. fraseri 'Robusta'**. This shrub bears large laurel-like leaves and the new growth is coppery red.

SITE & SOIL: Any reasonable garden soil will do, but avoid heavy clay. A sunny site is necessary.

PRUNING: Cut back new growth once it has lost its colour — new red growth will appear.

PROPAGATION: Plant cuttings in a cold frame in summer.

P. fraseri 'Robusta'

PIERIS Andromeda
Ⓔ

A splendid shrub which will succeed in gardens where rhododendrons thrive. The evergreen foliage is dense and in April or May the long sprays of blooms which look like lily-of-the-valley appear. However, the real glory of the most popular varieties is the bright red new growth in the spring. This slow-growing shrub needs little attention, but mulch with peat every spring.

VARIETIES: The best flower displays are provided by **P. japonica** (10 ft) and **P. taiwanensis** (6 ft), but it is better to choose one of the named varieties of **P. formosa forrestii**. **'Wakehurst'** is often recommended, but **P. 'Forest Flame'** is perhaps the best. There is also a white-and-green leaved variety — **P. japonica 'Variegata'**.

SITE & SOIL: Acid soil is essential — add peat at planting time. Shade from morning sun is beneficial.

PRUNING: Not necessary — remove dead flowers in May.

PROPAGATION: Sow seed under glass in spring or layer branches in early summer.

Pieris 'Forest Flame'

P. formosa forrestii

P. japonica

PITTOSPORUM Pittosporum
Ⓔ

This evergreen shrub is not particularly showy and will die in many gardens in a severe winter. It is not generally a good choice, but it is worth considering in two situations. If you are a keen flower arranger then P tenuifolium provides excellent foliage material and if you live on the southern coast then it will provide an attractive hedge.

VARIETIES: The most popular is **P. tenuifolium**. This slow-growing shrub will eventually reach 12 ft, its black twigs clothed with wavy-edged, pale green leaves. Textbooks talk of maroon flowers in spring but few are produced. For a flowering Pittosporum choose **P. tobira** — creamy, fragrant blooms in May and June.

SITE & SOIL: A warm and sheltered spot is essential — salt-laden air is tolerated. Good drainage is necessary.

PRUNING: Not essential — remove unwanted or damaged branches in spring.

PROPAGATION: Sow seed under glass in spring or plant cuttings in a cold frame in summer.

Pittosporum tenuifolium

P. tenuifolium

P. tobira

POTENTILLA Shrubby Cinquefoil
Ⓓ

There is nothing really spectacular about Potentilla. The flowers, though plentiful, are not large and the foliage is not particularly eye-catching. Nevertheless, this bush is indispensable in any shrub border, because it is in flower from May until September. Varieties are available in many colours and it will grow anywhere.

VARIETIES: All the garden forms are varieties of **P. fruticosa**. From the following list, choose the height and flower colour you want: **'Abbotswood'** (2½ ft, white), **'Elizabeth'** (3 ft, yellow), **'Jackman's Variety'** (4 ft, yellow), **'Katherine Dykes'** (5 ft, yellow), **mandschurica** (1 ft, white), **'Red Ace'** (2 ft, vermilion) and **'Tangerine'** (2 ft, coppery yellow).

SITE & SOIL: Any garden soil will do, but it should be well-drained. It will thrive in sun or partial shade.

PRUNING: Remove old and weak branches in March.

PROPAGATION: Easy — plant up self-sown seedlings or plant cuttings in a cold frame in summer.

Potentilla fruticosa

P. fruticosa mandschurica

P. fruticosa 'Tangerine'

P. fruticosa 'Jackman's Variety'

Prunus laurocerasus

PRUNUS

Prunus
Ⓓ or Ⓔ

The real glory of the Prunus group can be seen in the Tree section, but there are several shrubby forms which serve a useful purpose in the garden. They are mainly seen as hedges — the evergreen Laurels are the most popular but red-leaved deciduous varieties are also available for making high or low hedges. Not all the Prunus shrubs are grown for their foliage — there are flowering plums, almonds, peaches, cherries and apricots. All are reasonably easy to grow.

VARIETIES: There are two widely-used species of evergreen Prunus. **P. laurocerasus** (Cherry Laurel) is seen everywhere — large shiny leaves and candles of small white flowers in April. Left unpruned it will reach 15 ft — for ground cover grow the dwarf **P. laurocerasus 'Otto Luyken'**. More tolerant of chalk and smaller-leaved than the Cherry Laurel is **P. lusitanica**, the Portugal Laurel. Recognise it by its red leaf-stalks. A number of excellent deciduous hedging varieties are available. For a dwarf hedge, grow the coppery-leaved **P. cistena** — for a taller hedge, there is **P. cerasifera 'Pissardii'** with red foliage which turns almost black with age. If you are looking for beauty of flower rather than leaf then there is **P. tenella 'Fire Hill'** (4 ft, rosy red flowers in April), **P. triloba 'Multiplex'** (6 ft, double pink flowers in May) and **P. incisa** (9 ft, white or pale pink flowers in March).

SITE & SOIL: Any reasonable garden soil will do, but the site should be well-drained. Sun (deciduous types) or partial shade (evergreens).

PRUNING: Evergreens should be trimmed to shape in late spring — remove dead wood. Look up Prunus in the Tree Section for details of pruning the deciduous types.

PROPAGATION: Plant cuttings of evergreen varieties in a cold frame in summer. Deciduous types are generally propagated by grafting.

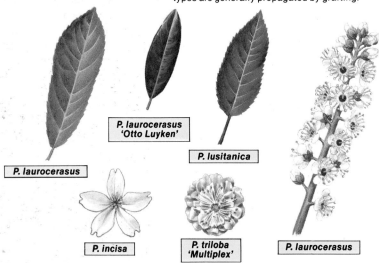

P. laurocerasus

P. laurocerasus 'Otto Luyken'

P. lusitanica

P. incisa

P. triloba 'Multiplex'

P. laurocerasus

Prunus cerasifera 'Pissardii'

Pyracantha coccinea 'Lalandei'

PYRACANTHA

Firethorn
Ⓔ

Clusters of small, white flowers appear in June, but this shrub is grown primarily for its massed display of berries in the autumn. In the open it forms a large bush, about 12 ft high, but it is more often grown as a wall shrub. It is rather similar to Cotoneaster, but the leaves are toothed and the stems are spiny. Plant container-grown specimens.

VARIETIES: The most popular Firethorn is **P. coccinea 'Lalandei'**, with branches covered in autumn by orange-red berries. **P. 'Orange Glow'** is more disease- and bird-resistant. For red berries choose **P. atalantioides** or **P. 'Watereri'**; for yellow berries there are **P. atalantioides 'Aurea'** and **P. rogersiana 'Flava'**.

SITE & SOIL: Any reasonable garden soil will do, including chalk. Thrives in sun and partial shade.

PRUNING: Immediately after flowering cut back unwanted shoots — take care not to spoil the berry display to come. Wear stout gloves!

PROPAGATION: Sow seed under glass in spring or plant cuttings in a cold frame in summer.

P. atalantioides

P. atalantioides 'Aurea'

RHODODENDRON

Rhododendron
Ⓔ

Thousands of different species and hybrids bear the latin name Rhododendron. It is usual to consider the Azaleas as a distinct group and they are described below. The average garden Rhododendron is about 6 ft tall and blooms in May, but there are many variations — heights range from 1 ft to 20 ft and the flowering time may be as early as February or as late as August. All the colours of the flowering plant kingdom are there, apart from true blue, but the foliage is always the same — evergreen and lance-shaped. Rhododendrons are shallow-rooted — mulch with peat each autumn and water copiously in prolonged dry weather.

VARIETIES: The Hardy Hybrids are the ones which are usually planted. Reds include **'Britannia'**, **'Cynthia'**, **'Doncaster'**, **'John Walter'** and **'Lord Roberts'**. The most popular pink variety is the large-flowered **'Pink Pearl'** which unfortunately grows too tall in many gardens — more compact pinks include **'Mrs G.W. Leak'** and **'Dr Tjebes'**. There is a bewildering array of purple varieties — the favourite is the late-flowering **'Purple Splendour'**. A good white variety is **'Sappho'**. More and more garden centres are offering dwarf Rhododendrons — **'Blue Tit'** (lavender), **'Bow Bells'** (pink) and **'Elizabeth'** (red) grow only 2–3 ft high. For something out of the ordinary look at the Rhododendron species — there is the prostrate **R. repens** (red), the tree-like **R. arboreum** (various colours) and the flat-flowered **R. quinquefolium** (white).

SITE & SOIL: Acid soil is essential. In limey soil the leaves turn yellow — water with Sequestrene if this happens. Add peat at planting time. Grow in partial shade.

PRUNING: Break off dead flowers with finger and thumb — make sure that buds at the base are not damaged. If stems have become leggy and bare, cut back hard in April.

PROPAGATION: The most reliable method is layering branches in summer, but it is usually better to buy new plants.

Rhododendron 'Mrs G. W. Leak'

R. 'Sappho'

R. 'Purple Splendour'

R. 'Pink Pearl'

R. 'Elizabeth'

R. 'Britannia'

Rhododendron 'Lavender Girl'

RHODODENDRON

Azalea
Ⓓ or Ⓔ

Azaleas are usually daintier than garden Rhododendrons but not always — there are 10 ft Azaleas and 1 ft Rhododendrons. The Evergreen or Japanese Azaleas are low and spreading, producing sheets of flowers in May. The Deciduous Azaleas are taller, reaching 6 ft or more. The flowers are followed by rich autumn foliage colours.

VARIETIES: The Evergreen Azaleas include the Kurume and Vuyk hybrids. Choose by colour — blue (**'Blue Danube'**), red (**'Addy Wery'**), orange (**'Orange Beauty'**), pink (**'Rosebud'**) or white (**'Palestrina'**). The Deciduous Azaleas include the Mollis, Exbury and Knap Hill hybrids. Favourite types include **'Koster's Brilliant Red'** (red), **'Cecile'** (pink), **'Lemonara'** (yellow) and **'Persil'** (white).

SITE & SOIL: Acid soil is essential — see Rhododendron above. Choose a sheltered site in partial shade.

PRUNING: Break off dead flowers with finger and thumb.

PROPAGATION: Sow seed under glass in spring or layer branches in summer.

Rhododendron 'Orange Beauty'

R. 'Cecile'

R. 'Palestrina'

RHUS
Sumach
<small>Ⓓ</small>

The Sumachs are grown for their brilliant autumn hues, the large palm-like leaves turning orange, red or purple. The flowers are insignificant, but the female plants bear 6 in. spikes of small crimson fruits in late summer. The shrub will grow anywhere but it should be pruned regularly or it will soon become leggy and bare.

VARIETIES: The Sumach you see everywhere is **R. typhina**, the Stag's Horn Sumach. Its branches will grow 12 ft or more if left unpruned and its prolific suckering habit makes it unsuitable for planting in the lawn. Try **R. typhina 'Laciniata'** with deeply cut, fern-like leaves. A smaller species is **R. glabra**, which also has a fern-leaf form (**R. glabra 'Laciniata'**).

SITE & SOIL: Any reasonable garden soil will do. Does best in a sunny site.

PRUNING: In February cut stems to 1 ft above the ground.

PROPAGATION: Remove and plant up rooted suckers in autumn or layer branches in spring.

R. typhina

RIBES
Ornamental Currant
<small>Ⓓ or ⓈⒺ</small>

The most popular Ribes by far is the Flowering Currant, its pink flowers in March or April providing early season colour in gardens everywhere. It is usually grown as a specimen plant but can be used for hedging. Easy, quick-growing but common-place — there are much less common varieties of Ribes from which you can choose.

VARIETIES: The Flowering Currants are varieties of **R. sanguineum**. The species grows about 7 ft high and produces insipid pink flowers — pick instead a named variety such as **'Pulborough Scarlet'** or **'King Edward VII'** (deep crimson). **R. odoratum** bears fragrant yellow flowers in April and the semi-evergreen **R. speciosum** carries fuchsia-like flowers in May.

SITE & SOIL: Any reasonable garden soil will do. It thrives in sun or partial shade.

PRUNING: After flowering, prune back shoots which have flowered. Cut out old, unproductive wood.

PROPAGATION: Plant 8 in. cuttings outdoors in autumn.

R. sanguineum

R. odoratum

ROMNEYA
Tree Poppy
<small>Ⓓ</small>

It is a pity that the Tree Poppy is not better known. The stems may be killed by frost in a severe winter but new growth is rapidly produced. At the tips of the stems white, poppy-like flowers the size of saucers appear from July until October. The decorative foliage is bluish grey. Romneya may be slow to establish after transplanting.

VARIETIES: The basic species of Tree Poppy is **R. coulteri**. The upright stems grow about 5 or 6 ft high and the fragrant blooms bear prominent golden stamens. In specialist nurseries you may find its close relative **R. trichocalyx** but there is very little difference between them. **R. hybrida** is a cross between the two species.

SITE & SOIL: Full sun and some shelter are necessary. Do not plant in cold, heavy soil.

PRUNING: In March cut stems to a few inches above the ground.

PROPAGATION: Remove and plant up rooted suckers in spring.

R. coulteri

Rosa 'Canary Bird'

ROSA   Rose Ⓓ

The Rose is both our national and favourite flower, but the Shrub Rose is certainly not a favourite in most gardens. Yet many of these Shrub Roses will thrive in soil and conditions which would not support a Hybrid Tea, and both pruning and upkeep are simple. The problem is that they are misunderstood — they are not "old-fashioned" (there are many modern hybrids) and they are not all giants (there are dainty 2 ft varieties). There is a Shrub Rose which is suitable for nearly every garden, and the choice is bewildering. For a comprehensive list and advice on this invaluable group of shrubs, see The Rose Expert (pages 61–72).

Shrubs for Flower Arranging

Buxus	Elaeagnus	Lonicera	Senecio
Chaenomeles	Euonymus	Mahonia	Skimmia
Chimonanthus	Fatsia	Philadelphus	Spartium
Choisya	Forsythia	Photinia	Spiraea
Cornus	Hamamelis	Pieris	Symphoricarpos
Cotinus	Kerria	Pittosporum	Syringa
Cotoneaster	Kolkwitzia	Pyracantha	Viburnum
Danae	Lavandula	Rhododendron — Azaleas	Vinca
Deutzia	Ligustrum	Ribes	Weigela

Rosmarinus officinalis

ROSMARINUS   Rosemary Ⓔ

The long, narrow leaves and pale blue flowers of Rosemary have been a familiar sight in British gardens for hundreds of years. Both fresh and dried leaves are used for flavouring meat and poultry. This dense, evergreen bush grows about 5 ft tall and it makes an attractive hedge. Grow it, but not if your soil is heavy and wet.

VARIETIES: There is one species — **R. officinalis**. The leaves are grey-green above, powdery white below, and the small flowers appear in clusters along the stems in April or May. Choose a named variety — **'Albus'** has white flowers and **'Miss Jessop's Upright'** is the popular blue one. In the rock garden you can grow the mat-like **prostratus**.

SITE & SOIL: The soil must be well-drained and not clayey. Full sun is necessary.

PRUNING: As soon as flowering is over, trim the bush lightly with garden shears.

PROPAGATION: Plant cuttings in a cold frame in summer.

R. officinalis

Rubus cockburnianus

RUBUS   Ornamental Bramble Ⓓ

Ornamental Brambles, like Dogwoods, are grown either for their colourful stems in winter or for the floral display which appears later in the year. It all depends on the variety you buy, so choose with care. Most of them have prickly stems and will grow almost anywhere. The right way to prune depends on the type grown — see below.

VARIETIES: The favourite decorative-stemmed type is **R. cockburnianus** — the Whitewashed Bramble. Arching stems, 8 to 10 ft long, are covered with a pure white bloom. The best of the flowering types is **R. tridel 'Benenden'** — tall, thornless stems bear masses of white, saucer-like flowers in May. The dwarf **R. illecebrosus** (Strawberry-Raspberry) is grown for its fruit.

SITE & SOIL: Any reasonable garden soil will do, in sun or partial shade.

PRUNING: With flowering types, cut back some older wood in autumn. Decorative stem types should have all old branches removed in early spring.

PROPAGATION: Plant cuttings in a cold frame in summer.

R. cockburnianus

R. tridel 'Benenden'

SALIX
Willow
Ⓓ

The word 'Willow' immediately suggests the graceful Weeping Willow or the silvery catkins of the Pussy Willow. You will find both of them in the Tree section of this book, but there are also several interesting Shrubby Willows. There are low-growing varieties for the rockery as well as bold, coloured-bark types for the larger garden.

VARIETIES: For coloured stems, grow **S. alba 'Chermesina'** (bright scarlet) or **'Vitellina'** (golden yellow) — cut back severely every second year. The dwarf varieties are useful but not often seen — **S. lanata** (Woolly Willow), 3ft high and spreading, has silvery green leaves and erect catkins. **S. 'Wehrhahnii'** (4 ft) bears icicle-like catkins.

SITE & SOIL: Does not like dry conditions — any loamy garden soil will do. Thrives in sun or partial shade.

PRUNING: Little or no pruning for dwarf types, but hard pruning is necessary for coloured-bark varieties.

PROPAGATION: Easy — plant cuttings outdoors in autumn.

S. alba 'Chermesina'

S. lanata

SAMBUCUS
Elder
Ⓓ

Everyone knows the green-leaved Elder, especially when the flat heads of tiny white flowers and the black berries appear above the large, divided leaves. It will grow anywhere and may reach 20 ft, but for garden use there are much better varieties. Their foliage is yellow or variegated and the leaves may be finely cut. June is the normal flowering period.

VARIETIES: The Common Elder is **S. nigra** — buy the variety **'Aurea'** for its golden foliage or choose the purple-leaved **'Purpurea'**. Even more attractive is **S. racemosa 'Plumosa Aurea'** — the feathery leaves are bright yellow and this 6 ft shrub bears red berries after the white flowers. Another fine Elder is **S. canadensis 'Aurea'**.

SITE & SOIL: Any garden soil will do, including clay. Yellow-leaved varieties need a sunny spot.

PRUNING: Prune hard in spring to ensure plenty of new growth.

PROPAGATION: Plant cuttings outdoors in autumn.

S. racemosa 'Plumosa Aurea'

SANTOLINA
Lavender Cotton
Ⓔ

If your soil is well-drained and there is an unshaded site available, Santolina will provide a splash of colour. You can use it as a specimen plant at the front of the border or as a low hedge, and the colour of this compact, mound-forming bush comes from the silvery grey foliage as well as from the yellow, button-like flowers which appear in summer.

VARIETIES: The popular variety is **S. chamaecyparissus**. It grows about 2 ft high and is densely covered with narrow, finely divided leaves which are strongly aromatic. The flowers appear from June to August. A smaller variety is **S. chamaecyparissus 'Nana'** (1ft) — a larger one is **S. neapolitana** (3 ft). The green-leaved variety is **S. virens**.

SITE & SOIL: Any reasonable soil will do, but it must be well-drained. A sunny spot is essential.

PRUNING: Trim after flowering — every 2 or 3 years cut back hard in April.

PROPAGATION: Plant 3 in. cuttings in a cold frame in summer.

S. chamaecyparissus

S. virens

SENECIO   Senecio
Ⓔ

The bright yellow, daisy-like flowers open in June, but most gardeners who grow this low and spreading shrub regard the distinctive foliage as its main charm. The leathery oval leaves are covered with silvery down when young. Senecio thrives in wind and salt spray but it is not completely hardy — choose a sheltered, sunny site.

VARIETIES: You will find the Common Senecio labelled either as **S. greyi** or **S. laxifolius** in the garden centre. There are small differences between these two species, but don't worry about them. The bush grows about 3 ft high and is quite hardy. Most other species, such as the white-flowered **S. hectori** and the pale yellow **S. reinoldii**, will not stand much frost.

SITE & SOIL: Any reasonable, well-drained soil will do — chalk is not a problem. Full sun is necessary.

PRUNING: Remove dead and straggly shoots in spring.

PROPAGATION: Plant 4 in. cuttings in a cold frame in summer.

Senecio greyi

S. greyi

SKIMMIA   Skimmia
Ⓔ

When you see a photograph of Skimmia there are red berries glistening above the oval leaves, and these fruits persist all winter. If you choose the most popular variety, however, you must grow male plants as well as females. The shrub is neat and compact, about 3 ft high, and the clusters of tiny white flowers appear in March or April.

VARIETIES: S. japonica is the common species. The variety **'Foremanii'** (female) is renowned for its large bunches of berries, **'Rubella'** (male) for its red flower buds and **'Fragrans'** (male) for its floral fragrance. If you want to grow only one shrub (Skimmia makes an excellent tub plant) choose a bisexual variety — there is **S. reevesiana**, also known as **S. fortunei**.

SITE & SOIL: Acid soil is essential. It succeeds best in partial shade.

PRUNING: Little or no pruning is required — merely remove damaged branches in spring.

PROPAGATION: Plant cuttings in a cold frame in summer.

Skimmia japonica

S. japonica

SPARTIUM   Spanish Broom
Ⓓ

A properly tended Spanish Broom is a beautiful sight in summer. A fountain of green and rush-like stems are clothed with yellow, pea-like flowers which are both large and fragrant. The more usual sight is different — a gaunt and leggy bush with few flowers. The cause is failure to prune properly or planting in a shady, wet site.

VARIETIES: S. junceum is the only species. The leaves are small and infrequent — it is the framework of green stems which provides the evergreen effect in winter. These stems may reach 9 ft or more, but they should be kept in check by regular pruning. There is a long flowering season, from early July until September, and Spartium makes an excellent cut flower.

SITE & SOIL: The soil should not be heavy and it must be well-drained. Full sun is necessary.

PRUNING: Dead-head faded blooms. In March cut back the previous season's growth to about 2 in. from the old wood.

PROPAGATION: Plant cuttings in a cold frame in summer.

Spartium junceum

S. junceum

SPIRAEA

Spiraea
Ⓓ

The Spiraeas are a popular group of quick-growing shrubs with a well-deserved reputation for easy cultivation and abundant flower production. The spring-flowering section bears tiny, white flowers which are massed in clusters on arching stems. The summer-flowering types are usually pink or red, the small blooms appearing in flat heads, round domes or upright spikes. There should be no problems, but some of the large suckering varieties can quickly form dense thickets. Another point to remember is that annual pruning is essential.

VARIETIES: The favourite spring-flowering Spiraea is the Bridal Wreath (**S. arguta**). It grows about 6 ft high with arching sprays of white flowers in April and May. The flowers of **S. thunbergii** appear earlier and the leaves remain on the bush nearly all year round. **S. prunifolia 'Plena'** bears small double flowers in May, the foliage turning bright red in autumn. The tall spring bloomer is **S. vanhouttei** (8 ft × 6 ft) which can be used for hedging. The summer-flowering section is dominated by **S. bumalda 'Anthony Waterer'** — the 2 ft bush with its flat heads of carmine-pink flowers is a common sight from July to September. Try its close relative **'Goldflame'** for a change — the young foliage is orange and yellow. Dwarf pink-flowering types are available for the rockery — choose **S. japonica 'Alpina'** or **'Bullata'**. The showiest in this summer-flowering section is **S. billardii 'Triumphans'** (8 ft, purple-rose spikes).

SITE & SOIL: Succeeds best in reasonably fertile soil. It will thrive in sun or partial shade.

PRUNING: Spring-flowering varieties should have old and weak stems removed when blooms have faded. Summer-flowering types should be pruned more severely — in early spring cut back the stems to a few inches above the ground.

PROPAGATION: Plant cuttings in a cold frame in summer or outdoors in autumn.

Spiraea arguta

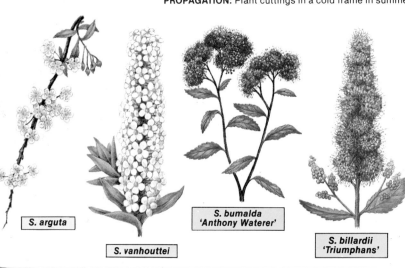
S. arguta
S. vanhouttei
S. bumalda 'Anthony Waterer'
S. billardii 'Triumphans'

Spiraea bumalda 'Anthony Waterer'

STEPHANANDRA

Stephanandra
Ⓓ

Many of the shrubs in this book are eye-catching plants with showy flowers. To frame these colourful specimens you need to intersperse them with a number of bushes which have attractive foliage. If your soil is moist then Stephanandra is a good choice — graceful, wide-spreading branches bearing bright green, deeply divided leaves which turn golden yellow in autumn.

VARIETIES: **S. incisa (S. flexuosa)** is the usual one. The zig-zagging stems reach 3 ft high and the shrub covers a width of about 7 or 8 ft. The leaves are deeply toothed and the insignificant, greenish yellow flowers appear in June. The dwarf form (**S. incisa 'Crispa'**) is a good ground cover — a 2 ft mound covered with crinkled leaves.

SITE & SOIL: A damp site is preferred — water in dry weather. Grow in partial shade.

PRUNING: Cut back old stems to ground level after flowering.

PROPAGATION: Divide clumps in autumn.

S. incisa 'Crispa'

Stephanandra incisa 'Crispa'

STRANVAESIA

Stranvaesia Ⓔ

Don't consider this vigorous, spreading evergreen unless you have plenty of space — it grows about 15ft tall. It will grow almost anywhere and needs little pruning — its usual purpose is to provide a screen or tall hedge. The white flowers which open in May are like Hawthorn — the bright berries which follow are like the fruits of Cotoneaster.

VARIETIES: The variety which is commonly available is **S. davidiana salicifolia.** The narrow leaves are olive green, the older ones turning red in autumn. The bright red berries are not eaten by birds — for yellow berries which also persist all winter, grow the variety **'Fructuluteo'.** Where space is restricted, pick the low-growing form **'Prostrata'.**

SITE & SOIL: Will succeed in any reasonable soil if it is well-drained. Thrives in sun or partial shade.

PRUNING: Not necessary. Cut back unwanted growth in spring.

PROPAGATION: Layer branches in spring or plant cuttings in a cold frame in summer.

S. davidiana salicifolia

Stranvaesia davidiana

SYMPHORICARPOS

Snowberry Ⓓ

The Common Snowberry is a rampant shrub which will grow anywhere — in full sun or in the dense shade under trees. It will cover large areas in the wilder parts of the garden, and its glory is the mass of large, marble-like berries which appear in October and persist for months. Good for indoor decoration and for hedging, but take care to keep it in check.

VARIETIES: S. albus (S. racemosus) is the Common Snowberry — 6 ft, pink flowers from June to August, berries large and pure white. **S. orbiculatus** (Coralberry) bears white flowers which are followed by large clusters of small purple berries. For the average-sized border pick one of the non-suckering Doorenbos Hybrids — **'Magic Berry'** (pink) or **'Mother of Pearl'** (white, flushed pink).

SITE & SOIL: Any reasonable garden soil in sun or shade.

PRUNING: Thin out unwanted shoots in early spring. Trim hedges in summer.

PROPAGATION: Remove and plant up rooted suckers or plant cuttings outdoors in autumn.

S. albus

S. doorenbosii 'Magic Berry'

Symphoricarpos albus

Shrubs to encourage Wildlife

🐝 Bees   🐦 Birds   🦋 Butterflies

Aucuba	Escallonia	Perovskia
Berberis	Euonymus europaeus	Potentilla
Buddleia	Fuchsia	Pyracantha
Callicarpa	Hebe	Rhus
Ceanothus	Hippophae	Ribes odoratum
Chaenomeles	Hypericum	Skimmia
Cistus	Ilex	Spiraea
Clerodendrum	Lavandula	Symphoricarpos
Cotoneaster	Ligustrum	Syringa
Cytisus	Mahonia	Ulex
Daphne	Olearia	Viburnum
Elaeagnus	Pernettya	Weigela

SYRINGA

Lilac
Ⓓ

The beloved Lilac — one of the mainstays of the British shrub border. The types you see brightening up gardens in May and early June are nearly always varieties of S. vulgaris, the Common Lilac. The flowering season is short, about three weeks, but the fragrance and size of the blooms compensate for it. These varieties will grow in all soils and many will reach 12 ft or more, but do not neglect them. Feed or mulch annually and remove both suckers and dead blooms. In the first season after planting pinch off flower buds as they form.

VARIETIES: You will find a wide choice of **S. vulgaris** varieties at any garden centre. Some are single-flowered — examples are **'Marechal Foch'** (carmine-rose), **'Souvenir de Louis Spaeth'** (wine red), **'Charles X'** (purple-red), **'Maud Notcutt'** (white), **'Primrose'** (pale yellow) and **'Esther Staley'** (pink). The remainder are double-flowered — popular ones include **'Charles Joly'** (deep purple-red), **'Katherine Havemeyer'** (lavender), **'Michel Buchner'** (lilac), **'Madame Lemoine'** (white) and **'Mrs Edward Harding'** (red). Syringa species are less well known than the large-flowered named varieties, but are worth growing. Try **S. microphylla** (5 ft, small leaves and small, open clusters of pink flowers) or **S. chinensis** (8 ft, drooping sprays of lavender flowers). Smallest of all is **S. velutina**, the Korean Lilac — a rounded bush, about 4 ft high, which bears lavender-pink flowers in May.

SITE & SOIL: All reasonable garden soils are suitable, but chalky ones are best. Choose a sunny site.

PRUNING: Cut out thin and unproductive branches immediately after flowering.

PROPAGATION: Nursery-raised plants of named varieties are generally grafted, but species can be propagated by planting cuttings in a cold frame in summer.

Syringa vulgaris

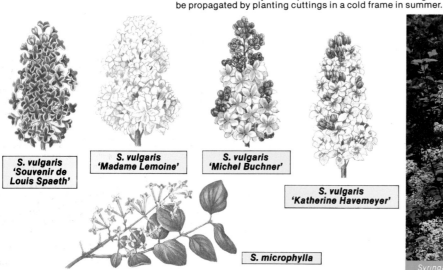

S. vulgaris
'Souvenir de
Louis Spaeth'

S. vulgaris
'Madame Lemoine'

S. vulgaris
'Michel Buchner'

S. vulgaris
'Katherine Havemeyer'

S. microphylla

Syringa microphylla

TAMARIX

Tamarisk
Ⓓ

You are not likely to confuse Tamarisk with any other shrub — when in bloom the delicate leaves combine with the plumes of tiny pink flowers to give a unique feathery effect. Despite its appearance it is not delicate — Tamarisk is a favourite subject for exposed coastal sites. You must prune this fast-growing shrub every year.

VARIETIES: T. tetrandra is the spring-flowering form. It will grow 12 ft high, the pale pink flowers appearing in May before the leaves. The common summer-flowering Tamarisk is **T. pentandra**. The leaves are darker and the flowers are a deeper pink — the scented blooms appear in August. The variety **'Rubra'** has red flowers. In coastal areas T. gallica is grown as a windbreak.

SITE & SOIL: Most well-drained soils will do — heavy clays are not suitable. Choose a sunny site.

PRUNING: With T. tetrandra cut back shoots with faded blooms immediately flowering is over. With T. pentandra cut back most of last year's growth in March.

PROPAGATION: Plant cuttings outdoors in autumn.

Tamarix tetrandra

T. pentandra

Ulex europaeus

ULEX   Gorse
Ⓔ

Gorse is an excellent garden shrub if the soil is right — it should be sandy or stony and there should be plenty of sun. If it is fertile and well-endowed with humus, this is not the shrub for you. All varieties of Gorse are densely spiny and bear bright yellow, pea-like flowers. It does not like transplanting — choose a small, container-grown specimen.

VARIETIES: You can buy Common Gorse (**U. europaeus**) — remember it is illegal to dig up a wild plant which you find growing in the countryside! It grows about 6 ft high, flowering in April and May and then on and off throughout the year. The semi-double form (**U. europaeus 'Plenus'**) is more compact and a better choice. There is an autumn-flowering dwarf variety (**U. gallii**), but you may have to go to a specialist nursery to find one.

SITE & SOIL: Avoid rich and moist soils. Needs full sun.

PRUNING: Trim back stems in May.

PROPAGATION: Plant cuttings in a cold frame in summer.

U. europaeus 'Plenus'

VIBURNUM   Viburnum
Ⓓ or Ⓔ

A large genus of garden shrubs with varieties to produce colour all year round and to suit almost every purpose — ground cover, screening, specimen plants and bushes for the shrub border. A wide assortment, but they do have a few features in common. All are easy to grow and will succeed in chalky soils. There is no need for regular pruning and all are hardy. The Viburnums are divided into three basic groups and each contains one or more garden favourites — the winter-flowering group, the spring-flowering group and the autumn berry/leaf colour group.

VARIETIES: The winter-flowering group contains the popular **V. tinus** (Laurustinus). A useful evergreen, 6 – 10 ft high, producing clusters of pink buds and then small white flowers between December and April. The old favourite **V. fragrans (V. farreri)** produces clusters of scented white flowers from November to February. For larger but equally fragrant flowers, grow **V. bodnantense**. The spring-flowering group usually have small white blooms clustered in large flat heads or 'snowballs'. There is the popular **V. carlesii** (4 ft, white fragrant flowers in tight domes in April and May), **V. burkwoodii** (6 ft, rather similar to carlesii but taller and evergreen), **V. rhytidophyllum** (10 ft, grown for its huge, heavily-veined evergreen foliage and red berries), **V. opulus 'Sterile'** (8 ft, white ball-like flower-heads) and **V. plicatum 'Lanarth'** (5 ft, white plate-like flower-heads). The final section is the autumn berry and leaf colour group — **V. opulus** has fiery foliage and red berries in autumn. **V. davidii** produces blue berries.

SITE & SOIL: Prefers well-cultivated soil containing ample humus. Most do best in full sun.

PRUNING: Not necessary — cut back old or damaged branches after flowering (deciduous types) or in May (evergreen types).

PROPAGATION: Layer branches in autumn or plant cuttings in a cold frame in summer.

Viburnum fragrans

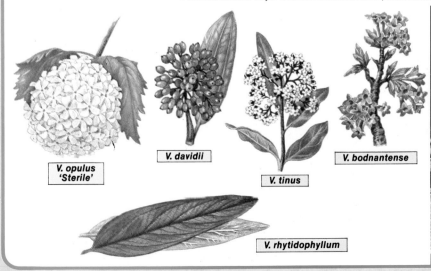

V. opulus 'Sterile'

V. davidii

V. tinus

V. bodnantense

V. rhytidophyllum

Viburnum opulus

VINCA
Periwinkle Ⓔ

The Periwinkle may be lowly in height and some authors may not even include it in their shrub books, but it is a highly regarded ground cover plant. It will grow in sun or shade, its stems rooting into the soil as they spread. Use it for covering banks or the bare ground under trees and you will be rewarded by flowers all summer long.

V. minor

VARIETIES: The big one is **V. major**, growing about 8 – 10 in. tall and producing large blue flowers from May to September. You can buy varieties with leaves splashed with yellow (**'Maculata'**) or white (**'Variegata'**). Less invasive and smaller is **V. minor** (2 – 4 in. high, blue or white flowers, green or variegated leaves).

SITE & SOIL: Any reasonable well-drained soil will do. Thrives in sun or shade.

PRUNING: Not necessary — cut back shoots in spring if spread is to be contained.

PROPAGATION: Divide plants or remove rooted side-shoots in late autumn or winter.

V. major

WEIGELA
Weigela Ⓓ

Weigela (sometimes listed as Diervilla) does best when pruned annually and grown in rich soil, but it will succeed almost anywhere and withstands the neglect it receives in millions of gardens. It does not grow very tall, 6 or 7 ft at the most, but it must be given space to show off its arching stems. The tubular flowers appear in May and June.

VARIETIES: If you can have only one, choose **W. florida 'Variegata'**. It is compact (slow-growing to about 4 ft) and bears pale pink flowers. When not in flower there are the decorative white-edged leaves. **W. florida** is taller (6 ft) and has rosy pink flowers. For brighter blooms choose a Weigela Hybrid — **'Bristol Ruby'** (ruby red) is the favourite.

SITE & SOIL: Any reasonable garden soil will do — succeeds in chalky soil. Thrives in sun or partial shade.

PRUNING: Immediately after flowering cut back shoots which bear faded blooms.

PROPAGATION: Plant cuttings outdoors in autumn.

W. florida 'Variegata'

YUCCA
Yucca Ⓔ

A plant to grow on its own so that its sword-like leaves and immense flower-heads can be enjoyed to the full. There are several fallacies — despite their tropical appearance the popular varieties are hardy in Britain, and it will bloom quite happily every year despite the old wives' tale of only one floral year in seven.

VARIETIES: The stemless varieties are the ones usually grown. Top of the list is **Y. filamentosa**, with a basal rosette of 2 ft high stiff leaves and a 4 – 6 ft flower stalk in August. The blooms are white and cup-shaped, and you can expect to see the first flowers about 3 years after planting. There is a variety (**'Variegata'**) with yellow-striped leaves.

SITE & SOIL: Needs good drainage and absence of heavy clay. Thrives in sun and partial shade.

PRUNING: Not necessary.

PROPAGATION: In spring remove rooted offsets growing at the base of the shrub.

Y. filamentosa

CHAPTER 3

TREES

Trees are a delight in the garden, and the larger the space you have available then the more you can enjoy them. There are far fewer tree varieties available than shrubs, and for the owner of an average-sized plot the choice is strictly limited. There are the Flowering Cherries and Crabs, of course, and the Laburnum to provide beautiful blossoms from early spring to early summer. The Mountain Ash displays its brilliant berries in autumn and the Hawthorn makes a useful hedge around many gardens. Silver Birch adds a graceful touch – much less frequently Robinia pseudoacacia 'Frisia' is used to provide sheets of bright yellow foliage throughout the growing season.

There are numerous other compact and attractive trees which can be used in the smaller garden, and the following pages describe some of them. Don't be frightened off by words like Maple, Horse Chestnut or Ash – they all have garden varieties. The tragedy is that all too often a woodland giant is planted in a small garden because it looked nice at the garden centre. This is the sorry tale of the Weeping Willow and the Horse Chestnut, the Copper Beech and the Large-leaved Lime. The problem is that we become sentimentally attached to the tree we planted 10 or more years ago and so we leave it to cast its deep shade over windows, flower beds and the neighbour's garden. The rule is never to buy a tree until you have checked on the height it is likely to reach in about 10 years' time.

Having chosen your tree, pick the planting site with care. Bearing in mind the mature height, never plant it close enough to the house for the roots to threaten the foundations. Also remember to leave enough room between trees to prevent the need for constant pruning when they are fully grown.

If you avoid these pitfalls then a carefully selected collection of trees can be a joy. We add height and colour to the garden and to some extent we screen ourselves off from the rest of the world. This screening is not only vital for us – in a world of ever-growing urbanisation it is every gardener's duty to plant trees where he or she can in order to maintain the bird population of this country.

It is a pity perhaps, that the choice is so often the same – Japanese Cherry, Hazel, Malus 'Profusion', Common Laburnum ... whether your garden is large or small, it is worth trying one or two which are less common. Grow the weeping Willow-leaved Pear, for example, or the Tupelo with its brilliant autumn colouring. Gleditsia triacanthos 'Sunburst' and Acer pseudoplatanus 'Worleei' produce lovely golden foliage – at the other end of the colour scale is the Purple Norway Maple and the Purple Birch.

In many cases we don't want a tree to fork too quickly which would result in a short or non-existent trunk. Nor do we want it to be 'feathered' with lateral branches arising from the main trunk. What we want is a straight and naked trunk which at the desired height produces a head of branches. This is a 'standard' tree and it will have to be trained to grow in this fashion. Read the section on Training (page 108). You will find several shrubs at your garden centre which have been trained as standard trees – these are extremely useful in small gardens where most natural trees would be unsuitable.

With all woody plants, careful selection, planting and pruning are vital to some extent. In the case of trees, both selection and planting need close attention but pruning is not generally an important task once the plants are established.

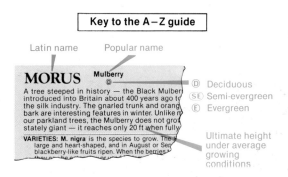

Key to the A – Z guide

Latin name · Popular name

MORUS Ⓓ Mulberry
A tree steeped in history — the Black Mulberry introduced into Britain about 400 years ago to [start] the silk industry. The gnarled trunk and orange bark are interesting features in winter. Unlike m[any] our parkland trees, the Mulberry does not gro[w into a] stately giant — it reaches only 20 ft when fully [grown.]

VARIETIES: M. nigra is the species to grow. The l[eaves are] large and heart-shaped, and in August or Sep[tember] blackberry-like fruits ripen. When the berries [...]

Ⓓ Deciduous
ⓢⒺ Semi-evergreen
Ⓔ Evergreen

Ultimate height under average growing conditions

ACER Maple
Ⓓ

The ordinary Sycamore is an Acer, but so are many excellent medium-sized trees with beautifully coloured foliage. The fruits (keys) are an attractive feature, and the Acers are tolerant of most soils and conditions.

VARIETIES: The quick-growing **A. negundo 'Variegatum'** is popular — it will eventually reach 25 ft. The Field Maple (**A. campestre**) is a native British tree which grows about 20 ft tall. Very tolerant, but unspectacular. Much more interesting is the Purple Norway Maple (**A. platanoides 'Goldsworth Purple'**) with dark purple leaves and red keys. Another colourful Norway Maple is **A. platanoides 'Drummondii'** (20 ft) with cream-edged leaves. The Sycamore **A. pseudoplatanus** is nobody's favourite, but it is extremely fast-growing and quickly reaches 30 ft or more. It has some fine varieties — **'Brilliantissimum'** (very slow-growing, 10 ft, young foliage bronzy pink) and **'Worleei'** (golden yellow foliage). There are Acers with attractive bark — **A. griseum** with peeling brown bark and **A. pensylvanicum** with 'snakeskin' bark.

SITE & SOIL: Any reasonable garden soil in full sun.

PRUNING: Not necessary — cut out dead and diseased wood in spring.

PROPAGATION: Named varieties with coloured foliage are generally grafted.

A. pseudoplatanus

A. platanoides 'Goldsworth Purple'

A. griseum

A. campestre

A. negundo 'Variegatum'

A. pensylvanicum

Acer pseudoplatanus 'Brilliantissimum'

AESCULUS Horse Chestnut
Ⓓ

The Common Horse Chestnut is a glorious sight when seen in May — large candles standing erect above the branches with each candle bearing white or pink flowers. But be warned — this is not the tree for you unless you have a large, open space available. The large leaves and spreading branches mean that little will grow underneath, and a 60 ft tree can shade out much of a modest garden.

VARIETIES: The Red Horse Chestnut (**A. carnea**) can grow 50 ft high, bearing pink flowers and nearly smooth seed cases. There is a more compact (20 ft) red-flowered variety — **A. carnea 'Briotii'**. The giant of the family is the popular Common Horse Chestnut, **A. hippocastanum**. Towering up to 80 ft when fully grown, its white candles are known to every adult and its spiny seed case is known to every conker-collecting child. The double-flowered form (**'Baumanii'**) does not produce conkers. For the average garden you must choose a much more modest variety — there is the white-flowering **A. parviflora** and **A. pavia**, a beautiful tree growing no more than 10 ft tall and bearing crimson flowers in late June.

SITE & SOIL: Any reasonable garden soil in full sun.

PRUNING: Not necessary — cut out dead and diseased branches in early spring.

PROPAGATION: Plant conkers in spring.

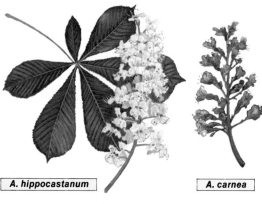

A. hippocastanum

A. carnea

Aesculus parviflora

AILANTHUS
Tree of Heaven
ⓓ

Tree of Heaven is a fanciful name for a rather ordinary tree, whose main claim to fame is its ability to withstand smoke and pollution to a remarkable degree. The ash-like leaves grow up to 3 ft long. Its speed of growth (it can reach 65 ft in 20 years) and its suckering habit may make it a nuisance in the average garden.

VARIETIES: A. altissima is the only species you are likely to find. The greenish-yellow male and female flowers are inconspicuous and are borne on separate trees — the female trees bear bunches of orange key-like fruits.

SITE & SOIL: Any reasonable garden soil in sun or partial shade.

PRUNING: Cut back hard each spring to ensure luxuriant foliage and to keep growth in check.

PROPAGATION: Remove rooted suckers from the base of the parent tree.

| A. altissima |

ALNUS
Alder
ⓓ

The Alder is a useful tree if you need a fast-growing screen or hedge in a boggy part of the garden — it is not suitable for chalky soils. In spring, attractive catkins hang from the branches, followed by fruits which are egg-shaped 'cones'.

VARIETIES: The Common Alder is **A. glutinosa**. One of the best varieties to grow is the Golden-leaf Alder (**A. glutinosa 'Aurea'**) — the leaves are pale yellow and the height of the tree rarely exceeds 12 ft. Rather similar in leaf colour and height is **A. incana 'Aurea'**. A much taller species is the Italian Alder (**A. cordata**), best known for its glistening leaves and large 'cones'.

SITE & SOIL: Damp or wet soil in sun or partial shade.

PRUNING: Not necessary — cut out dead wood in spring.

PROPAGATION: Plant cuttings outdoors in autumn.

Alnus cordata

| A. glutinosa |

BETULA
Birch
ⓓ

The Birch is quite rightly one of our favourite specimen trees. Its graceful growth habit is enhanced by attractive bark which is usually (but not always) white. Yellowish green male and female catkins are borne in the spring — the saw-edged diamond-shaped leaves flutter in the summer winds and turn yellow in the autumn. They are not difficult trees to grow — all are very hardy and thrive in a wide range of soil types — but you must remember that they are shallow-rooted. Do not underplant them and watering will be necessary during a period of prolonged drought.

VARIETIES: Silver Birch (**B. pendula**) is known to everyone — tall (up to 35 ft high), pendulous branchlets and white, peeling bark. It has several interesting varieties — **'Youngii'** (more compact and more weeping, the branches touching the ground), **'Tristis'** (tall and narrow with pendent branches), **'Purpurea'** (purple leaves and branches), **'Fastigiata'** (column-shaped; ideal for small gardens) and the Swedish Birch **'Dalecarlica'** (deeply cut, feathery leaves). There are other Birches apart from B. pendula — **B. albo-sinensis septentrionalis** has red, flaking bark and the bark of **B. ermanii** is pinkish white.

SITE & SOIL: Any reasonable soil in sun or partial shade.

PRUNING: Remove dead wood in early spring.

PROPAGATION: Sow seed in a cold frame in spring.

| B. pendula |

| B. pendula |

| B. pendula |

| B. albo-sinensis septentrionalis |

| B. pendula 'Purpurea' |

| B. pendula 'Dalecarlica' |

Betula pendula 'Youngii'

CARAGANA Pea Tree
D

There is little chance of finding the Pea Tree at your local garden centre, but you will find it in the catalogues of specialist tree nurseries. It came to us from the wastes of Siberia and is not surprisingly one of the toughest of all plants, growing in starved soil and windswept locations where little else could survive.

VARIETIES: C. arborescens grows to about 12 ft. In May the clusters of yellow, pea-like flowers appear and these are followed by slender pods. There are several varieties — **'Pendula'** has a weeping growth habit and **'Nana'** is a dwarf for the rockery.

SITE & SOIL: Any soil in sun or partial shade

PRUNING: Not necessary.

PROPAGATION: Sow seed under glass in spring.

C. arborescens

Autumn Foliage Colour

Acer campestre (gold and red)
Acer griseum (red)
Acer pensylvanicum (yellow)
Acer platanoides (gold and red)
Betula species (gold)
Carpinus betulus (gold and orange)
Crataegus prunifolia (red)
Fagus species (yellow and brown)
Koelreuteria paniculata (yellow)
Liquidambar styraciflua (gold, red and purple)
Liriodendron tulipifera (gold)
Nothofagus antarctica (yellow)
Nyssa sylvatica (gold and red)
Populus alba (yellow)
Populus canescens (yellow)
Populus tremula (yellow)
Prunus subhirtella (orange)
Quercus rubra (red in lime-free soil)
Robinia pseudoacacia (yellow)
Sorbus species (orange and red)

CARPINUS Hornbeam
D

The Common Hornbeam is a stately tree, but it has none of the popularity of the Common Beech. This poor relation keeps its leaves over the winter if grown as a hedge, and it has one or two advantages — unlike the Beeches it thrives in wet, sticky soils and the grey, fluted bark is an attractive feature.

VARIETIES: The Common Hornbeam (C. betulus) can easily be distinguished from a Beech tree — the leaves are saw-edged and the fruits are hop-like. It can be used for hedging or as a specimen tree, reaching about 40 ft in time. For the average garden choose the smaller and more upright C. betulus 'Fastigiata'.

SITE & SOIL: Any garden soil is suitable in sun or partial shade.

PRUNING: Not necessary.

PROPAGATION: Sow seed under glass in spring.

Carpinus betulus

C. betulus

CASTANEA Sweet Chestnut
D

This is a tree for the park rather than your plot — a well-grown specimen will tower upwards to about 70 ft. The first one came over with the Romans — since then it has earned a reputation for drought-resistance, long life and a good crop of edible nuts after a hot, dry summer.

VARIETIES: C. sativa (Spanish or Sweet Chestnut) grows well on most soils and is easily recognised by its shiny, lance-shaped leaves. The pale yellow catkins in July are eye-catching and the brown chestnuts which follow develop within spiny coats. The bark of a mature tree has deep spiral grooves.

SITE & SOIL: Any reasonable garden soil except chalky land in sun or partial shade.

PRUNING: Not necessary.

PROPAGATION: Gather chestnuts and plant in spring.

Castanea sativa

C. sativa

CATALPA
Indian Bean Tree
Ⓓ

Catalpa is an excellent summer-flowering tree — quick-growing, showy and capable of thriving in town gardens. It does, however, have its problems — it will not flower until it is about 10 ft high and it is not really suited to heavy soils and exposed sites.

VARIETIES: **C. bignonioides** grows about 20 ft tall with leaves which are large, soft and heart-shaped. The Horse Chestnut-like flowers in August are white, flecked with yellow and purple. In autumn long, pencil-thin pods appear. A handsome tree, but the boughs may break in strong winds. Choose **C. bignonioides 'Aurea'**, a yellow-leaved, slow-growing variety.

SITE & SOIL: Any well-drained soil in sun or partial shade.

PRUNING: Not necessary.

PROPAGATION: Sow seed under glass in spring.

C. bignonioides

Catalpa bignonioides

CERCIS
Judas Tree
Ⓓ

Cercis is a native of the eastern Mediterranean (legend has it that it is the tree on which Judas hanged himself) and it is not completely happy in our climate. It succeeds in the south east but it is not recommended for cold or clayey gardens.

VARIETIES: **C. siliquastrum** grows as a tall bush but can slowly become a rounded tree about 15 ft high. Clusters of pink, pea-like flowers appear on the bare branches in May before the heart-shaped leaves open. The flowers are followed by seed pods, tinted red when they ripen in July. A white-flowered variety (**C. siliquastrum 'Alba'**) is available.

SITE & SOIL: Well-drained in full sun.

PRUNING: Not necessary.

PROPAGATION: Sow seed under glass in spring.

C. siliquastrum

Cercis siliquastrum

CORYLUS
Hazel
Ⓓ

Hazel is a familiar, many-stemmed tree grown mainly for its nuts. It can be used to provide a screen on exposed sites and there are several decorative varieties, described below. The long, yellow catkins in February or March are a conspicuous feature.

VARIETIES: **C. avellana** (10 ft) is the Common Hazel or Cobnut. Interesting varieties include **C. avellana 'Aurea'** (6 ft, yellow leaves) and **C. avellana 'Contorta'**, the Corkscrew Hazel (10 ft, curiously twisted branches). **C. maxima** is the Filbert, with large nuts surrounded by a prominent husk. Choose **C. maxima 'Purpurea'** with purple leaves. The giant is **C. colurna**, the Turkish Hazel — a neat 30 ft pyramid.

SITE & SOIL: Any reasonable soil in sun or partial shade.

PRUNING: Cut out some old wood in early spring.

PROPAGATION: Layer or remove rooted suckers in autumn.

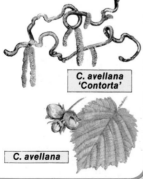

C. avellana 'Contorta'

C. avellana

Corylus avellana

Trees suitable for Seaside Areas

Acer platanoides	Populus canescens
Acer pseudoplatanus	Populus nigra 'Italica'
Castanea	Quercus ilex
Crataegus	Quercus robur
Fraxinus	Sorbus aria
Populus alba	Sorbus aucuparia

Trees suitable for Industrial Areas

Acer	Liquidambar
Aesculus	Liriodendron
Ailanthus	Malus
Alnus	Platanus
Betula	Populus
Carpinus	Prunus
Catalpa	Pyrus
Crataegus	Quercus
Davidia	Robinia
Eucalyptus	Salix
Fraxinus	Sorbus
Gleditsia	Tilia
Laburnum	Ulmus

CRATAEGUS Hawthorn
Ⓓ

Crataegus is a familiar sight in both hedgerows and gardens, and has acquired many common names over the years — May, Quickthorn, Hawthorn, etc. It is an excellent specimen tree for a lawn and can be used as a stout hedge. The general growth pattern needs little description — white, pink or red flowers appear in clusters in May or June and are followed by red or orange berries (haws) in autumn. The leaves often colour at the end of the season.

VARIETIES: Our native Hawthorn is **C. monogyna** (15 ft, scented white flowers, red berries). **'Stricta'** is a column-shaped variety. The varieties of **C. oxyacantha** are less spiny and less vigorous, but they are more popular — choose from **'Paul's Scarlet'** (double red), **'Rosea Flore Pleno'** (double pink) and **'Plena'** (double white). It may be berries rather than flowers which interest you — for a display which lasts into the New Year choose from **C. crus-galli** (fierce 3 in. thorns, red berries and fine autumn colours), **C. orientalis** (large, yellowish red berries) and **C. prunifolia** (fierce thorns, red berries, fine autumn colours).

SITE & SOIL: Any garden soil will do in sun or partial shade.

PRUNING: Not necessary — trim hedges in summer.

PROPAGATION: Buy named varieties from a garden centre.

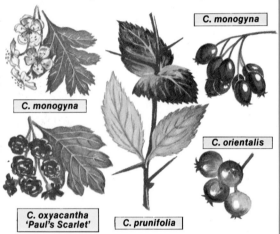

C. monogyna

C. monogyna

C. orientalis

C. oxyacantha 'Paul's Scarlet'

C. prunifolia

Crataegus oxyacantha 'Rosea Flore Pleno'

DAVIDIA Handkerchief Tree
Ⓓ

An exotic-looking tree which is completely hardy in this country. The common names (Handkerchief, Ghost or Dove Tree) all refer to the flower-heads which appear in May — two large bracts which surround the tiny blossoms. A good choice if you have space and patience — it can exceed 50 ft and the first flowers appear about 10 years after planting.

VARIETIES: **D. involucrata** is the only species. The leaves are similar to Lime, but they are hairy underneath. After the flowers large globular fruits appear turning purple with age. Specialist nurseries offer the hairless-leaved variety **D. involucrata vilmoriniana**.

SITE & SOIL: Any fertile garden soil will do. Thrives in sun or partial shade.

PRUNING: Not necessary.

PROPAGATION: Sowing seed is the usual method, but germination takes about 2 years.

Davidia involucrata

D. involucrata

EUCALYPTUS Gum Tree
Ⓔ

The popular Gum Tree of our gardens, E. gunnii, can be treated in two ways. It can be pruned back each spring to maintain its shrub form and display the distinctive juvenile foliage — round and waxy blue. Alternatively you can let it form a tree bearing adult foliage — lance-shaped and green. Buy a small, pot-grown plant

VARIETIES: **E. gunnii** grows very quickly — 3 to 6 ft a year. In time it may become a 50 ft graceful tree, but it is at risk in an abnormally cold winter. Young foliage is excellent for flower arranging. The Snow Gum (**E. niphophila**) is hardier and has beautiful 'snakeskin' bark.

SITE & SOIL: A well-drained site is necessary; both sandy and chalky soils should be avoided. Thrives in full sun.

PRUNING: Not necessary unless grown for juvenile foliage.

PROPAGATION: Sow seed under glass in spring.

Eucalyptus gunnii

E. gunnii

FAGUS Beech
Ⓓ

Beech trees play several roles — there are the stately specimens of Common Beech in parks and large gardens, there are beech hedges in every corner of Britain and there are colourful varieties for planting in lawns and large plots. Nearly all the varieties need a great deal of space and little will grow under their dense canopy of leaves.

VARIETIES: Our Common Beech is **F. sylvatica**. A mature specimen will grow 100 ft or more, with a multi-branched dome bearing shiny green leaves which turn yellow and then brown in autumn. This species is too tall to be grown as a specimen tree in the average garden, but it does make a good hedge — the brown leaves will remain over winter if you prune in midsummer. For garden use choose one of the varieties — there is **'Fastigiata'**, the Dawyck Beech which is column-shaped and takes up the least room of all. There is **heterophylla**, the Fern-leaved Beech and **'Pendula'**, the Weeping Beech. The most spectacular types are the coloured-leaved ones. There is the golden **'Aurea Pendula'**, but it is the Copper Beech **purpurea** which is usually bought. There is a small, mushroom-headed form (**'Purpurea Pendula'**) and for the brightest purple leaves of all choose **'Riversii'**.

SITE & SOIL: Any reasonable garden soil will do, but avoid heavy clays. Grow coloured-leaved varieties in full sun.

PRUNING: Trim trees and hedges in July.

PROPAGATION: Sow beech nuts outdoors in autumn.

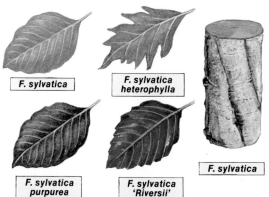

F. sylvatica

F. sylvatica heterophylla

F. sylvatica purpurea

F. sylvatica 'Riversii'

F. sylvatica

Fagus sylvatica

FRAXINUS Ash
Ⓓ

The ground underneath a Common Ash has none of the dense shade associated with Common Beech. The branches are widely spread and the leaves broken up into leaflets, but it is not suitable for the garden. It is late coming into leaf, the root system quickly covers a large area and the uppermost branches can reach 60 ft or more. In summer bunches of fruits (keys) hang from the twigs. The leaves do not change colour before falling in autumn.

VARIETIES: **F. excelsior** is the Common Ash — it is quick-growing and will thrive in almost any soil and situation. **'Jaspidea'** is a good garden variety, a 15 ft tree with yellow branches and foliage which is golden in both spring and autumn. Another garden variety of the Common Ash is **'Pendula'**, a large weeping tree which can grow about 25 ft high. There is a Flowering Ash (**F. ornus** or Manna Ash) — in May clusters of fragrant white flowers appear. None of the Ashes is particularly attractive as a specimen tree — perhaps the best one to choose is **F. oxycarpa 'Raywood'**. It is densely clothed with attractive glossy leaves which turn purple in autumn and its shape remains narrow for many years.

SITE & SOIL: Any reasonable soil in sun or partial shade.

PRUNING: Not necessary.

PROPAGATION: Sow seed outdoors in autumn.

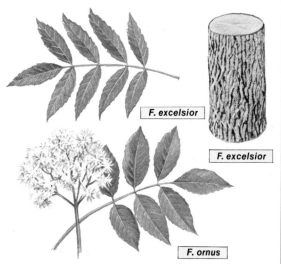

F. excelsior

F. excelsior

F. ornus

Fraxinus excelsior

GLEDITSIA Honey Locust
D

A graceful tree — popular in the U.S. but rare in Britain. It is grown for its attractive leaves, which appear late in the season, and its long seed pods. The leaves turn yellow in autumn — a good specimen tree but the branches are brittle and may break when strong winds blow.

VARIETIES: G. triacanthos is a tall, fast-growing tree which can reach 25 ft. Choose one of its varieties. The best one is **G. triacanthos 'Sunburst'** — thornless, golden foliage in the spring and shorter than its parent. Another variety is the feathery-leaved **G. triacanthos 'Elegantissima'**.

SITE & SOIL: Any well-drained garden soil in sun or partial shade.

PRUNING: Not necessary — remove dead wood in spring.

PROPAGATION: Sow seed under glass in spring.

G. triacanthos 'Sunburst'

Gleditsia triacanthos 'Sunburst'

JUGLANS Walnut
D

A fine shade tree with ash-like leaves and familiar edible fruits. These walnuts will not appear until the tree has been established for about ten years and a good crop depends on a mild spring. Always plant small, pot-grown specimens and choose a sheltered site.

VARIETIES: The Common Walnut is **J. regia**, a slow-growing plant which eventually forms a tall and spreading tree. The large, divided leaves appear in late spring. The variety **'Laciniata'** has drooping branches and deeply-cut leaves. The Black Walnut (**J. nigra**) is a fast-growing tree which may reach 100 ft.

SITE & SOIL: Deep, well-drained soil and full sun are necessary.

PRUNING: Remove unwanted wood in summer or autumn — never in spring.

PROPAGATION: Sow nuts outdoors in autumn.

J. regia

Juglans regia

KOELREUTERIA Pride of India
D

There are not many trees which bear bright yellow flowers in midsummer. If you have a sunny site and well-drained soil, then this unusual medium-sized specimen is worth considering. The leaves appear late and fall rather early, but they are colourful — reddish at first, bluish green later and finally yellow in autumn.

VARIETIES: K. paniculata is the only species. It grows about 20 ft high and bears long, pinnate leaves. The flower-heads which appear in July and August are full panicles of 4-petalled golden flowers. The bladder-like fruits turn pink as they mature in the autumn. Easy to grow, but it does need a good summer to make it flower freely.

SITE & SOIL: Well-drained soil and full sun are essential.

PRUNING: Not necessary.

PROPAGATION: Sow seed under glass in autumn.

K. paniculata

Koelreuteria paniculata

Trees suitable for Chalky Soil

Acer	Laburnum
Aesculus	Liriodendron
Ailanthus	Malus
Betula	Morus
Carpinus	Platanus
Catalpa	Populus
Corylus	Prunus
Crataegus	Pyrus
Davidia	Quercus
Fagus	Robinia
Fraxinus	Salix
Gleditsia	Sorbus
Juglans	Tilia
Koelreuteria	Ulmus

Trees suitable for Badly-drained Soil

Acer	Populus
Alnus	Pyrus
Carpinus	Quercus robur
Crataegus	Salix

LABURNUM
Golden Rain
Ⓓ

Laburnum is light and graceful, casting dappled shade in which other plants can grow. The long sprays of flowers appear in May or June. These are followed by brown pods which remain until midwinter, when the shiny, green branches are a characteristic feature. The often-stated precaution must be repeated — the leaves, twigs and especially the seeds are poisonous.

VARIETIES: L. watereri 'Vossii' is the one to buy. It is more up-right than Common Laburnum and the yellow tassels are exceptionally long — 10 to 20 in. is not unusual. The foliage is glossy and very few seeds are formed. The flowers appear in June — an advantage of the Common Laburnum (**L. anagyroides**) is that flowering starts about 2 weeks earlier. It grows about 15 ft high and has a weeping variety — **L. anagyroides 'Pendulum'**. Much less popular than the Common Laburnum is **L. alpinum** (Scotch Laburnum). The leaves are larger, the flowers appear later and the seeds are brown. A novelty rather than a thing of beauty is **L. adamii** (**Laburnocytisus adamii**), a laburnum/broom hybrid which bears yellow, purple and pink flowers on the same tree.

SITE & SOIL: Any reasonable garden soil in sun or partial shade. Protect from strong winds.

PRUNING: Remove dead or damaged wood after flowering.

PROPAGATION: Sow seed under glass in autumn.

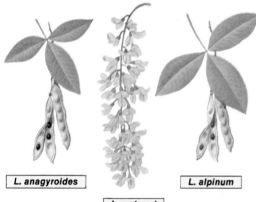

L. anagyroides | L. alpinum

L. watereri 'Vossii'

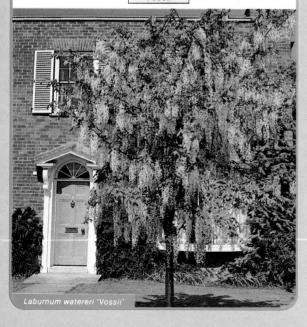

Laburnum watereri 'Vossii'

LIQUIDAMBAR
Sweet Gum
Ⓓ

A large conical tree which can be mistaken for a Maple at first glance. Look closely and you will see that the lobed leaves of the Sweet Gum are arranged alternately on the branch — Maple leaves are opposite. The corky bark is attractive but its real glory is in the autumn when the leaves turn red, purple or gold.

VARIETIES: L. styraciflua is the popular species. The large, star-like leaves are shiny and brightly coloured at the end of the season. The intensity of colour in autumn is heightened by adequate soil moisture and the absence of lime. The globular autumn fruits are woody and spiky.

SITE & SOIL: Any reasonable garden soil — preferably moist but definitely not chalky. Thrives in sun or light shade.

PRUNING: Not necessary.

PROPAGATION: Layer shoots in spring — wait 2 years before severing from the parent plant.

L. styraciflua

Liquidambar styraciflua

LIRIODENDRON
Tulip Tree
Ⓓ

A tall, stately tree with uniquely-shaped leaves — 4-lobed with a flattened tip. These large leaves flutter in the breeze and at the end of the season turn bright gold. The flowers do not begin to appear for about 25 years, and are never really conspicuous.

VARIETIES: L. tulipifera is the basic species — far too big for a suburban garden. The tulip-like flowers appear in June or July. For ordinary gardens there are much better varieties — **'Aureomarginatum'** is quite compact — **'Fastigiatum'** is tall but column-like.

SITE & SOIL: Any garden soil, including chalk, in full sun.

PRUNING: Not necessary.

PROPAGATION: Layer shoots in spring — wait 2 years before severing from the parent plant.

L. tulipifera

Liriodendron tulipifera

MALUS
Flowering Crab
Ⓓ

The most popular flowering trees are Prunus and Malus, lighting up our gardens each April and May with white and pink blossoms. Varieties of Prunus (the Flowering Cherries) are the usual choice, but do consider the advantages of Malus. Red-blossomed types are available, they are reliable in heavy soils and they produce fruits which are often large, colourful and suitable for jelly- and wine-making. A few tips — enrich the soil with peat or well-rotted compost before planting, stake firmly and spray against pests and diseases when necessary.

VARIETIES: M. 'John Downie' is the favourite variety — white flowers and then large conical fruits, orange-scarlet in colour and excellent for jelly-making. M. 'Montreal Beauty' has even larger fruits, but most eye-catching of all is M. 'Golden Hornet', a small tree with white flowers which are followed by bright yellow fruits. Some varieties are grown for the beauty of their shape rather than their fruits — M. floribunda (Japanese Crab) has long, arching branches and in April the red buds open to form pale pink flowers. The popular column-like variety is M. 'Van Eseltine'. The Purple-leaved Crabs are a distinct group with red flowers, coppery foliage and red fruit. Popular examples are M. 'Eleyi', M. purpurea and M. 'Lemoinei' — perhaps the best choice is M. 'Profusion'.

SITE & SOIL: Well-drained soil. Thrives best in full sun.

PRUNING: Remove damaged and straggly shoots in winter.

PROPAGATION: Named varieties are grafted on to specially selected rootstocks to produce standards or half-standards. Buy from a reputable supplier.

M. 'Golden Hornet'

M. 'John Downie'

M. floribunda

M. 'Lemoinei'

Malus 'Profusion'

MORUS
Mulberry
Ⓓ

A tree steeped in history — the Black Mulberry was introduced into Britain about 400 years ago to found the silk industry. The gnarled trunk and orange scaly bark are interesting features in winter. Unlike many of our parkland trees, the Mulberry does not grow into a stately giant — it reaches only 20 ft when fully grown.

VARIETIES: M. nigra is the species to grow. The leaves are large and heart-shaped, and in August or September the blackberry-like fruits ripen. When the berries turn dark red they can be eaten raw or used for jam-making. These fruits do not appear until the tree is many years old.

SITE & SOIL: Any reasonable soil in sun or partial shade.

PRUNING: Remove dead wood in winter — never prune unless it is necessary.

PROPAGATION: Plant 1 ft cuttings outdoors in autumn.

M. nigra

Morus nigra

Malus or Prunus?

In spring we see 'Flowering Cherries' everywhere, but on close inspection they may not be Cherries at all — they may be Flowering Crabs. You can tell them apart by looking at the leaves, flowers and fruit.

MALUS
Flowering Crab

PRUNUS
'Flowering Cherries'
including: Ornamental Plum
Ornamental Peach
Ornamental Almond
Ornamental Cherry

Leaf:

or

Flower:

5 styles

1 style

Fruit:

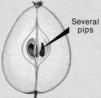

Several pips

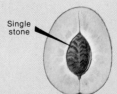

Single stone

NOTHOFAGUS Antarctic Beech

Nothofagus (literal translation 'False Beech') is gaining in popularity for street planting — it grows quickly at first but does not exceed 40 ft when mature. The fruits look like small beech masts, but the leaves are not like beech leaves — they are small, shiny and toothed.

VARIETIES: Several varieties are grown in Britain but **N. antarctica** is the only one you are likely to find. The leaves are only about 1 in. long and are crowded on the branches. They turn yellow in autumn — in winter the twisted trunk and lower branches are picturesque.

SITE & SOIL: Rather fussy — does not tolerate chalk and dislikes strong winds. Plant in full sun.

PRUNING: Not necessary — remove dead and damaged branches in winter.

PROPAGATION: Layer shoots in autumn.

N. antarctica

Nothofagus antarctica

NYSSA Tupelo

For most of the year the Tupelo is quite ordinary. The leaves, though glossy, are undistinguished and the flowers are inconspicuous. The berries are small and are quickly devoured by birds. It is only in the autumn that this tree stands out with its brilliant colouring.

VARIETIES: N. sylvatica (N. multiflora) is a slow-growing tree which is occasionally seen in large gardens in the southern counties. At first it is conical but spreads with age and may reach 30 ft. The glossy leaves turn golden in autumn and in some seasons continue to colour until they are all brilliant scarlet.

SITE & SOIL: Moist, lime-free soil is preferred. Choose a sunny or lightly shaded spot.

PRUNING: Not necessary — remove dead or damaged branches in autumn.

PROPAGATION: Sow seed under glass in autumn.

N. sylvatica

Nyssa sylvatica

PALMS

Nothing can quite rival palms for adding a tropical touch to the garden or patio. One or two of the hardier varieties are offered by many garden centres, but they are expensive and a severe winter will mean heavy losses.

VARIETIES: The best choice for a specimen tree is **Trachycarpus fortunei**, the Chusan or Chinese Windmill Palm. Large fan-shaped leaves are borne at the top of a thick trunk. It is hardy in many areas, but choose a sheltered spot. You may find **Chamaerops humilis** on offer, but it is only hardy in mild locations near the sea. The best choice as a tub plant is the Cabbage Tree (**Cordyline australis**).

SITE & SOIL: Well-drained soil in a sunny, sheltered spot.

PRUNING: Remove dead leaves.

PROPAGATION: Buy from a reputable supplier.

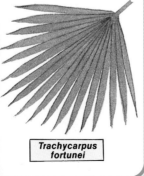

Trachycarpus fortunei

Cordyline australis

PAULOWNIA Paulownia

Spectacular is the only word to describe a well-grown Paulownia in full flower. Erect spikes of mauve, foxglove-like flowers stand above the giant leaves in May — a most unusual and exotic effect. But it's a gamble — a newly-planted Paulownia will not bloom for many years and flower buds are killed by sharp frosts.

VARIETIES: P. tomentosa (P. imperialis) grows about 25 ft tall with leaves 1 ft or more across. After a fine summer the flower buds appear in autumn — a mild winter will ensure a fine display in late spring.

SITE & SOIL: Fussy — it needs deep well-drained soil, full sun and shelter from strong winds.

PRUNING: Not necessary, but can be cut to ground level each March to keep it as a non-flowering shrub.

PROPAGATION: Sow seed under glass in autumn.

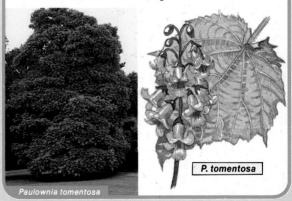

P. tomentosa

Paulownia tomentosa

PLATANUS Plane Ⓓ

For nearly all of us this is a tree to admire and not to grow — it would soon overwhelm the average garden. Easily recognised by the creamy patches beneath the flaking grey bark, Platanus is invaluable for planting in areas where air pollution is a problem.

VARIETIES: The London Plane has been with us for 300 years, but horticulturalists still can't decide whether to call it **P. hispanica** or **P. acerifolia**. It reaches about 80 ft and bears 5-lobed maple-like leaves and ball-shaped seed pods. The leaves of **P. orientalis** are more deeply lobed.

SITE & SOIL: Any deep garden soil will do, in sun or light shade.

PRUNING: Not necessary.

PROPAGATION: Plant 1 ft cuttings in a cold frame in late summer.

P. hispanica

Platanus hispanica

PYRUS Ornamental Pear Ⓓ

Few Ornamental Pears have been bred for decorative use in the garden — you are likely to find only a single variety at even a large garden centre. Although there is only one it is worth considering — the Willow-leaved Pear is unusual and easy to grow.

VARIETIES: P. salicifolia 'Pendula' is a beautiful weeping tree, reaching about 20 ft when it is fully grown. The leaves are slender, like willow leaves, and covered with silvery hairs until early summer. Creamy-white flowers open in April and are followed by small, inedible pears.

SITE & SOIL: Any reasonable garden soil will do. Thrives best in full sun.

PRUNING: Remove dead or damaged wood in winter.

PROPAGATION: Buy stock from a reputable supplier.

P. salicifolia 'Pendula'

Pyrus salicifolia 'Pendula'

POPULUS Poplar Ⓓ

It is usual to begin a description of Poplars with a few warnings. Their roots can damage drains, raise paving stones and undermine foundations. The brittle branches can be a hazard when they fall. Obviously the Poplar is not a plant for the small garden, but when grown well away from the house it can provide height in a new garden more quickly than almost any other tree, reaching 80 ft in less than 20 years.

VARIETIES: The White Poplar (**P. alba**) is easy to recognise — the woolly underside of the leaves is seen as the foliage flutters in the breeze. A tall tree (60–80 ft) which tolerates poor conditions. A column-like variety (**'Pyramidalis'**) is available. The Grey Poplar (**P. canescens**) is another widely planted species, growing up to 100 ft high. As with P. alba the leaves are variable in shape and size, but you can identify the Grey Poplar by its yellow-grey bark. Other Poplars include **P. candicans 'Aurora'** (30 ft, creamy white blotches on the leaves) and **P. nigra 'Italica'**, the Lombardy Poplar — one of the finest of all tall columnar trees. **P. tremula** is the Aspen, its rounded leaves constantly fluttering in even the gentlest breeze.

SITE & SOIL: Any reasonable soil in sun or light shade.

PRUNING: Remove dead or unwanted branches in summer. Do not prune in winter or spring.

PROPAGATION: Remove and plant up rooted suckers in early spring.

P. candicans 'Aurora'

P. alba

P. alba

P. nigra 'Italica'

P. canescens

P. canescens

Populus tremula

PRUNUS

Flowering Cherries
Ⓓ

The Shrubby Prunus varieties, so widely used for hedging, are described on page 46. Here we look at the unchallenged queen of the trees which bloom in the spring — the types of Prunus popularly known as 'Flowering Cherries'. Everyone is familiar with the common varieties — trees reaching about 20 ft when mature with a spreading, weeping or upright growth habit. Between March and May the clusters of blooms cover the branches — each 5-petalled flower white or pink, 1 or 2 in. across, single or double — combining with thousands of companions to provide the brightest plant in the spring garden.

There are, however, a wide range of flowering Prunus varieties. The Chinese Peach blooms in January — the Holly-leaved Cherry waits until June. The Dwarf Almond grows about 3 ft tall — the Wild Cherry can reach 60 ft or more. The 'Flowering Cherries' are made up of a bewildering assortment of species and varieties, and it is usual to split them up into the four groups described below.

Nearly all are easy to grow in reasonably fertile soil and an open, sunny location. Be careful not to plant too deeply nor in midwinter — early autumn is the best time. Stake firmly when planting and spray against pests and diseases when necessary.

SITE & SOIL: Any well-drained garden soil will do, preferably with some lime present.

PRUNING: Prune in late summer — never in winter. Cut out damaged and unwanted shoots.

PROPAGATION: Buy stock from a reputable supplier.

ORNAMENTAL ALMOND

P. dulcis

VARIETIES: The popular Common Almond (**P. dulcis** or **P. amygdalus**) is an erect tree growing about 25 ft high. Pink flowers open in March on the naked branches. It thrives in urban gardens, but do not expect almonds for the table. Choose **'Alba'** if you want white flowers or **'Erecta'** if you want column-like growth for a small garden. The most beautiful of all the Almonds is **P. amygdalo-persica 'Pollardii'**, a rounded 20 ft tree bearing 2 in. rich pink flowers in March and April.

ORNAMENTAL PLUM

P. blireana

VARIETIES: Purple or coppery foliage is a frequent feature — **P. blireana** has bronze-coloured leaves and bears double rose-pink flowers in April. The Cherry Plum or Myrobalan (**P. cerasifera**) can be grown as a hedge (see page 46) or as a spreading tree, reaching 25 ft x 25 ft. The variety **'Nigra'** has pink flowers and almost black leaves. Blackthorn or Sloe (**P. spinosa**) grows wild in the hedgerows; for garden use buy one of the cultivated varieties which will grow into a small tree — there is **'Plena'** (double white flowers in March) and **'Purpurea'** (single white flowers in March, purple leaves).

ORNAMENTAL PEACH

P. persica
'Klara Meyer'

VARIETIES: The Ornamental Peaches are not for every garden — they are rather short-lived, need a sunny but sheltered spot and are particularly susceptible to peach leaf curl. Despite the drawbacks, the Chinese Peach **P. davidiana** is a good choice because it provides such early blooms — single pink flowers in January. It will grow about 20 ft high — the variety **'Alba'** reaches the same height but bears white flowers. **P. persica** is the Common Peach, displaying its pale pink blooms in April and fleshy fruits later in the season. There are many named varieties — **'Klara Meyer'** is the popular double-flowered one.

ORNAMENTAL CHERRY

VARIETIES: The Ornamental Cherries are the stars of the flowering Prunus family and the choice is truly bewildering. They have pointed and toothed green leaves with individual flowers which are about 1½ to 2½ in. across. These flowers are borne in showy clusters between March and May, depending on the variety. You will find two basic groups in the catalogues — the Ordinary Cherries and the Japanese Cherries. Base your choice on the type of growth habit you want rather than on the nature of the flowers. There is an exception — **P. subhirtella 'Autumnalis'** is chosen because it produces its white flowers from November until March.

In the Ordinary Cherry group you will find the Bird Cherry **P. padus** (20 ft, almond-scented white flowers in May, rounded growth habit) and the Wild Cherry **P. avium** (40 ft, white flowers in April, attractive bark, pyramidal growth habit). There are many more — **P. hillieri 'Spire'** (25 ft, pink flowers in April, erect growth habit), **P. 'Pandora'** (20 ft, pink flowers in March, erect growth habit) and **P. subhirtella 'Pendula Rubra'** (15 ft, rose-pink flowers in April, weeping growth habit). For beautiful shiny bark choose **P. serrula**.

You will probably pick a Japanese Cherry. For a narrow tree, choose **P. 'Amanogawa'** (20 ft, pink flowers in May, column-like growth habit). At the other end of the scale is the favourite weeping variety **P. 'Kiku-shidare Sakura'**, better known as Cheal's Weeping Cherry (15 ft, pink flowers in April, pendulous branches). There are many more. The most popular is **P. 'Kanzan'**, also sold as **'Sekiyama'** and **'Hisakura'** (20 ft, double pink flowers in April, bronzy foliage, stiffly ascending branches). There is **P. 'Shirotae'** (20 ft, white fragrant flowers in April, spreading growth habit) and the Great White Cherry **P. 'Tai Haku'** (35 ft, large white flowers in April, spreading growth habit).

Prunus 'Kanzan'

Prunus 'Kiku-shidare Sakura'

QUERCUS
Oak
Ⓓ or Ⓔ

With its massive frame and broad, dome-shaped head, its wavy-edged leaves and neat acorns sitting in knobbly cups, the Oak is a basic part of our countryside. The leaves may be oval (Holm Oak) or long and narrow (Willow Oak). The acorn cups may be mossy (Turkey Oak) or the foliage may turn bright scarlet in autumn (Red Oak). Despite the variations many common family traits exist — large size, long life, foliage which casts filtered shade and a dislike of shallow soils.

VARIETIES: Q. robur (English or Common Oak) is by far the most widespread species. A superb stately tree, of course, but too tall for the average garden. A column-like variety (**'Fastigiata'**) is available. Q. robur is not our only native Oak — the very similar **Q. petraea** (Sessile Oak) is common in the west country. For large gardens exposed to the sea or on chalk soil, a good choice is the fast-growing Turkey Oak (**Q. cerris**). You can't miss it — the winter buds have long whiskers. The Red Oak (**Q. rubra**) grows quickly to form a large tree up to 80 ft high, and if grown in acid soil the leaves turn vivid scarlet at the end of the season. **Q. ilex** (Holm Oak) is one of our most stately evergreens — it can be kept clipped to form an imposing hedge.

SITE & SOIL: Any deep garden soil; thrives best in full sun.

PRUNING: Remove dead or damaged branches in winter.

PROPAGATION: Plant acorns in autumn.

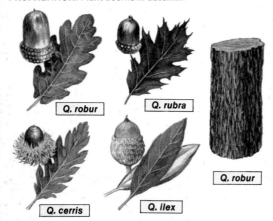

Q. robur   *Q. rubra*

Q. cerris   *Q. ilex*   *Q. robur*

Quercus robur

ROBINIA
False Acacia
Ⓓ

Pendulous sprays of fragrant, pea-like flowers appear in June, but the False Acacia is grown for its graceful shape and attractive leaves. It will grow almost anywhere and makes an excellent specimen tree, but avoid a wind-swept site as the branches are brittle.

VARIETIES: R. pseudoacacia is a large, upright tree which reaches 60 ft or more. The long leaves are made up of many small leaflets and the trunk is deeply furrowed. One of the most colourful of all foliage trees is the variety **'Frisia'** (25 ft) which bears spreading layers of foliage which remain golden yellow all season long.

SITE & SOIL: Not fussy — grows in all types of soils and atmospheric conditions. Thrives in sun or light shade.

PRUNING: Remove dead and damaged branches in summer, not spring.

PROPAGATION: Remove and plant rooted suckers in autumn.

Robinia pseudoacacia 'Frisia'

R. pseudoacacia

Flowers for Every Season

Many of the trees in this section are grown for their handsome shape or attractive foliage rather than their blooms, but it is still possible to use trees to provide flowers for every month of the year.

JANUARY
Prunus subhirtella 'Autumnalis'

FEBRUARY
Prunus davidiana

MARCH
Prunus (various)   Salix (various)

APRIL
Magnolia stellata   Prunus (various)
(see page 39)
Malus (various)   Pyrus

MAY
Aesculus (various)   Davidia involucrata
Caragana arborescens   Fraxinus ornus
Cercis siliquastrum   Paulownia tomentosa

JUNE
Crataegus (various)   Laburnum (various)

JULY
Koelreuteria paniculata   Liriodendron tulipifera

AUGUST
Catalpa bignonioides   Eucryphia (see page 26)

SEPTEMBER–OCTOBER
Magnolia grandiflora   Eucryphia (see page 26)
(see page 39)

NOVEMBER–DECEMBER
Prunus subhirtella 'Autumnalis'

SALIX Willow
ⓓ

One of the fine sights of gardening is to see a well-grown Golden Weeping Willow dipping its branches into the water of a large pond. One of the sad sights is to see a specimen newly planted in a small garden, knowing that in a few years time it will have to be hacked back constantly to keep it within bounds. All Willows have several features in common — they are quick-growing, very hardy and thrive best in moist soil. They bear catkins which may be decorative and the foliage appears early in the spring.

VARIETIES: S. chrysocoma has a host of alternative latin names but there is only one common name — Golden Weeping Willow. It grows very quickly, producing a wide-spreading tree about 40 ft high. The pendulous shoots are golden yellow. It has replaced the old-fashioned **S. babylonica**, but neither tree is suitable for a modest-sized garden. Choose instead **S. purpurea 'Pendula'** (15 ft, the American Weeping Willow with purplish branches) or **S. caprea 'Pendula'** (10 ft, the Kilmarnock Willow with 'pussy' willow catkins). For a non-weeper pick the Corkscrew Willow (**S. matsudana 'Tortuosa'**) with its twisted and contorted branches rising 25 ft in the air. Another non-weeper is the Purple Willow (**S. daphnoides**).

SITE & SOIL: Thrives best in deep loamy soil and full sun.

PRUNING: Trim back unwanted growth in winter.

PROPAGATION: Plant 1 ft cuttings outdoors in autumn.

Salix matsudana 'Tortuosa'

Salix chrysocoma

SORBUS Mountain Ash, Whitebeam
ⓓ

A large group of useful trees, ranging in size from the rare 10 in. S. pygmaea to the 50 ft S. 'Mitchellii'. The popular garden Sorbus is the Mountain Ash, a graceful and rather slender tree. It has one outstanding characteristic — season-long colour. This colour is not merely the splash of white or cream when the flower clusters open in May or June. There is also a dazzling display of berries amid leaves which take on the golds of autumn.

VARIETIES: There are two groups — the Mountain Ashes and the Whitebeams. The Mountain Ashes are the more important, and you can tell them by their compound leaves made up of a number of small leaflets. The basic species is **S. aucuparia**, our native Rowan (25 ft, bright red berries). Interesting varieties include **'Asplenifolia'** (25 ft, fern-like foliage) and **'Fastigiata'** (15 ft, column-like growth). **S. 'Joseph Rock'** is a good choice — it bears brilliantly coloured foliage in autumn and birds do not like its yellow berries. The Whitebeams have simple oval leaves — green above and grey below. Choose **S. aria 'Lutescens'** (35 ft, silvery young leaves, red berries) or the Swedish Whitebeam **S. intermedia** (30 ft, orange-red berries). For a small garden choose **S. hostii** (12 ft).

SITE & SOIL: Not fussy. Thrives in sun or partial shade.

PRUNING: Not necessary — remove dead branches in winter.

PROPAGATION: Sow seed under glass in autumn.

Mountain Ash group
example: S. aucuparia

Sorbus aucuparia

Whitebeam group
example: S. intermedia

Sorbus aria 'Lutescens'

TILIA Lime ⒟

It is the Common Lime (T. europaea) and not the mighty Oak or Beech which is the tallest British broad-leaved tree. Limes (or Lindens) have been popular garden plants for hundreds of years, their heart-shaped leaves unfolding early in spring and remaining on the branches until late into the autumn. Tiny, fragrant flowers appear in June or July and they are followed by hard, pea-like fruits. Aphids can be a problem. These insects produce sticky honeydew which falls from the tree and turns black and mouldy.

VARIETIES: The Small-leaved Lime (**T. cordata**) grows quickly to produce a handsome tree for the large garden. The Large-leaved Lime (**T. platyphyllos**) is more popular and can produce an even taller specimen — 100 ft or more. Its leaves are much larger (4–6 in. long) than those of T. cordata, they are densely hairy below and the branches do not arch downwards. It has some interesting varieties — **'Fastigiata'** has a column-like shape and **'Rubra'** produces red shoots. Perhaps the best choice is **T. petiolaris**. It is aphid-resistant, the branches are attractively pendulous and the white-backed leaves flutter in the breeze. Another aphid-resistant variety is **T. euchlora**. The American Lime (**T. americana**) cannot stand air pollution.

SITE & SOIL: Moist, well-drained soil in sun or partial shade.

PRUNING: Not necessary, but hard pruning will do no harm.

PROPAGATION: Remove and plant rooted suckers.

Tilia petiolaris

Tilia platyphyllos

ULMUS Elm ⒟

Dutch Elm Disease has swept away many of the Elms from the gardens and parks of Britain. If you own an Elm then keep careful watch. If a branch loses its leaves in summer, then it is infected. There is nothing you can spray to cure it — you will have to remove and burn the diseased branch. If the whole tree is affected, it will have to be felled and removed — don't leave dead wood in the garden.

VARIETIES: The Wych Elm (**U. glabra**), Dutch Elm (**U. hollandica**) and English Elm (**U. procera**) differ in their maximum height (90–120 ft), their shape and in some other details. But they all have the standard Ulmus leaf (oval, toothed and distinctly lop-sided) and the seed is surrounded by a yellowish petal-like wing. If you plan to buy an Elm, choose carefully. The most disease-resistant is the Chinese Elm **U. parvifolia** (40 ft, glossy leaves which stay on the tree until the New Year). With other Elms there is some risk of disease — **U. glabra 'Camperdownii'** is a popular Weeping Elm, **U. sarniensis 'Dicksonii'** is a fine golden-leaved form and for white-splashed leaves buy **U. procera 'Argenteo-variegata'**.

SITE & SOIL: Any reasonable and deep garden soil will do. Thrives in sun or light shade.

PRUNING: Remove unwanted branches in autumn. Cut out and burn diseased branches as soon as they are seen.

PROPAGATION: Buy from a reputable supplier.

Ulmus glabra 'Camperdownii'

Notable Tree Gardens

Many of the gardens open to the public have an arboretum (collection of trees grown as specimen plants) or a pinetum (collection restricted to conifers). Some examples are:

Bath Botanical Gardens, Avon
Batsford Park Arboretum, Gloucs.
Bedgebury Pinetum, Kent
Bicton Gardens, Devon
Bodnant Garden, Gwynedd
Botanic Garden, Cambridge
Botanic Garden, Oxford
Castlewellan, N. Ireland
Cragside, Northumberland
Crarae Woodland Garden, Strathclyde
Exbury Gardens, Hampshire
Hergest Croft Gardens, Hereford
Hillier Arboretum, Hampshire
Ickworth, Suffolk
Inverewe Garden, Highland
Knightshayes, Devon
Leonardslee, W. Sussex
Longstock Park Gardens, Hampshire

Mount Stewart, N. Ireland
Ness Gardens, Merseyside
Pencarrow, Cornwall
Penjerrick, Cornwall
Roath Park, Glamorgan
R.H.S. Garden, Wisley, Surrey
Royal Botanical Garden, Edinburgh
Royal Botanical Garden, Kew
Sandringham, Norfolk
Scone Palace, Perthshire
Sheffield Park, W. Sussex
Thorp Perrow, N. Yorkshire
Valley Gardens, Windsor, Berks.
Vivod Forest Garden, Clwyd
Wakehurst Place, W. Sussex
Weston Park, Shropshire
Westonbirt Arboretum, Gloucs.
Winkworth Arboretum, Surrey

CHAPTER 4

CLIMBERS

Climbers have many uses in the garden, but before discussing them it is necessary to know the difference between a climber and a shrub. It is not simply the difference between a plant which can be grown against a wall or trellis and one which is grown in the open garden. Some true climbers, such as Ivy, are often used as ground covers and some true shrubs, such as Forsythia suspensa, are a common sight growing up trellis-work alongside the front doors of houses throughout the country.

A climber is a plant which has some special mechanism for attaching itself to a support such as a wall, pole or wire. First of all there are the self-clinging climbers, such as Ivy (Hedera), Hydrangea petiolaris and Campsis which produce aerial roots and Virginia Creeper (Parthenocissus) which bears adhesive pads along the stems. Here are the climbers which will cling to walls and woodwork without the need for wires or any other form of support. The other climbers are not so adaptable and they do need something to which they can cling. Some, such as Aristolochia, Jasminum and Wisteria are twiners, their stems winding round wires, poles or the wooden strips of trellis-work. Others, such as Passiflora and Vitis, produce tendrils or, like Clematis, bear twining leaf stalks.

All these climbers, with their clinging or twining mechanisms, have several important roles to play in the garden. There are bare fences to cover, ugly objects to hide, arches and pergolas to clothe and pillars to climb. Above all, of course, there are house walls to decorate. Self-clingers like Ivy and Virginia Creeper are associated perhaps with old houses, but the stark lines of the modern house can be softened and enriched by Clematis or Wisteria. As gardens get smaller we should never lose this opportunity to extend the floral display upwards.

A few rules. Plant about 18 in. away from the wall and slope the roots away from the house. Prepare the site properly – never plant into builder's rubble. Choose with care – make sure that the plant chosen is recommended for your soil type and the direction the wall faces. There is no need to restrict your choice to climbers – there are many wall shrubs such as Ceanothus 'Burkwoodii', Magnolia grandiflora 'Exmouth', Pyracantha, Jasminum nudiflorum, etc. Some of these may need tying to a support, but one of them (Euonymus radicans) is a link between the true shrub and the true climber. In the open garden it is a neat and bushy ground-covering shrub – against a wall it produces aerial roots and grows as a self-clinging climber.

Walls, fences, arches, pergolas, outbuildings – there are many areas to be clothed by climbers in the garden. There is an additional one – trees which are either dead or unattractive. Rambler roses, Clematis, Celastrus, Actinidia chinensis, Hedera, Jasminum and Lonicera can all be used to climb or clamber up trees in order to provide attractive greenery or an eye-catching floral display.

If you don't grow climbers then they can open up a whole new world for you. There is the spectacular Wisteria, very slow to start but rampant once established. If you are less patient there are scores of Clematis varieties to choose from, each one holding the promise of a beautiful floral display quite soon after planting. The whole range of flower shapes are found amongst the climbers – the trumpets of Campsis, the flattened heads of Hydrangea petiolaris, the tubes of Honeysuckle, the trails of Wisteria and the intricacy of the Passion Flower.

But it's not just a matter of flowers. There is leaf colour too – the green and yellow patterns of Hedera helix 'Goldheart' and Lonicera japonica 'Aureoreticulata', the flaming reds of Virginia Creeper and the Ornamental Vine in autumn and the multicoloured mixture of Actinidia kolomikta. The A-Z guide on the following pages shows some of the enormous variety to be found in this group of plants.

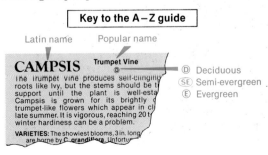

Key to the A – Z guide

Latin name — Popular name

CAMPSIS ⓓ Trumpet Vine

The Trumpet Vine produces self-clinging roots like Ivy, but the stems should be ti support until the plant is well-esta Campsis is grown for its brightly c trumpet-like flowers which appear in cl late summer. It is vigorous, reaching 20 t winter hardiness can be a problem.

VARIETIES: The showiest blooms, 3 in. long are borne by C. grandiflora. Unfortu

ⓓ Deciduous
ⓢⓔ Semi-evergreen
ⓔ Evergreen

ACTINIDIA

Actinidia
Ⓓ

Two species are available. They are both hardy twiners which lose their leaves in winter, but the similarity ends there. A. chinensis is a very vigorous plant which will cover an old tree or large wall with its extraordinarily large green leaves. A. kolomikta is a much smaller and more graceful plant grown for its colourful foliage.

VARIETIES: The stems of **A. chinensis** (Chinese Gooseberry) can reach 30 ft or more, bearing heart-shaped leaves nearly 1 ft across and cream-coloured flowers in midsummer. Plant a male and female close together for edible fruit. **A. kolomikta** is more popular — when planted against a sunny wall the upper part of the leaves on the 10 ft stems turns cream and pink.

SITE & SOIL: Any reasonable garden soil will do. Grow A. kolomikta in full sun.

PRUNING: Not necessary — remove unwanted stems in winter.

PROPAGATION: Plant cuttings in a propagator in summer.

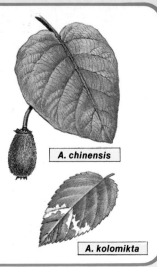

A. chinensis

A. kolomikta

Actinidia kolomikta

Fragrant Flowers and Ornamental Fruits

Actinidia chinensis: Cream-coloured fragrant flowers in July. Brown, gooseberry-like fruits; edible.

Celastrus species: Scarlet seeds revealed when orange-coloured capsules open.

Clematis montana: White flowers in May. Fragrance is generally not strong.

Jasminum species: White or pale pink flowers in summer. Fragrance is generally strong.

Lonicera periclymenum: Bright flowers from June to August. Fragrance is generally strong.

Passiflora caerulea: Orange, egg-shaped fruits; edible. Hot, dry summer is required.

Vitis vinifera: Bunches of small purple or black grapes; edible.

ARISTOLOCHIA

Dutchman's Pipe
Ⓓ

Most species of this group of vigorous twiners are too tender to grow outdoors in Britain, but the old favourite A. macrophylla is quite hardy. It produces curiously-shaped flowers which are a feature of the Aristolochias, but they are inconspicuous and this climbing shrub is grown for its dense foliage. It is the greenhouse varieties which bear eye-catching flowers.

VARIETIES: A. macrophylla (other names **A. durior, A. sipho**) will grow 20 ft high, rapidly covering trees or unsightly sheds. The heart-shaped leaves are 1 ft or more in length, hiding the pipe-shaped flowers which open in June. Each yellowish brown flower is about 1 in. long — a thing of interest rather than beauty.

SITE & SOIL: A fertile soil is required. Thrives in sun or partial shade.

PRUNING: Remove unwanted shoots in winter.

PROPAGATION: Layer stems in late summer or plant cuttings in a propagator in summer.

A. macrophylla

CAMPSIS

Trumpet Vine
Ⓓ

The Trumpet Vine produces self-clinging aerial roots like Ivy, but the stems should be tied to a support until the plant is well-established. Campsis is grown for its brightly coloured, trumpet-like flowers which appear in clusters in late summer. It is vigorous, reaching 20 to 30 ft, but winter hardiness can be a problem.

VARIETIES: The showiest blooms, 3 in. long in red and gold, are borne by **C. grandiflora**. Unfortunately it is also the least hardy and so should be avoided unless you live in the mild south west. Choose instead **C. radicans** (red and gold blooms, smaller than C. grandiflora) or the hybrid **C. tagliabuana 'Madame Galen'** (large, reddish salmon flowers).

SITE & SOIL: Plant in fertile soil in a sheltered spot. Full sun is essential.

PRUNING: In late winter cut back old stems which have flowered.

PROPAGATION: Layer stems in summer.

C. radicans

Campsis grandiflora

Celastrus orbiculatus

CELASTRUS
Bittersweet
Ⓓ

Celastrus is a vigorous twiner which will grow anywhere — the favourite uses are covering old trees and unsightly hedges. During the spring and summer it is an ordinary-looking climber bearing insignificant flowers in July. In autumn it is a colourful shrub — the foliage turns yellow and the orange seed capsules burst open to reveal bright red seeds. To ensure fruiting it is advisable to grow more than one plant.

VARIETIES: Choose **C. orbiculatus**. It will grow 30 ft or more up an old tree and the leaves will provide a dense, green cover. The capsules and seeds are plentiful and the winter display is striking. Cut and keep for indoor decoration. **C. scandens** is also available but it is not as vigorous and the seeds are not as plentiful.

SITE & SOIL: Any reasonable garden soil will do. Thrives in sun or partial shade.

PRUNING: Shorten stems in spring to increase fruiting.

PROPAGATION: Layer stems in summer.

C. orbiculatus

CLEMATIS
Virgin's Bower
Ⓓ or Ⓢ or Ⓔ

Clematis montana

The queen of the climbers, with a bewildering amount of advice in the textbooks and a host of varieties in the catalogues. Plant firmly in a spot where the soil around the roots will be shaded but the stems will be in the sun. The usual advice is to place stones or low shrubs around the base. It is the leaf-stalks and not the stems which twine, so provide adequate support. Each year mulch with compost and keep watch for clematis wilt. The affected stems suddenly die — cut out immediately.

VARIETIES: The large-flowered hybrids, growing about 10 ft high, are the popular group. The biggest blooms you are likely to see will be on **'W. E. Gladstone'** (lavender, June – September). Favourite varieties include **'Nelly Moser'** (pale pink, striped red, May – June and August – September), **'The President'** (purple, silver reverse, June – September), **'Jackmanii Superba'** (violet-purple, July – September), **'Ville de Lyon'** (red, deeper margin, July – October) and **'Vyvyan Pennell'** (violet-purple, double, May – July). The smaller-flowered species are easiest to grow — **C. montana** (30 ft, white, May) is the favourite one — a colourful form is **rubens**, with bronzy leaves and pink flowers. **C. tangutica** is quite different — yellow, bell-shaped flowers opening in August. **C. alpina** is a lovely spring-flowering species. The novelty variety **C. orientalis 'Orange Peel'** has thick and spongy 'petals'.

SITE & SOIL: Quite fussy — the soil must be fertile and moist. Chalk is beneficial. Sun is essential for the stems but not for the base of the plant.

PRUNING: Complicated. Some require light pruning — spring-flowering ones immediately after flowering and summer-flowering ones in early spring. Varieties which flower in late summer or autumn need harder pruning — in early spring cut back to within a few inches of previous year's growth.

PROPAGATION: Layer stems in spring or plant cuttings in a propagator in summer.

C. 'Ville de Lyon'

C. 'The President'

C. 'Nelly Moser'

C. montana

C. tangutica

C. alpina

C. montana rubens

Clematis 'Jackmanii Superba'

Hedera helix

HEDERA Ivy Ⓔ

Ivy is regarded by far too many gardeners as either a useful houseplant or a tree-damaging weed. If you choose the right variety and prune properly it is a reliable and colourful climber. The great benefit of Ivy is that it will grow anywhere and it is evergreen — a property shared by very few other climbers. Neither sound brickwork nor trees are damaged, but you should prune regularly so that the weight of the plant does not threaten the structure supporting it. Do not forget its use as a ground cover plant — the variegated forms will brighten up the space between deciduous shrubs in winter. The shape of the leaves of the climbing and flowering strains is often quite different. The flowers are inconspicuous.

VARIETIES: For ground cover choose the largest-leaved Ivy of all, the Persian Ivy (**H. colchica**). The variety **'Dentata Variegata'** has yellow-edged leaves. **H. canariensis 'Variegata'** is a rather similar plant with large, yellow-splashed leaves but the stems are red and it is not completely hardy in cold districts. For quick cover choose the vigorous Irish Ivy (**H. hibernica**). It grows about 12 ft x 12 ft and the glossy, dark green leaves effectively hide unsightly objects. The Common Ivy (**H. helix**) has many colourful varieties. For all-yellow leaves, choose **'Buttercup'**. For a yellow centre there is **'Goldheart'** and for white veins on a dark green leaf there is **'Caenwoodiana'**. Common Ivy certainly need not be a dull plant!

SITE & SOIL: Any garden soil will do. Thrives in shade, but the variegated types need some sunshine.

PRUNING: Keep in check by pruning in spring and summer. Do not let it grow into house gutters.

PROPAGATION: Remove and plant rooted runners.

H. canariensis 'Variegata'

H. colchica

H. colchica 'Dentata Variegata'

H. helix

H. hibernica

H. helix 'Goldheart'

Hedera helix 'Goldheart'

Hydrangea petiolaris

HYDRANGEA Climbing Hydrangea Ⓓ

Hydrangeas are best known as colourful bushes in the shrub border, but there is an excellent climbing species. Its finely-toothed leaves are glossy and no job is too big for it to tackle — in time an area of 70 ft x 70 ft can be covered. It is a very vigorous plant, but it is also a slow starter and can be disappointing for the first year or two.

VARIETIES: H. petiolaris is a self-clinging climber but this habit takes a few years to develop — provide some form of support during this early period. The best site is a shady wall — there is some evidence that wooden structures may be damaged. Large, white flower-heads of the 'Lacecap' type appear in June.

SITE & SOIL: Any well-drained garden soil will do. Thrives in sun or shade.

PRUNING: Not necessary — remove unwanted stems in winter.

PROPAGATION: Plant side growths in a cold frame in summer.

H. petiolaris

JASMINUM   Jasmine
Ⓓ

The popular Winter Jasmine (page 35) is usually grown against a wall or trellis but it is not a true climbing shrub. White Jasmine is a climber — its twining stems will quickly cover an old tree or a pergola. In summer the clusters of white, trumpet-shaped flowers appear. It is not completely hardy and will not survive in a cold, exposed site.

VARIETIES: **J. officinale** (Common White Jasmine) has been a cottage garden favourite for hundreds of years. An improved variety (**'Grandiflorum'**) is now available — between July and September pink buds open into fragrant flowers. The houseplant **J. polyanthum** is even more fragrant, but survives in only the mildest areas.

SITE & SOIL: A warm and sunny site is necessary. Any reasonable garden soil will do.

PRUNING: Not necessary — remove dead or unwanted stems after flowering.

PROPAGATION: Layer stems or plant cuttings in a cold frame in summer.

J. officinale

Jasminum officinale

LONICERA   Honeysuckle
Ⓓ or Ⓢ Ⓔ

The Honeysuckle has many virtues — it produces masses of colourful, tubular flowers and it often blooms over a long period. It is easy to raise from cuttings and will grow quite happily in partial shade, not demanding sun on its stems like Clematis. Above all there is the spicy fragrance but it also has one fault — Lonicera is a rather untidy shrub and therefore usually looks better if left to clamber over arches and fences or up trees and hedges rather than being clipped and tied into a neat shape against a house wall.

VARIETIES: Our native Honeysuckle or Woodbine (**L. periclymenum**) produces stems up to 20 ft long. The flowers appear from June to August — long trumpets which are reddish purple outside and cream within. The catalogues offer improved varieties — **'Belgica'** blooming in May and June, and **'Serotina'** blooming from July to October. **L. japonica** is a more vigorous Honeysuckle, usually keeping its leaves over winter but unfortunately often hiding its yellow flowers in the foliage. Choose the variety **'Aureoreticulata'** for its yellow-netted leaves. **L. americana** is a vigorous species which is excellent in every way. Some books recommend the red-flowering **L. brownii** (June–September) and the yellow-flowering **L. tellmanniana** (June–July) but they are not scented.

SITE & SOIL: Fertile, moist soil with some shade at the base of the plant. Thrives in sun or partial shade.

PRUNING: Remove unwanted stems when flowering is over — at the same time remove some of the old stems.

PROPAGATION: Layer stems or plant cuttings in a cold frame in summer.

Lonicera periclymenum

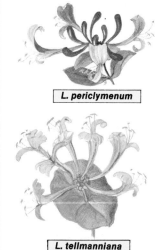

L. periclymenum

L. japonica 'Aureoreticulata'

L. tellmanniana

L. americana

L. brownii

Lonicera japonica 'Aureoreticulata'

Parthenocissus quinquefolia

PARTHENOCISSUS Virginia Creeper
ⓓ

Virginia Creepers are well known — tall and spreading vines growing on the sides of houses, the leaves turning bright red in autumn. Surprisingly there is a great deal of confusion over their names — you may find them listed under Ampelopsis or Vitis at the garden centre. They need some support at first, but soon become self-clinging.

VARIETIES: The most popular 'Virginia Creeper' is **P. tricuspidata**. Its proper name is Boston Ivy and it is seen everywhere. The shape of its leaves is variable, but the foliage is usually 3-lobed on a mature plant. The Large-leaved or True Virginia Creeper (**P. quinquefolia**) grows 20—40 ft high, each leaf being made up of 5 oval leaflets. The variegated **P. henryana** is the most colourful of all the Virginia Creepers.

SITE & SOIL: Fertile, free-draining soil is preferred. Thrives in sun or shade.

PRUNING: Remove unwanted growth in early spring.

PROPAGATION: Layer stems in autumn.

P. henryana

P. tricuspidata

Passiflora caerulea

PASSIFLORA Passion Flower
ⓓ

If you would like to grow something truly exotic in your garden, try this one. Frost will kill the top growth but new stems should arise from the base if you live in one of the milder districts. Plant it against a south or west wall — it climbs by means of tendrils so some form of support is necessary.

VARIETIES: Only one variety (**P. caerulea**) is sufficiently hardy to be grown outdoors in Britain. It can grow 20 ft high — a mass of tangled stems and lobed leaves. The flowers which appear between June and September are its glory — 3 in. across with an intricate pattern of purple, blue and white. There is an all-white variety (**'Constance Elliott'**).

SITE & SOIL: Free-draining soil, full sun and maximum protection from frost are essential.

PRUNING: In April cut back all frost-damaged and unwanted growth.

PROPAGATION: Layer stems in spring or plant cuttings in a cold frame in summer.

P. caerulea

Polygonum baldschuanicum

POLYGONUM Russian Vine
ⓓ

Russian or Mile-a-Minute Vine is the standard answer to the 'What-can-I-do-to-hide-an-eyesore' problem. Growing at the rate of 15 ft or more each year, hardly any other plant will cover old sheds, dead trees, unsightly walls or stumps quite so quickly. All summer long there are masses of flowers, but it does lose its leaves in winter. A commonplace climber but still very useful.

VARIETIES: **P. baldschuanicum** may reach 40 ft if left unpruned. The leaves are pale green and the small creamy flowers are usually tinged with pink. The floral sprays cover the upper part of the plant from July to October. Russian Vine has a twining growth habit, so some form of support is necessary.

SITE & SOIL: Any reasonable garden soil will do — thrives in sun or partial shade.

PRUNING: In spring cut back stems to keep growth in check.

PROPAGATION: Plant cuttings in a cold frame in summer.

P. baldschuanicum

SOLANUM Perennial Nightshade
SE

Two members of the Potato family can be grown as spectacular climbers in a sheltered garden. They are both vigorous and may quickly reach 15 ft or more. The leaves are semi-evergreen and the blue flowers are borne in clusters over a long period. Each flower has a prominent cone of yellow stamens.

VARIETIES: The species to choose is **S. crispum**, the Chilean Potato Tree. The flowers are a rich purple-blue and continue to appear from July until October. Choose the variety **'Glasnevin'** for extra hardiness and more flowers. If you live in a mild district you can try **S. jasminoides**. The flowers are pale blue — the variety **'Album'** has white flowers.

SITE & SOIL: Plant in full sun against a south or west wall. Any reasonable garden soil will do.

PRUNING: In April cut back all damaged and unwanted growth.

PROPAGATION: Layer stems in summer.

S. crispum

Solanum crispum 'Glasnevin'

VITIS Ornamental Vine
D

Vitis is usually grown for its fruit, but several types are offered for their ornamental value. Species of Vitis are not self-clinging — they climb by means of tendrils so some form of support is necessary. The main feature of these Ornamental Vines is the glowing colour of their autumn foliage, but a few bear clusters of edible grapes.

VARIETIES: The giant of the group is **V. coignetiae**, with lobed leaves more than 10 in. across and stems 40 ft long. In autumn the foliage turns golden and then crimson. **V. vinifera 'Brandt'** is a variety of the ordinary Grape Vine with green leaves which turn red before they fall. **V. vinifera 'Purpurea'** has red leaves which darken to purple before they fall.

SITE & SOIL: Any free-draining garden soil — the presence of chalk is beneficial. Thrives in sun or partial shade.

PRUNING: Cut back unwanted growth in summer.

PROPAGATION: Layer stems in April or plant cuttings in a cold frame in late summer.

V. coignetiae

Vitis vinifera 'Purpurea'

WISTERIA Wistaria
D

A very popular climbing plant — its twining stems covered with hanging trails of blue flowers are a familiar sight in May and June. It can be disappointing, however, if you don't take care in selection, planting and pruning. Use container-grown plants and choose a sheltered spot. The plant may remain dormant for several months after transplanting.

VARIETIES: The popular one is **W. sinensis** — a rampant grower with flower-trails about 9 in. long. It can get out of hand — not a good choice for a house wall as it often gets into gutters and under roofs. Choose instead the less vigorous **W. floribunda**. The variety **'Macrobotrys'** has lilac-blue flower-trails 2½ ft long.

SITE & SOIL: Any reasonable garden soil — dig in compost before planting. Requires full sun.

PRUNING: Cut back current year's side growths to about 6 in. in July.

PROPAGATION: Layer stems in spring or summer.

W. sinensis

Wisteria floribunda 'Macrobotrys'

CHAPTER 5

CONIFERS

When you visit a garden centre you can recognise a conifer immediately, and yet there is not a single feature you can rely upon to tell you that you are correct. To begin with, it is clothed with leaves in winter, but four well-known conifers (Larix, Taxodium, Metasequoia and Ginkgo) are deciduous. Then there are the leaves, which you would expect to be scale- or needle-like. This nearly always applies, but the foliage of Ginkgo biloba is flat and fan-shaped. They all form cones, even though some varieties are distinctly shy about producing them, but even these structures are occasionally difficult to recognise. The cones of Ginkgo look like small, yellow plums and Yew cones are red and fleshy.

Despite the vagaries of some unusual varieties, the conifer is easily distinguished from other woody plants by the average gardener and its value as a garden plant is just as widely recognised. To give a garden instant maturity you need a hardy evergreen tree. Few are available outside the conifers – it is to this vast group that you must turn to find the plant you want, a plant of almost any shape, size and colour.

Going back to the garden centre where we started this chapter, the conifer you picked up will almost certainly have all the family characteristics. It will be container-grown or ball-rooted, and in both cases the soil ball must not be disturbed at planting time. If it is ball-rooted you will have to plant it when there is some warmth in the soil, and that means September or April.

It will be hardy and have a long life expectancy, and after-care could not be simpler. There is no staking, spraying, dead-heading or leaf raking. Pruning is not necessary except in one special case – if a green-leaved branch appears on a golden or variegated variety it should be chopped out immediately.

Many features, then, that you can rely upon if it is a conifer but there is one vital feature that you just cannot predict – speed of growth and ultimate height. That little conifer can become an out-of-place giant in 10 years' time, as happens in countless gardens throughout Britain, or it can remain a frustrating dwarf when you

were hoping for a stately tree. Its *name* at the garden centre is the key to its rate of growth, not the *size* when you buy it. It may grow 4 ft a year, like Leyland's Cypress, or it may put on only an inch or two, like a dwarf conifer.

Most aspects of conifer growing are simple but the definition of size is not. A "dwarf" conifer can mean two quite separate things. It may describe a slow-growing variety like Chamaecyparis obtusa 'Nana Gracilis' which will have reached only 2 ft or less after 10 or 15 years, but will grow to an ultimate height of 10 ft or more. This ultimate height may take scores of years to reach – the record must go to Pinus aristata which takes 1500 years to reach its ultimate height! Apart from the slow growers, there are just a few varieties which are natural dwarfs and never grow taller than about 2 ft.

The interest in conifers is now greater than ever and new varieties continue to appear. You can buy a 1 ft midget or a plant which will reach 100 ft in time, you can choose a column, cone or spreading sheet of foliage, and you can pick a plant which is blue, grey, yellow, bronze or just plain green. You can find lime haters, such as Cryptomeria, Larix, Pinus and Taxodium or varieties which are happy in chalky soils, like some Junipers and Pines. If you live in an industrial area, remember that some conifers don't like polluted air – choose one of the tough types such as a Juniper or Yew. Wherever you live and whatever the size of your plot there are conifers for you, and your garden will not be really complete without them. The A-Z guide on the following pages illustrates only a small selection of the many types which are now available.

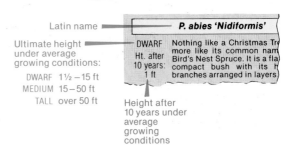

| Key to the A – Z guide |

Latin name

Ultimate height under average growing conditions:

  DWARF 1½ – 15 ft
  MEDIUM 15 – 50 ft
  TALL over 50 ft

P. abies 'Nidiformis'

DWARF
Ht. after
10 years:
1 ft

Nothing like a Christmas Tr[e] more like its common nam[e] Bird's Nest Spruce. It is a fla[t] compact bush with its [h] branches arranged in layers[.]

Height after 10 years under average growing conditions

ABIES Silver Fir Ⓔ

The typical True or Silver Fir is a tall conical tree, towering upwards for 100 ft in parkland or woodland. The straight trunk is unforked and the shape when young is almost perfectly symmetrical — the lower branches do not fall before the tree is about 30 years old. A classical Christmas Tree, but unfortunately very few of these splendid specimens are small enough to grow in the average garden. They like deep, moist soil — shallow soils and smoke-polluted air are not suitable. The cones may be green, brown or purple — they generally do not appear until the tree is many years old and they are usually borne on the highest branches, well away from the gardener's gaze.

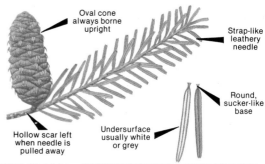

Oval cone always borne upright

Strap-like leathery needle

Round, sucker-like base

Hollow scar left when needle is pulled away

Undersurface usually white or grey

A. balsamea 'Hudsonia'

DWARF
Ht. after 10 years: 1 ft

A dwarf form of the Balsam Fir — slow-growing and a compact shape which makes it ideal for the rock garden. The foliage is aromatic. Can survive in chalky soil.

A. koreana

MEDIUM
Ht. after 10 years: 6 ft

The Korean Fir is a good choice. The needles of this neat, slow-growing tree are dark green above and white below. The cones, violet-purple in colour, appear from an early age.

A. grandis

TALL
Ht. after 10 years: 10 ft

The Giant Fir is Britain's tallest tree, growing to an eventual height of 100-150 ft. The foliage is borne in two distinct ranks — each leaf is strongly aromatic when crushed.

A. arizonica 'Compacta'

DWARF
Ht. after 10 years: 2 ft

A useful garden tree which reaches only about 7 ft when fully grown. It has a dense, conical shape and the leaves are blue-grey in colour. The bark is soft and corky.

A. pinsapo

TALL
Ht. after 10 years: 7 ft

The Spanish Fir is a large conifer with short prickly needles clothing the stems. It is the best Fir for chalky soil. Choose the variety 'Glauca' for its blue-grey foliage.

A. delavayi forrestii

MEDIUM
Ht. after 10 years: 6 ft

An excellent garden conifer which can reach 30 ft when fully grown. The young shoots are rusty red, the leaves dark green and the winter buds snowy white. The cones are black.

ARAUCARIA   Monkey Puzzle
Ⓔ

The common names of this conifer indicate its origin and shape. Chile Pine refers to its native home amongst the Araucarian Indians in Chile and Argentina. Its more usual name refers to the peculiar arrangement of its sharp, closely-set leaves which clothe the branches — "it would puzzle a monkey to climb that tree" was said by a long-forgotten dignitary at a tree-planting ceremony. Always buy a container-grown plant and provide the conditions it will require — full sun, moist acid loam and regular feeding. Remember that it will form a large tree in time — far too many Victorians planted Araucaria in tiny gardens. The lower branches fall with age — this occurs quickly in smoky or shady locations.

Globular cone borne upright on female tree. Takes 2–3 years to ripen

Thick, triangular and sharp-pointed leaves arranged spirally around the stem

A. araucana

TALL
Ht. after 10 years: 5 ft

Slow-growing at first, then develops rapidly to an eventual height of 70 ft or more. Open growth habit with branches which look like thick, curved ropes.

CEDRUS   Cedar
Ⓔ

A mature Cedar growing in spacious parkland is a magnificent sight, its massive trunk supporting the tiered branches layer upon layer up to a height of 80 ft. Unfortunately most of the Cedar varieties sold by garden centres belong in such a setting — they are quite out of place in the suburban garden. So choose with care — there are compact and weeping varieties which will not get out of hand. Always buy container-grown specimens and plant in a well-drained site which receives plenty of sun. The growth habit is conical at first, but with age the plants often become flat-topped.

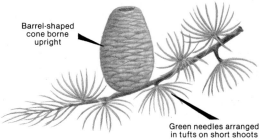

Barrel-shaped cone borne upright

Green needles arranged in tufts on short shoots

C. atlantica 'Glauca'

TALL
Ht. after 10 years: 10 ft

The Blue Cedar is a beautiful conifer, widely grown as a specimen tree in lawns where the blue-green foliage can be seen to its best advantage. Stake firmly after planting. A poor choice where space is limited — this tree can soon get out of hand. The weeping C. atlantica 'Glauca Pendula' and the yellow-leaved C. atlantica 'Aurea' are much less robust.

C. deodara

TALL
Ht. after 10 years: 10 ft

The Deodar is a graceful conifer, easily recognised by the drooping growth habit of its branches and leading shoot. Once established the Deodar grows vigorously and may reach 80 ft or more. This Cedar is not for the small garden — if the site is sheltered you can grow the much smaller C. deodara 'Aurea' which bears golden foliage in the spring.

C. libani

TALL
Ht. after 10 years: 6 ft

The Cedar of Lebanon requires little description — it is seen in parks and large gardens everywhere. Although slow-growing it reaches 80 ft or more in time and it has no place in the average garden. There are much smaller forms, such as C. libani 'Comte de Dijon' or C. brevifolia, or you can try C. libani 'Nana' or the weeping C. libani 'Sargentii'.

CHAMAECYPARIS   False Cypress
E

Chamaecyparis is the most popular evergreen tree in Britain. Even a modest-sized garden centre will offer a dozen or more different varieties — a specialist nursery may list a hundred or more. They come in all shapes, sizes and foliage colours — dwarfs for the rockery, compact types for the smaller garden and large trees to grow as showy specimens or dense screens. Only a selection of the better-known varieties can be shown here — many others are available. Remember to check the ultimate height before buying. The old name Cupressus is still sometimes used, but there are important differences between the two — the Chamaecyparis branchlets are flat, the cones are tiny and the plants are hardier and easier to transplant. But they do not like windy, exposed sites and they do need moist, well-drained soil.

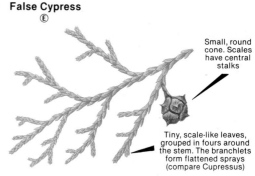

Small, round cone. Scales have central stalks

Tiny, scale-like leaves, grouped in fours around the stem. The branchlets form flattened sprays (compare Cupressus)

C. lawsoniana 'Allumii'

MEDIUM
Ht. after
10 years:
6 ft

A popular blue Lawson variety — the growth is compact and the upright branches bear flattened sprays of blue-grey foliage. It is an excellent specimen tree for the lawn and it is also useful for hedging.

C. lawsoniana 'Columnaris'

MEDIUM
Ht. after
10 years:
6 ft

One of the best column-shaped conifers. The upright branches form a narrow pillar which makes a splendid specimen in the lawn or shrub border. The foliage is blue-grey and the eventual height is about 25 ft.

C. lawsoniana 'Ellwoodii'

DWARF
Ht. after
10 years:
5 ft

'Ellwoodii' is perhaps the most popular of all the Lawson varieties. The grey-green foliage turns steely blue in winter, and this slow-growing, upright bush can be seen in tubs, rockeries and borders everywhere.

C. lawsoniana 'Ellwood's Gold'

DWARF
Ht. after
10 years:
4 ft

A sport of 'Ellwoodii', which it resembles in shape and growth habit. It is slower-growing, however, and the tips of the green branchlets are golden yellow. The effect is eye-catching and it is very popular.

C. lawsoniana 'Minima Aurea'

DWARF
Ht. after
10 years:
1 ft

One of the best of all dwarf conifers. The tightly-packed foliage forms a rounded pyramid, very slow-growing with an ultimate height of about 4 ft. The leaves are bright yellow — an outstanding rockery plant in winter.

C. lawsoniana 'Fletcheri'

MEDIUM
Ht. after
10 years:
6 ft

A broadly columnar variety with feathery grey-green foliage. It is often planted in rockeries, but it is really too tall for this purpose. Grow it as a tub plant or as a hedge. Responds well to clipping in the spring.

CHAMAECYPARIS continued

C. lawsoniana 'Minima Glauca'

DWARF
Ht. after
10 years:
1 ft

A rounded bush with dense sprays of green foliage. It grows very slowly and is a popular choice for rockeries and small shrub borders. C. lawsoniana 'Nana' is very similar with an ultimate height of 3–4 ft.

C. lawsoniana 'Lane'

MEDIUM
Ht. after
10 years:
6 ft

There are three popular golden Lawson varieties in the medium height range — 'Lane', 'Lutea' and 'Stewartii'. The brightest is 'Lane', the feathery sprays on the conical tree remaining golden all year round.

C. nootkatensis 'Pendula'

TALL
Ht. after
10 years:
8 ft

A spectacular tree, the most pendulous of all the tall conifers. Long branchlets hang like streamers from the branches. The leading shoot must be trained vertically after planting. The foliage is dull green.

C. obtusa 'Nana Gracilis'

DWARF
Ht. after
10 years:
2 ft

A very popular rockery conifer. Shell-shaped sprays of branchlets radiate from the compact bush and the foliage is dark and glossy. It is slow-growing, taking many years to reach its ultimate height of 10 ft.

C. pisifera 'Boulevard'

DWARF
Ht. after
10 years:
3 ft

This favourite dwarf conifer is easily recognised — neat and conical, the feathery foliage is silvery blue in summer and purplish blue in winter. It is slow-growing, but in time it can reach 10 ft or more.

C. pisifera 'Filifera Aurea'

DWARF
Ht. after
10 years:
3 ft

A straggly, untidy bush when first planted, but after a couple of years it develops into a broadly conical plant with spreading branches. From these hang bright yellow thread-like branchlets. The variety 'Filifera' is green.

CRYPTOMERIA Japanese Cedar
Ⓔ

Cryptomeria japonica is part of the Japanese landscape — it is grown in parks and around temples throughout the country. This stately tree reaches 150 ft or more in its native home, and it is obviously completely unsuitable for the average British garden. The popular variety over here is C. japonica 'Elegans', which is very slow-growing and takes many years to reach its maximum height of 30 ft. There are several dwarf varieties — the most compact is 'Vilmoriniana' which grows to only 1 ft after 10 years and its foliage turns reddish purple in winter. All Cryptomerias like acid, moist soil and full sun — they are susceptible to damage if heavy snow is left on their branches.

Needles long and feathery at juvenile stage, short and awl-shaped at adult stage

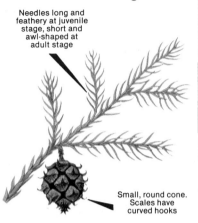

Small, round cone. Scales have curved hooks

C. japonica 'Elegans'

MEDIUM
Ht. after
10 years:
6 ft

C. japonica bears adult leaves which are small and awl-shaped. The variety 'Elegans' maintains its soft and feathery juvenile foliage throughout its life. The browny-green leaves on this bushy tree turn reddish bronze in winter.

CUNNINGHAMIA Chinese Fir
Ⓔ

Most of the varieties described in this Conifer section are both well known and reliable, but Cunninghamia is neither popular nor completely hardy. You will have to go to a specialist nursery to find the Chinese Fir (C. lanceolata) and it will need full sun, an acid soil and a site which is protected from cold winds. If you like plants which are out of the ordinary then Chinese Fir will provide you with an unusual and attractive specimen tree. When young it forms a pyramid of branches which are densely clothed with bright green and lustrous leaves which give the tree a 'Monkey Puzzle' appearance. With age this plant tends to become gaunt and unattractive, as dead leaves and branches do not fall.

Narrow, lance-shaped leaves, about 2 in. long

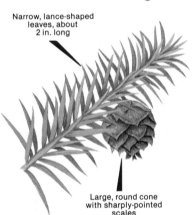

Large, round cone with sharply-pointed scales

C. lanceolata

TALL
Ht. after
10 years:
8 ft

The long, narrow leaves are arranged spirally around the branches, each one marked below with two white bands. The foliage turns brown in autumn. Once established it grows quickly to produce a sparsely branched, narrowly conical tree.

CUPRESSOCYPARIS Leyland Cypress
Ⓔ

In 1888 a chance cross occurred between a Nootka Cypress and a Monterey Cypress. Mr Leyland raised the seedlings on his estate and Cupressocyparis leylandii was born. It was not until quite recently that it became popular, and it is now the most widely used conifer for hedging and screening. The Leyland Cypress has replaced Chamaecyparis lawsoniana for this purpose as it has many advantages — it withstands hard pruning and tolerates windswept conditions, and it grows more rapidly (4 ft per year) than any other conifer. It is not a universal hedging plant — C. leylandii needs a minimum height and spread of 8 ft and cannot be used to replace a shoulder-high privet hedge around a small garden.

Pea-sized, round cone

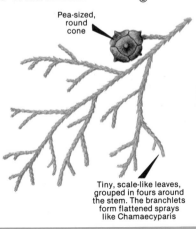

Tiny, scale-like leaves, grouped in fours around the stem. The branchlets form flattened sprays like Chamaecyparis

C. leylandii

TALL
Ht. after
10 years:
30 ft

A columnar tree which can reach 75 ft if left unpruned. Grows in all types of soils and situations but make sure you can buy small plants — maximum height 3 ft. Tall specimens establish very slowly. Growth is lax at first, dense and drooping later.

CUPRESSUS Cypress Ⓔ

The true Cypress is a splendid stately tree, and every gardener who has travelled in the Mediterranean region must have admired the dark green columns of C. semper-virens reaching up into the sky. Several forms, such as C. sempervirens 'Stricta', are available from specialist nurseries but all these Italian Cypresses are damaged in severe winters. Hardier varieties are listed below, but Cupressus is not an easy plant to grow like the closely-related and much more popular Chamaecyparis. They do not like transplanting — always plant a small specimen which has been either pot- or container-grown. Do not prune and remember to stake securely for the first couple of years.

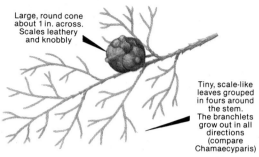

Large, round cone about 1 in. across. Scales leathery and knobbly

Tiny, scale-like leaves grouped in fours around the stem. The branchlets grow out in all directions (compare Chamaecyparis)

C. arizonica

MEDIUM
Ht. after 10 years: 7 ft

The botanists tell us that the Smooth Arizona Cypress is in fact C. glabra. Nurserymen and gardeners, however, will continue to call it C. arizonica. The variety generally on offer is 'Conica' or 'Pyramidalis' — there is no real difference between them. The shape is conical, the foliage blue-grey. The purple bark is attractive.

C. macrocarpa

TALL
Ht. after 10 years: 15 ft

The Monterey Cypress (C. macrocarpa) was a popular Victorian tree, but it has now been replaced by the much more reliable Leyland Cypress. It withstands the salt-laden air of coastal districts but it will not withstand garden shears, which means that it is useless for hedging. It loses its bottom branches with age — not a good choice.

C. macrocarpa 'Goldcrest'

MEDIUM
Ht. after 10 years: 8 ft

This cultivar of the Monterey Cypress was raised less than 40 years ago, and is the best Cupressus to choose. It is hardier and more compact than its parent, reaching no more than 25 ft when mature. The outstanding feature is its golden yellow foliage, a narrow conical tree shining brightly in the winter garden. Full sun and staking are essential.

GINKGO Maidenhair Tree Ⓓ

There is nothing about this tree which would make you think that it is a conifer. No needle-like or tiny foliage — the fan-shaped leaves are large, pale green at first and then golden yellow before falling in autumn. There are no cones — instead there are small, plum-like fruits. Ginkgo is represented by a single species — G. biloba — the sole survivor of a family of trees which flourished 200 million years ago. Conical at first, it later becomes a graceful spreading tree. Several varieties are available — there are the column-like 'Fasti-giata' and the weeping 'Pendula'. Despite its exotic appearance Ginkgo is easy to grow — happy in any reasonable garden soil.

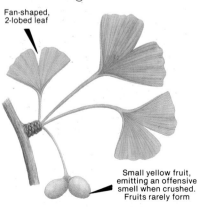

Fan-shaped, 2-lobed leaf

Small yellow fruit, emitting an offensive smell when crushed. Fruits rarely form

G. biloba

TALL
Ht. after 10 years: 10 ft

Slow-growing at first, it can reach 60 ft or more when mature and is seen at its best in parks and large gardens in the southern counties. Lower branches are retained.

JUNIPERUS Juniper Ⓔ

A useful group of conifers with many attractive low-growing varieties which spread to form effective ground covers. These ground-hugging Junipers have long been favourite plants in America and are now becoming very popular in Britain. Not all Junipers are low-growing — there are medium-sized shrubs and tall-growing trees. An advantage of all the varieties is their hardiness and tolerance of poor conditions. They will grow in chalky and gravelly soils, and will withstand drought better than most conifers. Junipers respond well to pruning — cut back hedges and trim prostrate forms in midsummer. The leaves are aromatic when crushed — both the adult and juvenile forms of foliage may occur on the same branch.

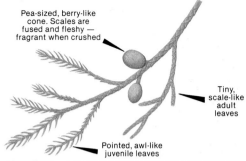

Pea-sized, berry-like cone. Scales are fused and fleshy — fragrant when crushed

Tiny, scale-like adult leaves

Pointed, awl-like juvenile leaves

J. communis 'Compressa'

DWARF
Ht. after 10 years: 1 ft

An excellent choice if you want a miniature column-like tree in the rock garden. Its greyish green branches are closely packed and it will not exceed 2 or 3 ft when fully grown.

J. communis 'Depressa Aurea'

DWARF
Ht. after 10 years: 1 ft

The Golden Canadian Juniper is a wide-spreading prickly bush, golden in summer and bronze in winter. It is not truly prostrate — an old specimen is about 2 ft tall. Full sun is essential.

J. chinensis 'Pyramidalis'

DWARF
Ht. after 10 years: 5 ft

A slow-growing conical Juniper with blue-green foliage which is almost entirely juvenile. A good choice if you want a small specimen tree — it may be listed as J. excelsa 'Stricta'.

J. horizontalis 'Glauca'

PROSTRATE
Ht. after 10 years: 1 ft

A ground-hugging plant which produces long branches with whipcord-like tips. A steely blue carpet is formed which builds up with age. The ultimate spread is 9 ft or more.

J. media 'Old Gold'

DWARF
Ht. after 10 years: 3 ft

A recent introduction which is rather similar to J. media 'Pfitzerana Aurea' — it differs by having a more compact growth habit and keeping its bronzy gold colour throughout the winter. The ultimate spread is 8 ft.

J. media 'Pfitzerana'

DWARF
Ht. after 10 years: 4 ft

One of the most popular of all conifers, the Pfitzer has strong branches rising at an angle of 45° with tips which droop gracefully. Wide-spreading, shade-resistant — an excellent choice.

JUNIPERUS continued

J. sabina tamariscifolia

PROSTRATE
Ht. after
10 years:
1 ft

The Spanish Juniper is an old favourite. The horizontal branches bear feathery foliage which is greyish green when young. When mature it is about 10 ft across.

J. squamata 'Meyeri'

DWARF
Ht. after
10 years:
4 ft

The ascending branches of this shrub are covered with steely blue leaves, the branch tips drooping downwards. Prune it regularly to prevent brown patches from appearing at the base.

J. virginiana 'Skyrocket'

MEDIUM
Ht. after
10 years:
6 ft

One of the narrowest of all conifers, bearing erect branches and blue-grey foliage. In time it will grow 15 ft or more, a tall 'pencil' which makes an ideal specimen plant for the lawn.

LARIX

Larch
Ⓓ

The Larch is one of the few conifers which loses its leaves in the winter at that time you can recognise it by its knobbly branches. In spring the bright green tufts of young leaves appear. Rose-red female flowers ('larch roses') are followed by brown cones. There are several species — L. decidua (Common Larch), L. kaempferi (Japanese Larch) and so on, and all are attractive — graceful trees with downswept branches and leaves which turn golden in autumn. But none is suitable for the average garden — they are quick-growing forestry trees which reach 80 ft or more.

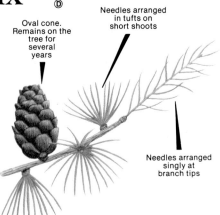

Oval cone. Remains on the tree for several years

Needles arranged in tufts on short shoots

Needles arranged singly at branch tips

L. decidua

TALL
Ht. after 10 years: 15 ft

Conical at first but with age the bottom branches are lost. It needs light, space and chalk-free soil. An important forestry tree, as is the Hybrid Larch and Japanese Larch.

LIBOCEDRUS

Incense Cedar
Ⓔ

In its native home in the western states of the U.S. the Incense Cedar is indeed a noble sight, towering upwards for 120 ft or more. The cultivated form of L. decurrens grown in the parks and gardens of Britain is also spectacular because it is narrower than the wild form — it is one of the slimmest and most elegant of all our large trees. The leaves when crushed and the wood when burnt emit an incense-like aroma, and the growth is slow enough to make this conifer an excellent choice for the garden. You may find the Incense Cedar listed in the catalogues as Calocedrus.

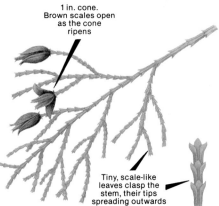

1 in. cone. Brown scales open as the cone ripens

Tiny, scale-like leaves clasp the stem, their tips spreading outwards

L. decurrens

TALL
Ht. after 10 years: 6 ft

Broadly conical at first, becoming tall and column-like with age. The bottom branches are not lost. For a slower-growing type with gold-splashed leaves, choose 'Aureovariegata'.

METASEQUOIA

Dawn Redwood
Ⓓ

The romantic story of the Dawn Redwood has been told many times. This prehistoric tree, known only from fossils, was discovered in the grounds of a Chinese temple in 1941. It first appeared in British gardens in 1948 and the earliest planted specimens are now 60 ft high. It is a quick-growing, narrowly conical tree which grows best in moist, free-draining soil. The Dawn Redwood is really only suitable for the park and the large estate, but a young specimen will provide a living fossil for the average-sized garden. The foliage is pale green in summer, turning orange in the autumn.

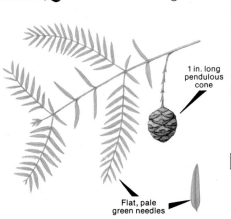

1 in. long pendulous cone

Flat, pale green needles

M. glyptostroboides

TALL
Ht. after 10 years: 15 ft

The foliage is feathery — in winter both the needles and the branchlets fall. No trees have yet reached maturity in Britain; the ultimate height is expected to be 100 ft. Closely related to Taxodium.

PICEA Spruce Ⓔ

Most Piceas look like Christmas Trees — in fact the cut trees you see for sale every December are almost certain to be the Common or Norway Spruce, P. abies. The typical Picea is tall and conical with its branches neatly arranged in whorls. The needles are usually stiff and dark green, and little or no pruning is needed to maintain the symmetrical shape. Fortunately for the gardener there are many variations — bushy and dwarf forms with grey, yellow or blue foliage. The Spruces are often praised for their tolerance of poor conditions — they will indeed succeed in wet and cold soils but they can be fussy when young. Late frosts can be damaging; so can dry, chalky and shallow soils.

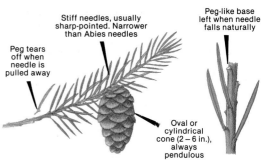

Stiff needles, usually sharp-pointed. Narrower than Abies needles

Peg tears off when needle is pulled away

Peg-like base left when needle falls naturally

Oval or cylindrical cone (2 – 6 in.), always pendulous

P. abies

TALL
Ht. after 10 years: 10 ft

The much-loved Christmas Tree, but not a good choice for the garden. There are many varieties of P. abies which are better, but the best Christmas Tree of all is P. omorika.

P. abies 'Nidiformis'

DWARF
Ht. after 10 years: 1 ft

Nothing like a Christmas Tree, much more like its common name — the Bird's Nest Spruce. It is a flat-topped, compact bush with its horizontal branches arranged in layers.

P. brewerana

TALL
Ht. after 10 years: 5 ft

Perhaps the most beautiful Spruce of all — a tall conical tree with long pendulous branchlets which give it a weeping appearance. The shining leaves are blue-green.

P. glauca albertiana 'Conica'

DWARF
Ht. after 10 years: 2 ft

One of the best and most popular rockery conifers — a perfect cone which grows very slowly to reach its maximum height of 6 ft. The tips are bright green in spring.

P. omorika

TALL
Ht. after 10 years: 10 ft

The Serbian Spruce should be your choice if you want a conical Picea which can be allowed to spread to ample proportions in the garden. The branches curve upwards at the tips.

P. pungens 'Koster'

MEDIUM
Ht. after 10 years: 6 ft

There are many forms of Blue Spruce — P. pungens 'Koster' is the most popular. It is a conical tree which may reach 25 ft. Its outstanding feature is the intense silvery blue foliage.

PINUS

Pine
Ⓔ

Pines are part of our countryside, and in parks and forests you will find the Scots Pine (our only large native conifer), the Corsican Pine, Austrian Pine and so on. At first they are conical or rounded in shape but as big trees they are usually flat-topped and irregular. These species are far too large for the average garden, but there are dwarf and slow-growing varieties which can be used very successfully. Unfortunately you will not find many on offer — Pines are not as popular as Cypresses, Junipers or Spruces. Grow one as a change from all those best-selling conifers — the leaves are much larger and the tree or shrub will grow in sandy soil and on exposed sites. Pick a dwarf Scots Pine or a Mountain Pine and remember the two pet hates — shade and polluted air.

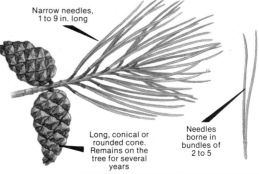

Narrow needles, 1 to 9 in. long

Long, conical or rounded cone. Remains on the tree for several years

Needles borne in bundles of 2 to 5

P. mugo 'Gnom'

DWARF
Ht. after 10 years: 2 ft

An excellent variety of the Mountain Pine which forms a globular compact mound suitable for the rock garden. The dark green leaves are borne in pairs and it will grow in all soils including chalk.

P. nigra

TALL
Ht. after 10 years: 10 ft

A good choice for a large garden where a tall specimen is required. The Austrian Pine has dark green leaves and makes a fine windbreak in maritime areas. For a slow-growing dwarf choose 'Hornibrookiana'.

P. strobus 'Nana'

DWARF
Ht. after 10 years: 2 ft

This is the popular dwarf form of the Weymouth Pine. It is a spreading plant, with an ultimate height of about 6 ft. Its outstanding feature is the colour of the foliage — silvery blue-green.

P. sylvestris

TALL
Ht. after 10 years: 12 ft

A familiar tree which reaches 80 ft or more when mature. You can easily recognise it by its reddish bark and twisted needles. These leaves are borne in pairs and are grey-green.

P. sylvestris 'Beuvronensis'

DWARF
Ht. after 10 years: 2 ft

A dwarf form of the Scots Pine, with a spread which is about twice its height. It is a compact and densely branched plant, highly recommended for the rock garden.

P. wallichiana

TALL
Ht. after 10 years: 10 ft

The Bhutan Pine is one of the most beautiful of all the large Pines. It retains its lower branches and the young foliage is bluish green. Often listed as P. griffithii.

PSEUDOTSUGA
Douglas Fir
Ⓔ

The mighty Douglas Fir (P. menziesii) is one of our tallest trees, grown mainly as a forestry tree for its timber. The trunk is corky and deeply furrowed, the lower branches bending upwards and the narrow conical shape providing a most impressive sight. Out of the question for the ordinary garden, but it can be grown as a tall hedge as it responds to clipping. A much better choice are the dwarf forms, not often seen for sale but worth looking for. Pseudotsuga can be mistaken for Abies but there are important differences — the cones hang downwards and the soft needles do not have sucker-like bases. The growth buds are spindle-shaped, like Beech. It needs deep soil in full sun — chalky land is unsuitable.

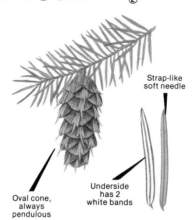

Strap-like soft needle

Underside has 2 white bands

Oval cone, always pendulous

P. menziesii 'Fletcheri'

DWARF
Ht. after 10 years: 2 ft

A low-growing form of the Douglas Fir, not widely known but a good choice for the larger rockery. Flat-topped when mature, with blue-green 1 in. long needles.

Conifers for the Rockery

Abies balsamea 'Hudsonia'
Chamaecyparis lawsoniana 'Ellwoodii'
Chamaecyparis lawsoniana 'Minima Aurea'
Chamaecyparis lawsoniana 'Minima Glauca'
Chamaecyparis obtusa 'Nana Gracilis'
Juniperus communis 'Compressa'
Picea glauca albertiana 'Conica'
Pinus mugo 'Gnom'
Pinus sylvestris 'Beuvronensis'
Pseudotsuga menziesii 'Fletcheri'
Thuja occidentalis 'Hetz Midget'
Tsuga canadensis 'Pendula'

Conifers which Change Colour

One of the few criticisms of conifers is that they never change colour and so there is no variety with the seasons. This is not strictly true — a few evergreens and all the deciduous varieties do take on autumn hues.

Cryptomeria japonica 'Elegans' Ⓔ
(green, changing to reddish bronze in winter)
Cunninghamia lanceolata Ⓔ
(green, changing to brown in autumn)
Ginkgo biloba Ⓓ
(pale green, changing to gold in autumn)
Larix decidua Ⓓ
(green, changing to gold in autumn)
Metasequoia glyptostroboides Ⓓ
(pale green, changing to gold in autumn)
Taxodium distichum Ⓓ
(pale green, changing to bronzy yellow in autumn)
Thuja occidentalis 'Rheingold' Ⓔ
(old gold, changing to copper in winter)
Thuja orientalis 'Aurea Nana' Ⓔ
(gold, changing to bronzy green in winter)
Thuja orientalis 'Rosedalis' Ⓔ
(gold in spring, green in summer and purple in autumn)

SCIADOPITYS
Umbrella Pine
Ⓔ

Perhaps you like to impress your friends with a plant they have never seen before. If so, choose Sciadopitys but you will have to go to a specialist nursery to buy one. There is just one species (S. verticillata), which is the sole survivor of this once-flourishing group of trees. The arrangement of the needles is unique — between ten and thirty are arranged in whorls like the ribs of an umbrella, hence the common name. It has none of the tolerance and hardiness of many of the conifers — it does not like shallow soil and it should be grown in a sheltered spot in partial shade. The soil must be lime-free. The oval cones are about 4 in. long, green at first and brown when ripe.

Pine-like needles arranged in whorls

S. verticillata

MEDIUM
Ht. after 10 years: 3 ft

An extremely slow-growing specimen tree, reaching a height of only 30 ft in 50 or 60 years. The 5 in. long needles are glossy, and the mature tree is broadly conical.

SEQUOIA   Californian Redwood
Ⓔ

Everything about the Californian Redwood (S. sempervirens) is astonishing. In its native home in the western region of the U.S. it is the world's tallest tree, the record standing at 366 ft. Some are more than 2000 years old but not everything about it is the biggest or the oldest. The cones are unusually small — less than 1 in. across, and this tree has the remarkable ability for a conifer of throwing up new shoots if it is cut down to ground level. Obviously it is a tree for the large park, where its column-like shape and drooping branches can be admired and is not suitable for the garden. But there are dwarf forms — these small varieties begin by growing slowly but will often revert and become tall trees if not pruned each year.

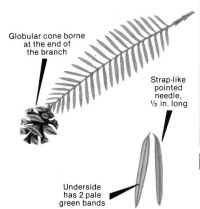

Globular cone borne at the end of the branch

Strap-like pointed needle, ½ in. long

Underside has 2 pale green bands

S. sempervirens 'Adpressa'

DWARF
Ht. after 10 years: 4 ft

You may find this dwarf variety of the Californian Redwood listed as 'Albos-pica' in the catalogue. It is slow-growing and the growing tips are creamy white. Prune it regularly to prevent reversion.

SEQUOIADENDRON   Wellingtonia
Ⓔ

Like its fellow giant, the Sequoia, this tree is full of interest. Its latin name comes from an Indian, Sequoyah, who never saw it and its common name is derived from the Duke of Wellington, who also never saw it. The Wellingtonia (S. giganteum) is the world's largest living thing — although less tall than the Sequoia it has a greater girth — imagine a tree 80 ft around! In California there are specimens over 3000 years old but the first one was planted in England less than 150 years ago. Since then it has been widely planted in grand gardens throughout the country, and this columnar tree with its curved branches is a familiar sight. A small form ('Pygmaeum') is available, but for nearly all of us Wellingtonia is a tree to admire and not to plant.

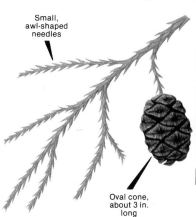

Small, awl-shaped needles

Oval cone, about 3 in. long

S. giganteum

TALL
Ht. after 10 years: 18 ft

A stately giant, well suited to the large estate but not the average garden. The leaves are blue-green. A much smaller column-like variety with pendent branches ('Pendulum') is available.

TAXODIUM   Swamp Cypress
Ⓓ

The Swamp Cypress is a beautiful and graceful tree, conical when young and rounded when mature. Its delicate, feathery foliage, light green in summer, turns bronzy yellow before it falls in the autumn. The remarkable feature of Taxodium is that it will thrive in wet soil, and it is certainly the conifer to choose if you have swampy ground. Wet conditions are not essential — it will grow in any chalk-free loamy soil. Several varieties of Taxodium can be purchased from specialist nurseries but there is only one common species — T. distichum. It is an excellent tree to plant next to a pond, but it will need space and full sun if it is to flourish.

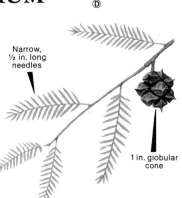

Narrow, ½ in. long needles

1 in. globular cone

T. distichum

TALL
Ht. after 10 years: 15 ft

A large tree with fern-like foliage and reddish, fibrous bark. It can grow 100 ft high — mature specimens produce above-ground growths from the roots ('cypress knees') in wet conditions.

TAXUS Yew ℮

The usual leaf colour of Yew is blackish green, and it is thought of as a slow-growing conifer for hedging old gardens and churchyards. Many varieties do make ideal hedges but there are other uses and other leaf colours. Golden varieties are available, and shapes range from prostrate sheets to 40 ft column-like trees. Yew is less demanding than most conifers — it will grow in shade and does not mind smoky air, but it does not like poorly-drained soil. Nearly all varieties are slow-growing, especially at first, but they are long-lived. The male and female flowers are borne on separate plants and the usual warning must be made — the leaves and seeds are poisonous.

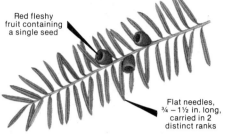

Red fleshy fruit containing a single seed

Flat needles, ¾ – 1½ in. long, carried in 2 distinct ranks

T. baccata

MEDIUM
Ht. after 10 years: 6 ft

The Common Yew is a native conifer, widely planted around gardens for centuries. As a tree it may in time reach 40 ft, but it is usually kept clipped as an evergreen hedge.

T. baccata 'Fastigiata'

MEDIUM
Ht. after 10 years: 5 ft

The familiar upright Irish Yew, a narrow column when young but spreading a little with age. The leaves are blackish green and the ultimate height is about 15 ft.

T. baccata 'Fastigiata Aureomarginata'

MEDIUM
Ht. after 10 years: 5 ft

The Golden Irish Yew is a colourful version of the well known 'Fastigiata'. The leaves are edged yellow — the tree is dull gold in winter. A smaller version is T. baccata 'Standishii'.

T. baccata 'Repandens'

PROSTRATE
Ht. after 10 years: 1 ft

A low-growing Yew which can be used for ground cover, with a spread of 10 ft or more when fully grown. The long branches droop at the tips. This plant thrives in sun or shade.

T. baccata 'Elegantissima'

DWARF
Ht. after 10 years: 4 ft

This is the most popular of the Golden Yews. It is a small version of the Common Yew, its leaves being all-yellow when young, later changing to green with yellow margins.

T. baccata 'Semperaurea'

DWARF
Ht. after 10 years: 2 ft

Perhaps the brightest of the Golden Yews — this wide-spreading bush has ascending branches clothed in bright yellow leaves every spring. It is a male plant and does not bear berries.

THUJA   Arbor-vitae ⓔ

It is quite easy to mistake a Thuja for the much more popular Chamaecyparis. In both cases the branches are clothed in tiny, scale-like leaves and there is a wide variation in size, shape and leaf colour. To tell the difference crush a branchlet — Thuja has aromatic foliage. Another sign is that Thuja branches often show brownish areas in winter, but the easiest way to tell them apart is to look at the cones. Thuja cones are elongated with the tips of the scales opening outwards. Chamaecyparis cones are quite different — see page 83. All the Thujas are easily grown — their only major dislike is badly-drained soil. They will tolerate some shade but the yellow varieties need full sun. Like Chamaecyparis, many make excellent hedges.

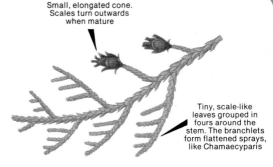

Small, elongated cone. Scales turn outwards when mature

Tiny, scale-like leaves grouped in fours around the stem. The branchlets form flattened sprays, like Chamaecyparis

T. occidentalis 'Hetz Midget'

DWARF · One of the smallest of all conifers. It
Ht. after forms a small, dark green globe which
10 years: will fit into a sink garden or a small
¾ ft rockery. It is extremely slow-growing and is a true miniature.

T. occidentalis 'Rheingold'

DWARF A popular rounded or conical shrub. It
Ht. after is noted for the old gold colour of its
10 years: summer foliage which turns coppery
3 ft in winter. It is widely recommended for planting amongst heathers.

T. orientalis 'Aurea Nana'

DWARF An oval-shaped bush with crowded
Ht. after upright branches. In summer it is
10 years: golden yellow, changing to bronzy
2 ft green in winter. The neat shape makes it an excellent specimen shrub.

T. orientalis 'Rosedalis'

DWARF Here we have a novelty — the soft
Ht. after juvenile foliage of this oval-shaped
10 years: dwarf changes from golden yellow in
2 ft the spring to pale green throughout the summer and then to purple in the autumn.

T. plicata

TALL The Western Red Cedar is one of the
Ht. after taller Thujas, a pyramid-shaped
10 years: specimen tree for the large garden or
16 ft trimmed as a high hedge. The glossy leaves are carried in drooping sprays. Not fussy about soil type.

T. plicata 'Zebrina'

TALL Similar in shape to T. plicata but
Ht. after slower-growing and with green foliage
10 years: which is banded creamy yellow. In late
12 ft spring the whole plant is golden. An excellent specimen tree for a large lawn.

TSUGA

Hemlock
Ⓔ

The Hemlocks are broadly conical trees, noted for their graceful appearance and arching branchlets. There are two species grown in Britain — the Western Hemlock (T. heterophylla) and the Eastern Hemlock (T. canadensis). Both are tall and elegant conifers which are far too large for the average garden, but there are fortunately several cultivars of T. canadensis which are compact enough for a small plot. 'Bennett' is a semi-prostrate bush which reaches a maximum height of 3 ft — even smaller is the ground-hugging 'Cole'. The most popular garden variety is 'Pendula', described on the right. All these forms are easy to grow, thriving in chalky soil and in shady conditions.

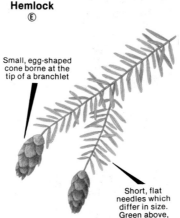

Small, egg-shaped cone borne at the tip of a branchlet

Short, flat needles which differ in size. Green above, white below

T. canadensis 'Pendula'

DWARF
Ht. after
10 years:
2 ft

A wide spreading mound of overlapping and drooping branchlets. Grow it in a large rock garden where it can cascade over the stones — the eventual spread may be 15 ft or more.

CHAPTER 6
BUYING & PLANTING

The trees and shrubs you are about to buy will cost considerably more than the price a few years ago, but they should last for many years. Care taken at the buying and planting stages will save money and problems later on.

These days there are several ways to buy plants and the planting material will be one of four distinct types – each source of supply and type of planting material has its good and bad points.

Planting should take place as soon as practical once the new shrub or tree has arrived at your home. There is much more to this than just digging a hole and dropping it in. Read this chapter *before* you begin... not afterwards to see what you did wrong!

Sources of supply

THE MAIL ORDER NURSERY

Despite the rapid spread of garden centres in recent years, the reputable mail order nursery still remains an important source of supply. The golden rules are to try to buy from a company you know or one which has been recommended and to order as early as you can. Fill out the order form carefully.

Advantages

● Many mail order nurseries produce excellent catalogues which enable you to choose trees and shrubs in the quiet and comfort of your own home. Each selection can be carefully considered and its requirements checked before you commit yourself.

● Unusual and rare varieties as well as the popular ones can be obtained. Some nurseries specialise in particular groups of plants, such as rhododendrons or heathers — look for their addresses in the classified advertisement pages in the gardening magazines.

● The nursery is only as far away as your nearest postbox, as their advertisements keep telling us. This is a distinct advantage if you can't get to a large garden centre.

Drawbacks

● You cannot see what you are buying and so you must take quality on trust.

● You cannot take your order home with you, which means that the plants may arrive when the weather is unsuitable for planting or when you are too busy to deal with them.

● One or more of your selections may be out of stock, and you won't know for some time after placing your order.

● The delivery charge for container-grown and balled plants is high.

● Transport to you may well have involved some stress to the plants. With mail order it is doubly important to plant as soon as possible.

If something goes wrong
If one or more of the plants fail and you are confident that it is not your fault, write to the company and explain what happened. Many nurseries will return your money if they feel your complaint is a genuine one.

THE BARGAIN OFFER NURSERY

National newspapers frequently have advertisements for 'bargain' offers and 'wonder' plants. Good value offers do, of course, occur but such advertisements must be viewed with caution. Above all, avoid taking some of the more glowing descriptions too literally – 'everlasting-blooming', 'a continuous sheet of yellow' and 'an impenetrable hedge within a year' are more hopeful than factual.

Advantage

● If money is short and you have a large space to fill, a 'bargain' collection is an inexpensive way of filling the border. The plants offered are usually old favourites which are noted for their toughness and vigour. Many new gardens have been partly or wholly furnished with basic shrubs in this way.

Drawback

● Bargains do not exist. If the plants on offer are very cheap — much cheaper than you could buy them locally, then almost certainly there is a reason. The shrubs or trees may be small, rooted cuttings, which can take some time to produce a worthwhile display in your garden, or they may be substandard stock.

If something goes wrong
If the plants fail and you are confident that it is not your fault, write to the company. If the stock is dead or badly diseased on arrival or the plants are not what you ordered, complain bitterly and send a copy to the newspaper which carried the advertisement. However, if the plants are healthy but are much smaller than expected you have no grounds for complaint ... it was a 'bargain' offer.

Sources of supply *continued*

THE GARDEN CENTRE

A visit to the local garden centre has become one of the established pleasures of gardening. You can wander around and look at the trees and shrubs, knowing that at almost any time of the year you can pick up a container-grown specimen and plant it in your own garden. Selecting a plant is easy but getting it home may be difficult – never bend or twist the stems to get it into the car; it is much better to ask the garden centre to deliver it. Also remember that a plant can get roasted in the boot or windburnt if left next to an open window in a moving car. Buying shrubs and trees from the garden centre is almost trouble-free, but there are still several golden rules. Try to go at the start of the planting season, when the largest selection will be available, and try to go midweek to avoid the weekend crowds. Don't buy on impulse unless you really know your plants – it is much better to take a list, and buy the best specimens you can find. There's an art in picking out good stock – pages 99-100 tell you the secrets. If you see some plants which appeal to you but are not on your list, make a note of their names and check when you get home whether they can be expected to succeed in your garden. If so, buy them on your next visit.

Advantages

● You can see exactly what you are buying. Whenever possible make your selection when the plant is at its maximum display stage — flowering shrubs in bloom, berrying shrubs in fruit, etc.

● You can buy container-grown stock which you can plant straight away. If your requirement is not available, you can immediately choose something else.

● In most cases you can take the plants home with you — no delays, no transport charges.

● Advice is always on hand, but do check the advice in the A–Z guides!

Drawbacks

● The varieties on offer are usually the more popular varieties — you cannot expect a garden centre to stock a wide range of rarities which might not sell.

● Garden centres are usually out of town, which means that your local one may be inaccessible if you don't have a car.

● Numbers of each variety may be limited, so if you are planning a massed planting or a long hedge you may have to order from a large mail order nursery.

● The main stock-in-trade, the container-grown plant, is generally expensive.

If something goes wrong

If one or more of the plants fail and you are confident that it is not your fault, take it back to the garden centre and explain what has happened. You will need proof of purchase — always keep your receipt when buying plants. If the garden centre is a member of the International Garden Centre Association (you will see the IGC symbol on display) then it guarantees to replace any container-grown tree or shrub which has failed within 6 months of purchase, if reasonable care has been taken.

THE HIGH ST. SHOP

The popular varieties of shrubs are available from autumn until early spring in many High St. shops. In hardware stores, garden shops, department stores, greengrocers and supermarkets you will find bare-rooted plants pre-packaged in polythene bags, colourfully labelled with names and instructions.

Advantages

● You can pick up a shrub without having to make a special trip to the garden centre — many people have bought their Forsythia and Lilac at the same time as their Fish Fingers and Lingerie!

● The pre-packaged plants are inexpensive, so that you can buy many common varieties very cheaply.

Drawbacks

● Warm conditions in the shop can lead to drying out and premature growth. You must always shop carefully when buying store-housed plants. A golden rule is to buy High St. plants at the beginning of the planting season.

● The selection is very limited — only fast-moving lines can be stocked and that means the most popular ones.

If something goes wrong

There are no general rules to follow. You can try complaining to the shop but the response depends on the policy of the store. Most assistants in a large department store know very little about the plants sold and you cannot expect them to deal knowledgeably with your complaint.

Types of planting material

THE CONTAINER-GROWN PLANT

A container-grown tree or shrub is a plant which has been raised as a seedling, cutting or grafted variety and has then been potted on until it is housed in the whalehide, plastic or metal container you see on display. It should *not* have been lifted from the open ground and its roots and surrounding soil stuffed into the container prior to sale. Unfortunately this does happen and such plants will disappoint or may fail completely when planted out – always apply the No 1 test, described below.

Next, check that the plant is both healthy and sturdy. Judge it by the number of stems and the density of the leaf cover. The presence of flowers and flower buds will tell you that the plant has reached flowering size, but the number of blooms does not necessarily indicate the quality of the shrub or tree. Look at the roots which may be growing through the container – this can be a good or bad sign, depending on their size and position.

The container-grown plant has one great advantage – it can be planted at any time of the year, provided the ground is suitable. It is not, however, a fool-proof way of raising trees and shrubs – choose badly or plant badly and you are going to be disappointed.

No 1 test
Pull gently to see if the plant readily moves out of the container. If the soil ball comes up easily, the plant is not well-established and should not be chosen

Size
Don't buy the biggest size you can afford. Large old shrubs and trees take a long time to establish and are often overtaken by young, vigorous and much less expensive specimens. Don't buy the smallest size — these could be recently rooted cuttings and would take some time to become established in the garden. However, cheap rooted cuttings in small pots can be a good buy — see below

Roots

Bad sign
Thick root growing downwards from the base of the container into the bed indicates starvation or that the plant has been in the container too long

Bad sign
Thick, exposed roots on the surface indicate that the plant has been in the container too long

Good sign
Small roots peeping through the container indicate that the plant is well-established

Leaves and Stems

Bad sign
Pests or disease. Shrivelled leaves, shrivelled or cankered stems

Bad sign
Leafless, leggy stems

Bad sign
Discoloured, undersized leaves. Marginal scorch, browning or reddish tints may indicate starvation

Bad sign
Pruning cuts which indicate that the plant has been drastically cut back

Bad sign
Distinctly one-sided growth

Soil

Bad sign
Dry soil and wilting leaves

Bad sign
Dense weed growth

Good sign
A few weeds or green algal growth on the surface indicates that the plant is well-established

Bad sign
Split container

The Pot Plant
The cheapest way to buy many shrubs and conifers is as rooted cuttings in small pots. They will take a few years to become properly established, but if you are prepared to wait then pot plants are a good buy. Plant out between October and March so that roots will have had a chance to spread into the garden soil before the dry days of summer arrive. Water during dry spells in the first year or two to prevent wilting or leaf loss.

Types of planting material *continued*

THE BARE-ROOTED PLANT

Bare-rooted plants are dug up at the nursery and then transported without soil. Damp material, such as peat, is packed around the roots to prevent drying out – at no stage should the roots be allowed to become dry.

Planting takes place during the dormant season and it must be timed before the leaf buds start to break. In most gardens the best time is between mid October and late November – in cold, wet sites and on heavy clay March planting is usually preferred. Bare-rooted plants are less expensive than their container-grown counterparts and it is not true that they are always more difficult to establish – some shrubs establish more readily when planted as bare-rooted stock.

THE PRE-PACKAGED PLANT

The pre-packaged shrub is the standard planting material sold by hardware shops, supermarkets and department stores. It is a bare-rooted plant with moist peat around the roots and the whole plant housed in a polythene bag and/or box. Planting instructions and illustration of the plant in flower are included. The comfort of the shop is its advantage and its drawback – it is readily available to the shopper but in the warm conditions, away from the cold benches of the garden centre, premature growth may occur.

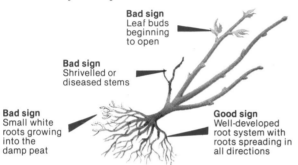

Bad sign
Leaf buds beginning to open

Bad sign
Shrivelled or diseased stems

Bad sign
Small white roots growing into the damp peat

Good sign
Well-developed root system with roots spreading in all directions

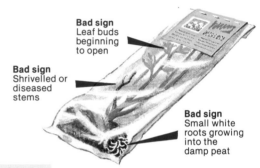

Bad sign
Leaf buds beginning to open

Bad sign
Shrivelled or diseased stems

Bad sign
Small white roots growing into the damp peat

THE BALLED PLANT

Evergreen trees and shrubs, including conifers, are often sold as balled plants. The tree or shrub is dug up and the soil around the roots is left intact, the soil ball being tightly wrapped with hessian sacking, nylon netting or polythene sheeting. The ball should be firm and comparatively large, and it should not have been allowed to dry out. Always carry a balled plant by holding it under the sacking – do not use the stem as a handle. You may find that the balled conifers at the garden centre are available in a variety of sizes. A good rule is to buy tall-growing conifers as young specimens – they will establish much more quickly than mature ones. Dwarf conifers can be bought as older plants.

Bad sign
Lop-sided growth, large patches of brown foliage

Good sign
If the balled plant is an evergreen, the stems should be sturdy and well-clothed with healthy leaves

Bad sign
Girdling roots growing horizontally around the stem at the top of the soil ball. You can feel these girdling roots through the wrapping

Bad sign
Dry soil or a broken soil ball

Timing

CONTAINER-GROWN PLANTS

JULY	AUG	SEPT	OCT	NOV	DEC	JAN	FEB	MARCH	APRIL	MAY	JUNE

BALLED EVERGREENS   BARE-ROOTED PLANTS & PRE-PACKAGED PLANTS   BALLED EVERGREENS

Soil conditions are as important as the calendar. The ground must be neither frozen nor water-logged. Squeeze a handful of soil — it should be wet enough to form a ball and yet dry enough to shatter when dropped on a hard surface.

Getting the soil ready

The most expensive shrub or tree you can buy will only grow as well as the soil allows. Very few soils are naturally ideal, but almost all can be transformed into a satisfactory home for the plant with some spadework (especially in clayey gardens) and humus (especially in sandy soils). Chalky soils can be a problem – do not plant trees and shrubs which require acid soil and avoid digging too deeply.

STEP 1

DOUBLE DIGGING is recommended to aerate the topsoil and break up the subsoil. The first step is to dig out a trench 18 in. wide and 12 in. deep at one side of the border and transport the soil to the other. Fork over the trench left by the removal of A, again incorporating compost or peat. Turn over strip B and so on, until a final trench is formed which is then filled with the soil from the first one. Do not remove small stones, as they are beneficial in a dry season. Roots of perennial weeds should be removed during digging. Fork 4 oz of Bone Meal per sq. yard into the topsoil, and then let the ground settle for several weeks before planting. If the top-soil is very shallow and the subsoil is composed of heavy clay, the simplest plan is to avoid digging and grow shrubs in a raised bed with added topsoil.

STEP 2

Getting the plants ready

BARE-ROOTED and PRE-PACKAGED PLANTS

IF PLANTING IS TO BE DELAYED FOR 3 or 4 DAYS — Leave the plants in an unheated but frost-proof cellar, garage or shed. The moist peat around the roots must be left intact — add more water if it is dry.

IF PLANTING IS TO BE DELAYED FOR MORE THAN 3 or 4 DAYS — 'Heel-in' the plants by digging a V-shaped trench and then spreading the plants as a single row against one side of it. Cover the roots and lower part of the stems with soil and tread down. Label with some form of permanent tag — paper labels attached by the supplier may rot away.

WHEN YOU ARE READY TO BEGIN PLANTING — Carefully unpack and place the packing material, sacking, etc. over the roots. Then prepare the plants as shown in the adjoining diagram.

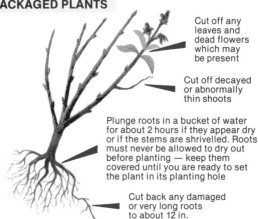

Cut off any leaves and dead flowers which may be present

Cut off decayed or abnormally thin shoots

Plunge roots in a bucket of water for about 2 hours if they appear dry or if the stems are shrivelled. Roots must never be allowed to dry out before planting — keep them covered until you are ready to set the plant in its planting hole

Cut back any damaged or very long roots to about 12 in.

BALLED PLANTS

Balled plants can be left unplanted for several weeks provided the soil ball is kept moist

To prevent the plant from toppling over, secure the stem to a firm support if planting is to be delayed

Do *not* remove the covering at this stage

Keep the soil ball moist until you are ready to plant. If the delay is to be prolonged, cover the soil ball with damp peat, compost or soil

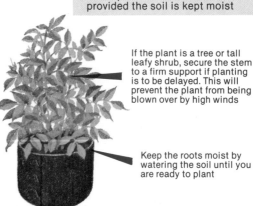

CONTAINER-GROWN PLANTS

Container-grown plants can be left unplanted for several weeks provided the soil is kept moist

If the plant is a tree or tall leafy shrub, secure the stem to a firm support if planting is to be delayed. This will prevent the plant from being blown over by high winds

Keep the roots moist by watering the soil until you are ready to plant

Planting

BARE-ROOTED and PRE-PACKAGED PLANTS

The first step is to mark out the planting stations with canes to make sure that the plants will be spaced out as planned. Next, the planting hole for each shrub or tree must be dug, and the commonest mistake is to dig a hole which is too deep and too narrow. Use the soil mark on the stem as your planting guide. Planting shrubs is a one-person job, but for large shrubs and trees you will need someone to assist you.

Planting Mixture
Make up the planting mixture in a wheelbarrow on a day when the soil is reasonably dry and friable — 1 part topsoil, 1 part moist peat and 3 handfuls of Bone Meal per barrow load. Keep this mixture in a shed or garage until you are ready to start planting.

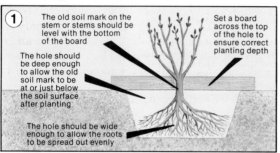

1

The old soil mark on the stem or stems should be level with the bottom of the board

The hole should be deep enough to allow the old soil mark to be at or just below the soil surface after planting

The hole should be wide enough to allow the roots to be spread out evenly

Set a board across the top of the hole to ensure correct planting depth

2

Work a couple of trowelfuls of the planting mixture around the roots. Shake the plant gently up and down and add a little more planting mixture. Firm this around the roots with your fists. Do not press too hard.

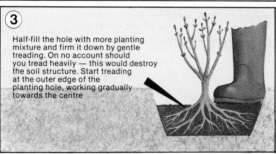

3

Half-fill the hole with more planting mixture and firm it down by gentle treading. On no account should you tread heavily — this would destroy the soil structure. Start treading at the outer edge of the planting hole, working gradually towards the centre

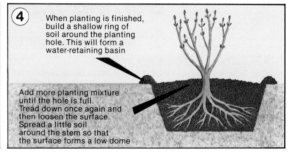

4

When planting is finished, build a shallow ring of soil around the planting hole. This will form a water-retaining basin

Add more planting mixture until the hole is full. Tread down once again and then loosen the surface. Spread a little soil around the stem so that the surface forms a low dome

BALLED and CONTAINER-GROWN PLANTS

Never regard container-grown plants as an easy way to plant trees and shrubs. If the environment surrounding the soil ball is not right then the roots will not grow out into the garden soil. This means that it is not enough to dig a hole, take off the container, drop in the plant and replace the earth.

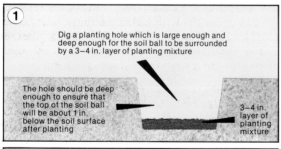

1

Dig a planting hole which is large enough and deep enough for the soil ball to be surrounded by a 3–4 in. layer of planting mixture

The hole should be deep enough to ensure that the top of the soil ball will be about 1 in. below the soil surface after planting

3–4 in. layer of planting mixture

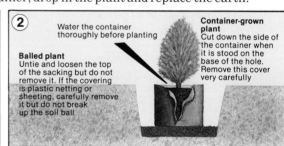

2

Water the container thoroughly before planting

Balled plant
Untie and loosen the top of the sacking but do not remove it. If the covering is plastic netting or sheeting, carefully remove it but do not break up the soil ball

Container-grown plant
Cut down the side of the container when it is stood on the base of the hole. Remove this cover very carefully

3

Container-grown plant
Examine the exposed surface of the soil ball. Very gently cut away circling or tangled roots but never break up the soil ball

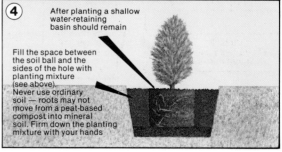

4

After planting a shallow water-retaining basin should remain

Fill the space between the soil ball and the sides of the hole with planting mixture (see above). Never use ordinary soil — roots may not move from a peat-based compost into mineral soil. Firm down the planting mixture with your hands

Staking

A tree or tall spindly shrub can be rocked by strong winds if its roots are not able to anchor it firmly in the ground. A newly-planted specimen does not have this anchorage, so it can be dislodged or blown over. Staking is the answer – it is a job to do at planting time and not after the damage has been done.

BARE-ROOTED TREES

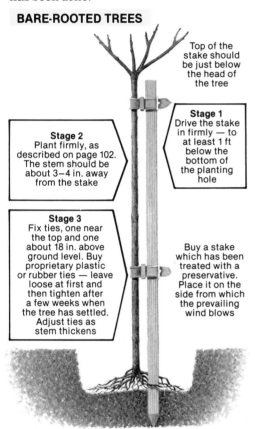

Top of the stake should be just below the head of the tree

Stage 1
Drive the stake in firmly — to at least 1 ft below the bottom of the planting hole

Stage 2
Plant firmly, as described on page 102. The stem should be about 3–4 in. away from the stake

Stage 3
Fix ties, one near the top and one about 18 in. above ground level. Buy proprietary plastic or rubber ties — leave loose at first and then tighten after a few weeks when the tree has settled. Adjust ties as stem thickens

Buy a stake which has been treated with a preservative. Place it on the side from which the prevailing wind blows

BALLED and CONTAINER-GROWN TREES

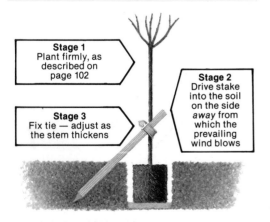

Stage 1
Plant firmly, as described on page 102

Stage 2
Drive stake into the soil on the side *away* from which the prevailing wind blows

Stage 3
Fix tie — adjust as the stem thickens

Spacing

Text books on roses always provide a clear guide to the correct planting distances between the various types, but shrub books generally ignore the subject. This is surprising, because planting too closely is perhaps the commonest fault in the shrub garden.

It is easy to see why people plant too closely. The plants from the garden centre or nursery are usually small, and it is hard to imagine at this stage what they will look like when they are mature. But they *will* reach maturity, and if you have planted them too closely there are only two alternatives – you can either dig out some of the cramped shrubs (which is the more sensible but the less popular choice) or you can hack them back each year, which destroys so much of their beauty.

Of course, the better plan is to start correctly:

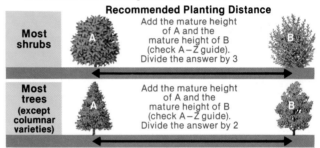

Recommended Planting Distance

Most shrubs — Add the mature height of A and the mature height of B (check A–Z guide). Divide the answer by 3

Most trees (except columnar varieties) — Add the mature height of A and the mature height of B (check A–Z guide). Divide the answer by 2

When you plant at these distances the border will look bare and unattractive. You can plant a little closer, but that is not really the answer. One solution is to plant a number of 'fill-in' shrubs between the choice shrubs and trees which you regard as permanent residents. These 'fill-in' shrubs, such as Forsythia, Ribes, Spiraea, Mahonia, etc., can be bought cheaply as 'bargains' and will soon provide a colourful display. They are progressively removed as the choice shrubs develop and require more room. A second alternative is to fill the space between widely-spaced shrubs with bulbs, annuals, herbaceous perennials and ground cover plants. Whichever plan you follow, the result will be much better than the over-crowded effect you can see in countless gardens.

After planting

Proper after-care is just as important as good planting. Once the new tree or shrub is in place it should be watered in thoroughly. Cut back the branches of bare-rooted shrubs to about two-thirds of their length; container-grown and balled plants should not need trimming.

Evergreens pose a problem. Winter browning can take place when they are planted in autumn – protect choice specimens with a screen made out of polythene sheeting. When spring arrives, spray the leaves with water on warm days and apply a mulch around the stems.

Do not let grass grow closer than 1 ft from the base of trees until about two years after planting.

CHAPTER 7
TREE & SHRUB CARE

The labour-saving aspect of growing trees and shrubs is one of the main reasons for the ever-increasing popularity of this group of plants. The gardener is spared the constant round of annual soil preparation and planting, regular feeding and spraying, autumn lifting and so on. For most of us it is just a matter of cutting away unwanted branches and occasionally hoeing and watering.

There is a little more to tree and shrub care than that. Keeping growth in check and pruning to increase the floral display calls for cutting in the proper season and in the proper way. Mulching and training have an important part to play. Trees and shrubs *are* labour-saving, but saving too much labour by ignoring an essential task can mean a great deal of extra work later on.

PRUNING

The purpose of pruning is threefold. Firstly, there is the need to remove poor quality wood, such as weak twigs, dead or diseased branches and damaged stems. Next, there is the need to shape the tree or shrub – this calls for the removal of good quality but unwanted wood so that the vigour of the plant is directed as required. Finally, trees and shrubs are pruned to regulate the quality and the quantity of flower production over the years.

In order to achieve these benefits it is generally necessary to prune each year. Some will require virtually no cutting at all – others will need fairly drastic treatment if their beauty is to be maintained. There are a few general rules and they are listed in this section but there is only one golden rule: *Check the A-Z guides and follow the instructions given for the plant in question.*

INFORMAL SHAPING
This is the style of pruning for specimen plants and for trees and shrubs in the border. The natural growth habit is maintained — the important pruning method is **thinning**

FORMAL SHAPING
This is the style of pruning for topiary and for neatly trimmed hedges. An artificial but attractive growth habit is maintained — the important pruning method is **heading back**

The Tools for Pruning

TWO-BLADED SECATEURS
will cut cleanly for many years with proper care. The cut must be made at the centre of the blades — maximum diameter ½ – ¾ in.

GARDEN SHEARS
are required for trimming hedges and tidying-up in the border. Buy a good pair and make sure they are properly set — keep them clean, dry and sharp

GLOVES
are necessary to protect your hands from prickles and thorns. Buy a stout and flexible pair

PRUNING SAW
is useful if you have stems over ½ in. across to be cut

LONG-HANDLED PRUNER
for stems ½ – 1½ in. across — many gardeners prefer them to a pruning saw for dealing with thick stems. Essential for tall shrubs and trees

ELECTRIC HEDGE TRIMMER
will take the hard work out of hedge trimming — a good buy if you have a large stretch to keep under control

PRUNING KNIFE
is useful for cleaning up ragged pruning cuts. Excellent for pruning thin branches, but only if you are experienced in its use

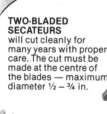

The Types of Pruning

HEADING BACK

The ends of the branches are removed. This stimulates the buds below the cuts to burst into growth.

The long-term effect is to produce a shrub which is smaller and denser than one left unpruned.

Special Types of Heading Back

TRIMMING

The growing points with only a small amount of stem attached are removed *en masse* by cutting with shears or an electric trimmer. This technique is used to maintain the shape of hedges and topiary.

PINCHING

The growing points with only a small amount of stem attached are removed one at a time by nipping out with the finger tips. This technique is used to make small plants bushier.

THINNING

Entire branches are removed back to a main stem. This diverts extra energy to the remaining branches.

The long-term effect is to produce a shrub which is larger and more open than one left unpruned.

Special Type of Thinning

LOPPING

The removal of a large branch from the trunk of a tree. Call in a tree surgeon if the job is larger than your experience.

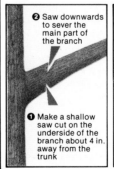

❷ Saw downwards to sever the main part of the branch

❶ Make a shallow saw cut on the underside of the branch about 4 in. away from the trunk

Saw off the stub — make the cut almost flush with the trunk

Pare away the rough edges with a pruning knife. Paint the cut surface with Arbrex

The Types of Wood

OLD WOOD
THIRD YEAR WOOD (growth made the year before last)

OLD WOOD
SECOND YEAR WOOD (last year's growth)

NEW WOOD
FIRST YEAR WOOD (this year's growth)

Lateral Bud

Terminal Bud

Step-by-Step Guide to Annual Pruning

STEP 1

Pick the right time. It is essential that pruning takes place at the correct growth stage of the tree or shrub — cutting back severely at the wrong time often leads to the loss of a whole season's flowers and occasionally it leads to the death of the plant.

The best plan is to look up the particular tree or shrub in the A – Z guides — the following timing rules are only a general guide and there are exceptions:

Deciduous Trees and Shrubs which bloom before the end of May	As soon as flowering has finished — do not delay
Deciduous Trees and Shrubs which bloom after the end of May	Between January and March — do not wait until growth starts
Flowering Cherries	Late summer
Broad-leaved Evergreens	May
Conifers	Autumn

STEP 2

Cut out dead wood. It is quite natural for the lower branches of some shrubs and trees to die under the dense canopy of the upper leaves. Prune back to where the dead branch joins the stem from which it arose.

STEP 3

Cut out damaged and diseased wood. All branches which have been broken by wind or snow should be removed and all badly diseased or cankered wood should be cut out. The pruned surface should not bear tell-tale brown staining.

STEP 4

Cut out weak and overcrowded wood. Prune all very thin and weak stems — then stand back and look at the network of branches. If there is a tightly packed arrangement of criss-crossed stems at the centre of the bush, some thinning of the old wood will help to open the shrub and improve its vigour and appearance.

STEP 5

Remove suckers. With grafted plants the suckering growth produced from the rootstock will weaken the plant and may allow the wild plant to take over if left unchecked. Some shrubs which grow on their own roots may also produce suckers, and these too should be removed if you want to keep the plant within bounds. Failure to remove the suckers can lead to a dense thicket of stems within a few years.

STEP 6

Cut back overgrowth. Once again stand back and look at the plant. Are some of the branches awkwardly placed? Is it becoming too invasive? Are the stems overhanging the path? Remember that overgrowth should be tackled *every* year and not left until major surgery is required.

STEP 7

Prune (if necessary) for floral display. Many but not all flowering shrubs and trees require pruning each year to ensure a regular and abundant supply of flowering stems. Look up the plant in the A – Z guides — the following rules are only a general guide and there are exceptions:

Deciduous Trees and Shrubs which bloom before the end of May. Examples: Ribes, Forsythia, Philadelphus, Winter-flowering Jasmine, Weigela and Deutzia	Flowers are produced on old wood. Cut back all the branches which have borne blooms. In most cases this calls for cutting back to a point which is close to where the branch joins the stem. New, vigorous growth will develop and this will bear flowers next season
Deciduous Trees and Shrubs which bloom after the end of May. Examples: Fuchsia, Potentilla, Tamarix, Buddleia davidii	Flowers are produced on new wood. Cut back all old wood hard. New, vigorous growth will develop and this will bear flowers this season
Flowering Cherries	No further pruning needed
Broad-leaved Evergreens	No further pruning needed. With some of these shrubs, such as Buxus, Rhododendron and Santolina, hard pruning can be used to regenerate bushes with leggy and bare lower branches
Conifers	No further pruning needed

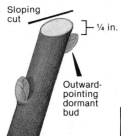

Sloping cut

¼ in.

Outward-pointing dormant bud

The Pruning Cut

All pruning cuts must be clean — pare off any ragged parts. Sharp secateurs are essential — press downwards, don't just squeeze. Cuts more than ½ in. across should be painted with Arbrex to protect them from frost and damp. It is impossible to avoid making some wrong cuts when pruning and as a result snags of dead wood will form above some of the new shoots. Cut off these dead bits as they develop.

Pruning Hedges

There are special rules for pruning newly-planted and established hedges — see page 114.

MULCHING

A mulch is a layer of bulky organic material placed on the soil surface around plants. Placed around shrubs and trees it provides five distinct benefits:

- The soil is kept moist during the dry days of summer.
- Weeds are greatly reduced.
- Soil structure is improved as humus is added to the soil.
- Plant foods are provided by some mulching materials.
- Frost penetration into the soil is reduced in winter.

Suitable materials are moist peat, good garden compost, well-rotted manure, Bio Humus and leaf mould. Grass clippings are often recommended and used, but a word of caution is necessary. Add a thin layer at a time and stir occasionally — do not use them if they are weedy or if a weedkiller has been applied.

The standard time for mulching is late April or early May. Success depends on preparing the soil surface before adding the organic blanket — remove debris and weeds, and then water if the surface is dry. Spread a 2 to 3 in. layer around but not touching the stems. Rhododendron, Azalea, Magnolia and Camellia respond particularly well to mulching.

WINTER PROTECTION

The snow and frost of an average winter usually does little or no harm to the trees and shrubs in the garden, but an abnormally severe winter can cause heavy losses. Newly-planted stock will benefit from some form of frost protection, especially if it is evergreen and known to be rather tender. You can either build a plastic screen (make sure that the bottom of the plastic sheeting is pinned down to prevent draughts) or you can put a large plastic bag over the specimen on nights when a heavy frost is forecast.

Established plants are more resistant than newly-planted ones to frost, but they are more liable to damage by the other winter enemy — snow. The weight on large conifer branches can cause them to break — if heavy snow is forecast it may be worth tying the branches of a choice evergreen with twine.

HOEING

The main purpose of hoeing is to keep down weeds, such as couch grass, which are not smothered by mulching. For this purpose hoeing must be carried out at regular intervals so that the underground parts of the weeds will be eventually starved. Hoeing should not go deeper than an inch below the surface, or shallow roots may be damaged. Do not bother to hoe as a way of conserving moisture — the old idea of creating a 'dust mulch' is of little value.

FEEDING

Trees and shrubs, like all living things, require food. The production of stems, leaves and roots is a drain on the soil's reserves of nitrogen, phosphates, potash and other nutrients, but regular feeding is not usually necessary. The extensive rooting system of the established plant can effectively tap the resources in the soil, but there are times when applying fertilizer is recommended:

- A newly-transplanted tree or shrub has not had time to develop a wide-spreading rooting system. You should therefore incorporate a slow-acting fertilizer in the soil which surrounds the limited supply of roots. The best plan is to add Bone Meal to the planting mixture — see page 102.

- Many people apply a routine dressing of Growmore around their trees and shrubs each spring, but there are times when root feeding is not effective, as in shallow and impoverished soils, prolonged dry weather, etc. In these cases use the foliar feeding technique, which involves spraying the leaves with a dilute fertilizer — the nutrients are readily absorbed into the sap stream. The response by the plant is extremely rapid and root activity is increased. Use a hose-end dilutor such as the Bio Hoser, and a suitable foliar feed like Instant Bio or Fillip. Do not feed trees and shrubs after the end of July.

- Shrubs with large flower-heads and/or a prolonged flowering season, such as Lilac and Roses, do require feeding each year. Use a proprietary rose food.

TRAINING & SUPPORTING

Supporting and training are not quite the same thing. **Supporting** involves the provision of a post, stake or framework to which weak stems can be attached — **training** involves the fixing of branches into desired positions so that an unnatural but desirable growth habit is produced.

When a tree has outgrown its stake it may still require support. This can be provided by fixing a collar to the middle of the trunk and then securing it to the ground by means of three strong wires. Some shrubs with lax spreading stems may require some form of support after a few years. If the plant is not growing against a wall or frame, use three or more unobtrusive stakes with a band joining the top of each stake — never rely on a single ugly pole and twine.

Many trees, especially weeping ones, require training from an early stage if a mass of untidy branches is to be avoided. Select the branch which will form the trunk and attach it to an upright stake — trim away all low-growing side branches. Remove side growths as they appear. At the desired height let this main branch fork to produce the head — this produces a standard tree with a trunk which is waist high (short standard), shoulder high (half standard) or head high (standard). Even a climber such as Wisteria can be trained as a weeping standard in this way.

Climbers must be trained from the outset to ensure that they remain attached to their support and grow in the desired direction. This does not mean that the main stems should all be trained vertically — spreading them at an angle (fan-trained) or horizontally (espalier) can dramatically increase the display.

CUTTING

Cutting flowers and decorative leaves to take indoors for arranging is, of course, one of the pleasures of gardening. This form of spring or summer pruning generally does no harm but there are pitfalls. During its first season in your garden the plant needs all the stems and green leaves it can muster, so only cut a few flowers and do not remove many leaves.

DEAD-HEADING

It is, of course, quite impractical to remove the dead flowers from most trees and shrubs, but there are a few large-flowering varieties which must be dead-headed. The trusses of Hybrid Tea and Floribunda Roses should be cut off once the blooms have faded and the dead flowers of Rhododendrons should be carefully broken off with finger and thumb — take care not to damage the buds below. Cut off the flower-heads of Lilac once the blooms have faded.

WATERING

During the first couple of years of a tree or shrub's life in your garden, copious watering will be necessary during a prolonged dry spell in late spring or summer. Once established the plant will need watering much less often, as trees and shrubs usually remain fresh and green when the annuals and vegetables have started to flag.

The need to water, however, cannot be ignored. If the weather is dry, look at the trouble spots. Climbers growing next to the house, shrubs in tubs and all plants growing in very sandy soil will probably need watering. Then there are the shallow-rooted plants which can quite quickly suffer even in good soil once the dry spells of summer arrive. Birch trees and Rhododendron bushes are well-known examples of plants which suffer in drought, but there are others.

Once you decide to water, then water thoroughly — a light sprinkling can do more harm than good. As a rough guide use 1 gallon for each small shrub and 4 gallons for each large one. A watering can is often used, but a hose-pipe is a much better idea unless your garden is very small. Remember to water slowly close to the base of the plant.

Trickle irrigation through a perforated hose laid close to the bushes is perhaps the best method of watering. A quick and easy technique popular in America is to build a ridge of soil around each bush and then fill the basin with a hose.

CHAPTER 8
INCREASING YOUR STOCK

There are three basic reasons for raising new shrubs and trees in your own garden. First of all, there is the satisfaction of having plants which are actually home-grown and not raised by somebody else. Next, it is the only way to reproduce a much-admired variety which is not available from a nursery and lastly, but certainly not least, there is the purely practical reason of saving money.

Not all trees and shrubs can be raised at home and the ease with which new plants can be produced varies from child's play to near impossible. There are several techniques — the one most likely to succeed for each plant is given in the A-Z guides. Every gardener should try his or her hand at layering, division or taking cuttings — there is nothing to lose and much to gain.

DIVISION

Some small shrubs form clumps which can be lifted and then split up like herbaceous perennials into several rooted sections. Each section should be planted firmly and then watered in thoroughly.

Best time: Early winter

Examples: Ceratostigma   Lavender
Daboecia   Vinca

Many shrubs spread by means of suckers, which are shoots arising from an underground shoot or root. Removing and planting suckers is one of the easiest of all methods of propagation.

Best time: Early winter for deciduous plants; April or September for evergreens

Examples: Bamboo   Mahonia
Cornus alba   Pernettya
Hazel   Rhus typhina
Kerria   Snowberry

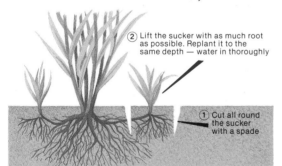

② Lift the sucker with as much root as possible. Replant it to the same depth — water in thoroughly

① Cut all round the sucker with a spade

LAYERING

Shrubs with flexible stems can be raised very easily by layering — some plants (e.g. Rhododendron, Magnolia) produce new plants naturally by this method. To layer a shrub or climber, a stem is pegged into the ground and left attached to the parent plant until roots have formed at the base of the layered shoot. This takes about 6 to 12 months.

Best time: Spring or autumn

Examples: Berberis   Honeysuckle
Camellia   Japonica
Clematis   Lilac
Forsythia   Magnolia
Heather   Rhododendron

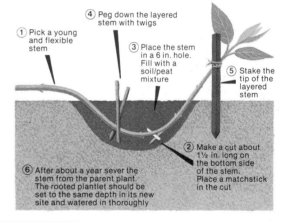

④ Peg down the layered stem with twigs

① Pick a young and flexible stem

③ Place the stem in a 6 in. hole. Fill with a soil/peat mixture

⑤ Stake the tip of the layered stem

② Make a cut about 1½ in. long on the bottom side of the stem. Place a matchstick in the cut

⑥ After about a year sever the stem from the parent plant. The rooted plantlet should be set to the same depth in its new site and watered in thoroughly

SEED SOWING

Seed sowing is the standard method of raising flowers and vegetables, but it is not widely used for propagating shrubs and trees at home. Germination is not always straight-forward — some seeds take many months to germinate and others need exposure to months of cold weather before they start to grow. It may be several years before the seedling is large enough to be decorative and many varieties will not breed true. Despite the drawbacks, there are several shrubs which can be readily raised from seed:

Examples: Cistus   Genista   Leycesteria
Clerodendrum   Hippophae   Potentilla

Spring is the best time. Fill a pot with Seed & Cutting Compost; firm lightly with the fingertips and water gently. Sow seed thinly — space out each seed if they are large enough to handle. Cover large seeds with a layer of compost; small seeds not at all. Place a polythene bag over the container and secure with a rubber band.
Stand the pot in a shady place, a temperature of 65°–70°F is ideal. As soon as the seeds have germinated move them to a bright spot, away from direct sunlight. Remove the cover, keep the surface moist and turn the pot regularly to avoid lop-sided growth. As soon as the seedlings are large enough to handle they should be pricked out into small pots filled with Potting Compost.

TAKING CUTTINGS

Autumn cuttings outdoors

Most trees and shrubs are propagated from cuttings, and hardwood cuttings planted outdoors in late autumn are the easiest ones to raise. Unfortunately, fewer uncommon varieties can be increased in this way than by striking cuttings under glass in summer.

Best time:	November

Examples:

Aucuba	Forsythia	Philadelphus	Salix
Buddleia	Honeysuckle	Populus	Sambucus
Buxus	Jasminum	Potentilla	Snowberry
Cornus	Kerria	Privet	Spiraea
Deutzia	Laburnum	Ribes	Weigela

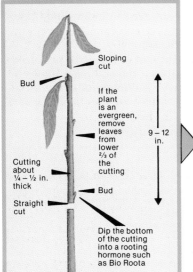

Sloping cut

Bud

If the plant is an evergreen, remove leaves from lower ⅔ of the cutting

9 – 12 in.

Cutting about ¼ – ½ in. thick

Straight cut

Bud

Dip the bottom of the cutting into a rooting hormone such as Bio Roota

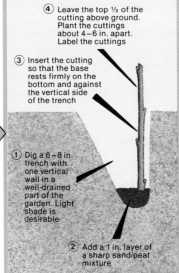

④ Leave the top ⅓ of the cutting above ground. Plant the cuttings about 4 – 6 in. apart. Label the cuttings

③ Insert the cutting so that the base rests firmly on the bottom and against the vertical side of the trench

① Dig a 6 – 8 in. trench with one vertical wall in a well-drained part of the garden. Light shade is desirable

② Add a 1 in. layer of a sharp sand/peat mixture

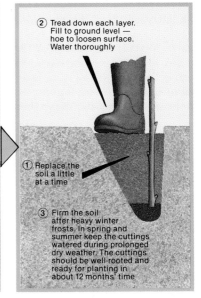

② Tread down each layer. Fill to ground level — hoe to loosen surface. Water thoroughly

① Replace the soil a little at a time

③ Firm the soil after heavy winter frosts. In spring and summer keep the cuttings watered during prolonged dry weather. The cuttings should be well-rooted and ready for planting in about 12 months' time

Summer cuttings under glass

The most important method of propagating trees and shrubs is to strike semi-ripe cuttings in summer. Sturdy side shoots are usually chosen, and the cutting should be soft and green at the top but somewhat stiff at the base. The cuttings must be planted quickly and not left to dry out, and some form of glass or plastic cover will be required.

Best time:	July and August

Examples:

Berberis	Daphne	Laurus	Santolina
Buddleia	Escallonia	Lilac	Senecio
Ceanothus	Euonymus	Pernettya	Skimmia
Cistus	Hebe	Pieris	Spiraea
Cotoneaster	Honeysuckle	Potentilla	Viburnum
Cytisus	Hydrangea	Rhododendron	Weigela

Stem-tip cutting

Cut off leaves from lower half of the cutting

1 – 6 in. depending on the size of the parent plant

Leaf joint

Straight cut

Dip bottom ½ in. of the cutting into a rooting hormone such as Bio Roota

or
Heel cutting

Cut off leaves from lower half of the cutting

Pull off side shoot with a heel attached. Dip bottom 1 in. of the cutting into a rooting hormone such as Bio Roota

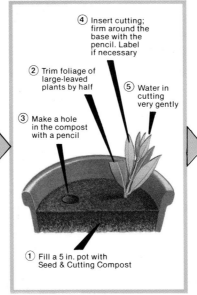

④ Insert cutting; firm around the base with the pencil. Label if necessary

② Trim foliage of large-leaved plants by half

⑤ Water in cutting very gently

③ Make a hole in the compost with a pencil

① Fill a 5 in. pot with Seed & Cutting Compost

Polythene bag method

① Place 4 canes in the pot and drape a polythene bag over them. Secure with a rubber band. Stand pot in a bright spot away from direct sunlight

② See below

or
Cold frame method

① Place pots in the cold frame — shade glass and ventilate on hot days — water when necessary. In frosty weather cover glass with sacking

② Pick off leaves which turn yellow or start to rot. In spring the rooted cuttings should be planted out in a corner of the garden. Move them to their permanent quarters at the end of the season

CHAPTER 9
USING TREES & SHRUBS

The word 'shrub' conjures up a picture of a spring- or summer-flowering, leafy bush for the back of the border. A 'climber' is a plant for clothing the wall by the front door and a 'tree' is a large, green cornerstone for a distant part of the garden. There is some truth in all of these stereotyped pictures, of course, but there are many more uses for the thousands of trees, shrubs, climbers and conifers which are now available to us.

Here are plants which will cover the ground and so reduce the constant battle we have to wage against the weeds, and here are plants to change the environment in the garden – reducing noise, protecting tender plants in winter, providing privacy and so on. Shrubs and trees can blot out eyesores, create eye-catching focal points and provide year-round floral and foliage material for indoor decoration. Every rockery needs its small shrubs and conifers and many fences need to be clothed. Trees and shrubs have many, many uses and the secret is to pick the right one for the job you want it to do.

Specimen Plants

A specimen tree or shrub is a plant grown to be admired on its own as distinct from being grouped with other plants. In the border, the bare stems of a neglected shrub may be hidden by other plants and the drab appearance of some shrubs when not in flower can be overcome by the bright display of neighbouring plants. But a specimen plant has to stand on its own. Its role is to be a focal point, adding interest to the scene and diverting attention away from less attractive features. Because of the role it has to play there are special rules for its selection and care.

● Choose a tree or shrub which will be worth looking at for most if not all of the year. Fine foliage and a pleasing shape are vital; an evergreen nature may be desirable but is by·no means essential. A fine floral display is of course an important bonus, but a specimen tree should not be chosen for that feature alone. In many specimen trees colour is obtained from the leaves, berries or bark rather than from the flowers.

● Choose the right shape and size. A small shrub in a large lawn looks out of place. A large tree in a very small lawn not only looks out of place — it may also be positively harmful to the gardening efforts of you and your neighbours by robbing the land of sun, water and food. If you want a tree rather than a bush and your garden is small, consider a shrub or rose grown as a standard. As a general rule for the smaller garden, the taller the specimen you choose, the narrower its growth habit should be.

● Proper maintenance is especially important. Follow the pruning rules given in this book — leaving it unpruned may well lead to a gaunt, unproductive shrub or tree in a few years' time. Feed it annually if it is a flowering deciduous tree or shrub and spray against pests when necessary.

Choosing a Specimen Plant

Within the rules above there is a very wide choice, and the one you pick should be the plant which appeals to you. As a guide, the following list includes specimen trees and shrubs which are widely recommended and grown.

Weeping habit
Betula pendula 'Youngii'
Laburnum anagyroides 'Pendulum'
Prunus 'Kiku-shidare Sakura'
Salix chrysocoma

Columnar habit
Chamaecyparis lawsoniana 'Columnaris'
Juniperus virginiana·'Skyrocket'
Populus nigra 'Italica'
Prunus 'Amanogawa'
Taxus baccata 'Fastigiata Aureomarginata'

Red/Purple leaves
Acer palmatum 'Atropurpureum'
Fagus sylvatica 'Purpurea'
Malus 'Profusion'

Golden/Yellow leaves
Catalpa bignonioides 'Aurea'
Chamaecyparis lawsoniana 'Stewartii'
Gleditsia triacanthos 'Sunburst'
Robinia pseudoacacia 'Frisia'
Sambucus racemosa 'Plumosa Aurea'
Thuja occidentalis 'Rheingold'

Variegated leaves
Elaeagnus pungens 'Maculata'
Ilex altaclarensis 'Golden King'
Liriodendron tulipifera 'Aureomarginatum'
Yucca filamentosa 'Variegata'

Blue-green leaves
Cedrus atlantica 'Glauca'
Chamaecyparis pisifera 'Boulevard'
Picea pungens 'Koster'

Miscellaneous
Aesculus hippocastanum
Amelanchier canadensis
Aralia elata
Corylus avellana 'Contorta'
Eucryphia nymansensis
Ginkgo biloba
Laburnum watereri 'Vossii'
Magnolia soulangiana
Pieris formosa
Rhododendron species
Rhus typhina
Sorbus aucuparia

Ground Cover Plants

A ground cover shrub is a low-growing and spreading plant which forms a dense, leafy mat. The purpose of these shrubs is clear cut — to cover the ground with a green or coloured carpet and to prevent weeds. However, the dividing line between ground cover and dwarf shrubs is much less clear cut. In this book the term 'ground cover' is restricted to wide-spreading shrubs which have an ultimate height of 3 ft or less.

There are numerous uses for ground covers — they provide greenery beneath taller shrubs and trees, hide stumps and manhole covers, edge shrubberies, clothe low walls and cover banks. They should never be regarded as eliminators of established weeds — before planting ground covers always remove every bit of perennial weed root from the soil.

Choosing a Ground Cover Plant

There are three factors to consider — the height of the plant (this can range from a few inches to 3 ft), the soil type (some are lime haters) and the location (choose shade-tolerant types for planting under shrubs and sun-lovers for clothing exposed banks).

Berberis candidula	Hypericum calycinum	Prunus laurocerasus 'Otto Luyken'
Calluna species	Juniperus horizontalis	Santolina chamaecyparissus
Cotoneaster horizontalis	Juniperus media	Senecio greyi
Erica species	Lavandula species	Taxus baccata 'Repandens'
Euonymus radicans	Pachysandra terminalis	Viburnum davidii
Hedera species	Pernettya mucronata	Vinca species

Tub Plants

Tub-grown trees and shrubs have their place in the garden. A colourful bush adds interest to a patio or balcony or against the house wall if direct planting is not possible. A Yucca or Cordyline in a pot provides a tropical touch and carefully trained and trimmed Box and Bay trees are familiar sights.

The first step is to pick a suitable container. Wooden tubs are the traditional choice, but there are many other types to select from — metal, stone, clay, plastic, fibreglass and so on. The essential feature is a drainage hole or holes. The tub should be stood on blocks to allow free drainage, and a 1 in. layer of crocks placed in the bottom. Fill it with a soil-based compost (*not* ordinary soil) or, if weight is a problem, a peat-based compost. Plant firmly and stake if necessary. Regular watering in dry weather is essential.

Choosing a Tub Plant

There are several types of tub plant. Firstly, many ordinary shrubs and compact conifers can be used to provide the sort of display they produce in the open garden. Secondly, you can choose one of the varieties which will stand regular pruning and grow it as a geometrically-shaped shrub. Next, there are many flowering shrubs which you can buy as standards and finally there are the tender exotics, such as Orange trees, which will need protection indoors during the winter months.

Arundinaria viridistriata	Hydrangea paniculata 'Grandiflora' (standard)
Berberis species	Juniperus chinensis 'Pyramidalis'
Buxus sempervirens	Juniperus media 'Old Gold'
Caragana arborescens 'Pendula' (standard)	Juniperus squamata 'Meyeri'
Chamaecyparis lawsoniana 'Ellwoodii'	Laurus nobilis
Chamaecyparis pisifera 'Boulevard'	Palms
Cotoneaster salicifolius (standard)	Prunus cistena (standard)
Euonymus radicans 'Silver Queen'	Rhododendron species
Fatsia japonica	Viburnum carlesii (standard)
Forsythia 'Lynwood' (standard)	Yucca filamentosa

Rockery Plants

Conifers and shrubs give the rock garden a permanent living form in winter, and all year round they provide columns, small bushes or coloured carpets here and there to add interest to the flat sheets of flowers and green foliage provided by the more usual rockery plants.

The coloured leaf types of Heather are, of course, extremely useful but most of the shrubs grown in the rockery are miniature forms of large plants such as Willow, Spiraea, Hypericum and Philadelphus.

Careful choice is vital, of course. A few shops sell small rooted cuttings of conifers as 'rockery conifers' whereas they are really immature forms of tall-growing varieties.

Choosing a Rockery Plant

There are numerous shrubs (see page 14) and conifers (see page 92) which are suitable for the rock garden. Occasional trimming may be necessary to keep them from becoming too invasive.

The Shrub Border

A Shrub Border is an area planted entirely with shrubs and perhaps some trees. This area is designed to be viewed from the front.

Shrubs are used in many ways in the garden, but the traditional place for them is in the Shrub Border or Shrubbery. Here a variety of shrubs and trees are planted along one side of the garden to provide a green and solid-looking feature.

Green and solid-looking — these were the essential properties of the Victorian-style Shrubbery. Privet, Aucuba, Box and Yew provided a dull, 6 ft wide band of evergreens, and even today you will find many of these old-fashioned borders.

A Shrub Border, however, should be a much more interesting feature, and the secret is to plan it properly from the start. You will want to achieve a tiered effect — tall shrubs with perhaps some trees at the back, medium-sized shrubs in the middle and then short, dwarf and ground-covering shrubs at the front. This instruction must not be taken too literally — you certainly don't want to achieve a regular and consistent slope right across the border. Break up the line occasionally by planting a medium-sized columnar or conical plant close to the front.

Shrub Border

Start your plan with the back row — this is the most important area to get right. Most Shrub Borders have an additional job apart from looking decorative — they may have to act as windbreaks or provide privacy. The general rule is to choose plants with a maximum height which will fulfil this secondary job, but which are no higher than required to do it. For the average border this means choosing a back row which will be about 6–8 ft tall, with taller shrubs and trees here and there.

Once the background plants have been decided, choose the smaller ones for the front. Never plant in straight rows. Planting distances are determined by the size the plant will be when mature and not by the size of the specimens you have bought — look at the guide on page 103.

You have hundreds and hundreds of shrubs from which to make your choice. Your aim should be to achieve variety — when you look at the border at any time of the year there should be a pleasing mixture of shapes and colours. Read the Mixed Border section below for more general information on plant selection, and then study the A–Z guides.

Single Group Border

A special form of the Shrub Border is the **Single Group Bed** or **Border**. The favourite types are the Heather Border and the Rhododendron Border. Never attempt to plant a Single Group Border until you have proved that your soil is suitable by growing a few examples in the garden. A large area of a single variety is spectacular, but it can be boring — the usual pattern is to plant clumps of varieties which contrast in a pleasing way with their neighbours.

The Mixed Border

A Mixed Border is an area planted with shrubs and other plants, such as roses, perennials, bulbs, etc. This area is designed to be viewed from the front.

Most gardens cannot afford the luxury of having a border devoted entirely to shrubs and trees, and so the Mixed Border is much more popular than the Shrub Border. The same general rules apply but in the Mixed Border there are pockets or bays in which non-woody plants are grown.

The permanent framework is provided by shrubs and occasionally trees, and great care must be taken over their selection. First of all, seek an all-year-round effect — this calls for some leaves and colour during every month of the year. To ensure the presence of foliage you will need to grow evergreens as well as deciduous shrubs. To achieve colour we need flowers, but there are several other ways to brighten up a border. There are coloured-leaved varieties and there are types with coloured bark or berries. The basic colour of the border should be green, but ensure some colour during every season and do not rely on flowers alone.

Mixed Border

Secondly, ensure a variety of shapes — a border consisting entirely of rounded bushes is usually rather dull. Make use of weeping varieties and ground covers, and plant conifers of various forms.

Within this framework of shrubs and trees the other plants are grown. Make sure that the pocket or bay is large enough to give the bold effect required. Bulbs, of course, and herbaceous perennials such as Iris, Hemerocallis, Michaelmas Daisy, etc. Do not forget roses — both Shrub varieties for the back of the border and Hybrid Tea and Floribunda varieties to provide summer-long colour for the middle and front of the border. And then there are the annuals — potentially bold and bright but often suffering very badly in the dense shade cast by the surrounding shrubs.

Woodland Garden

A special form of the Mixed Border is the **Woodland Garden**. Here trees rather than shrubs are dominant and it is an area for walking through rather than admiring from outside. If you have an overgrown wooded area, try to turn it into a Woodland Garden rather than clearing it away. Remove dense shade trees, leaving those which cast a dappled shade. Plant Rhododendrons, Hypericum, Ferns, Camellias and other shade-tolerant types below them.

Hedges

A formal hedge is a continuous line of shrubs or trees in which the individuality of each plant is lost. An informal hedge is a line of shrubs or trees in which some or all of the natural outline of the plant is preserved. Unlike a plant-covered screen or fence, a hedge requires little or no support.

The purpose of a hedge in most gardens is to mark the boundary and to provide some degree of privacy and protection. But there are other roles it can play — it can divide one area of the garden from another, hide unsightly objects, provide wind protection, etc. The job the hedge has to do is a vital factor in the correct choice of planting material — so is the degree of formality and the desired height. The blessings of a tall and dense hedge are obvious, but do remember the drawbacks. Shade will be a problem for nearby plants and so will the drain on both the water and food resources in the soil.

Pruning & Trimming

Initial pruning For a dense, formal hedge it is essential to build up a plentiful supply of shoots at the base, and this calls for hard pruning after planting. Bare-root plants should be cut back to about ½ of their height — container-grown plants to about ⅔ of their original height. Do not prune the plants again during their first growing season in the garden.

Second year pruning Clip the hedge lightly on about four occasions between May and August. Do not leave it uncut because it has not yet reached the height required — the purpose of this second year pruning is to increase the density and to create the desired shape *before* the requisite height is reached.

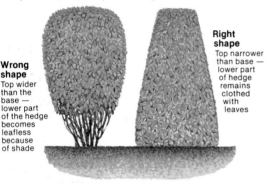

Wrong shape
Top wider than the base — lower part of the hedge becomes leafless because of shade

Right shape
Top narrower than base — lower part of hedge remains clothed with leaves

Trimming the mature hedge Once the hedge has reached the desired height, trimming should take place between May and August whenever the plants look untidy. This may involve a single clipping during the season or it may mean cutting every 6 weeks to produce a neatly manicured Box or Privet.

The correct tool is a pair of garden shears or an electric hedge trimmer. Lay down a sheet of polythene at the base of the hedge — this will make removal of the fallen clippings a much easier task. Cut back to a little above the last cut, leaving about ¼ in. of new growth. In this way the density of the hedge is improved and ugly bare spots are avoided.

Planting a Formal Hedge

Your first job is to decide the planting line, and this is not quite as straightforward as it seems. The edge of the pavement or along your neighbour's fence may seem the right place at planting time, but in a few years there is the serious problem of encroachment onto his property or the overhang across the street. Having decided on the planting line, dig a 3 ft wide strip. Follow the soil preparation rules on page 101.

Single row planting is recommended where economy is a vital factor and where quick screening is not essential

Double row planting is recommended for spindly shrubs such as Privet, and where maximum screening is required as quickly as possible

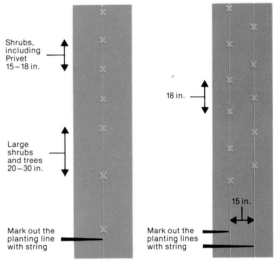

Shrubs, including Privet 15–18 in.

Large shrubs and trees 20–30 in.

Mark out the planting line with string

18 in.

15 in.

Mark out the planting lines with string

Plant out as described on page 102. After planting stretch a wire tightly along the young plants and attach them to it with ties. Remember to avoid this wire when pruning and trimming. Keep the plants well watered during the first season.

Choosing a Hedge

It is usual to plant just one variety, but this is not always desirable. The all-green types of Holly or Privet can be mixed with the variegated forms to produce a more colourful hedge, and green-leaved Beech can be intermixed with the purple-leaved variety.

If you want a densely-clothed, formal hedge which will provide privacy then choose a Traditional Hedge (see page 115). Some of these hedges do bear flowers or berries but they are generally grown for their leafiness and impenetrability. If strict formality is not required you can grow a Flowering Hedge, which is usually informal as regular clipping would reduce or remove the floral display. For dividing areas within the garden a Low-growing Hedge will be required, made up of shrubs which do not exceed 3 ft or are kept below that height by regular pruning.

The Traditional Hedge — formal and dense

CARPINUS (Hornbeam)
Similar to Beech, but much less popular. In most cases it retains its dead leaves over winter like its rival, and has the added advantage of being reliable in heavy and wet soils. The hedge should be trimmed in August. Hornbeam will quite quickly attain a height of about 8 ft or more.

CRATAEGUS (Hawthorn)
The most popular farm hedge, but not highly recommended for garden use. It is tough, quick-growing and forms an impenetrable barrier, but it looks rather untidy when grown on its own. The usual recommendation is to plant it as a mixed hedge with Beech, Privet, Holly or Hornbeam.

CUPRESSOCYPARIS (Cypress)
C. leylandii (Leyland Cypress) is the quickest-growing of all hedges — it can reach a height of 10 ft in 5 or 6 years. Young plants are spindly — keep them staked and regularly trimmed for the first few years. The mature hedge can be maintained by trimming twice a year.

FAGUS (Beech)
Deciduous, but the brown leaves persist over the winter. Both the green-leaved and purple-leaved varieties can be kept trimmed to produce a tall, formal hedge which will serve as an excellent windbreak. Beech tolerates chalky soil and exposed sites. Trim the hedge in August — tackle any hard pruning in February.

ILEX (Holly)
An excellent hedge for both sunny and shady sites. It forms a secure and dense barrier which is colourful when berries are present or a variegated type has been chosen. Alternate male and female varieties to ensure berry production and if practical trim with secateurs rather than shears.

LIGUSTRUM (Privet)
Much despised, but the Privet hedge is quick-growing, tolerant of poor conditions and hardy. Choose a variety of L. ovalifolium. The leaves are usually retained over winter. It is essential that new plants are cut back hard. Its drawback is that not many plants can thrive in its company.

PRUNUS (Laurel)
Two species are commonly used for hedging — P. laurocerasus (Cherry Laurel) and P. lusitanica (Portugal Laurel). Both of them make fine, tall hedges which are shiny-leaved and dense, but do not grow a Laurel hedge unless you have plenty of room. If possible prune with secateurs rather than shears.

TAXUS (Yew)
Do not be put off by the near-black specimens you see in churchyards — there are bright golden varieties of T. baccata available these days. Yew is an excellent dense hedge which can be kept quite narrow. Its drawback is you must wait many years for a satisfactory hedge.

The Flowering Hedge — informal and colourful

BERBERIS (Barberry)
B. stenophylla produces a splendid informal hedge. Its slender arching branches are clothed with narrow, evergreen leaves. In spring the yellow flowers appear, and once they fade the hedge should be trimmed. Berries appear if the plants are left untrimmed.

ESCALLONIA (Escallonia)
The evergreen E. macrantha is a popular hedge in coastal districts as it is tolerant of salt-laden air. The red flowers appear in June — trim immediately after the flowers fade to encourage a second flush to appear. It succumbs to heavy frost.

LONICERA (Honeysuckle)
L. nitida (Chinese Honeysuckle) is widely used for hedging. The leaves are shiny and Box-like, the flowers are small but they are followed by prominent, black berries. Stout support is usually necessary.

PYRACANTHA (Firethorn)
The popular P. coccinea can be used for hedging but the Firethorn which is usually recommended is P. rogersiana. The leaves are small and the berries are abundant. It grows well in chalky soils and on exposed sites. Prune lightly after flowering.

ROSA (Rose)
Some Shrub and a few vigorous Floribunda roses make excellent hedges, but the hedge will have to be an informal one as these plants cannot stand constant clipping back. Choose R. rugosa as a boundary hedge if maximum protection is required.

SPIRAEA (Spiraea)
The Spiraea generally used for hedging is S. vanhouttei. The arching branches bear lobed leaves which colour well in autumn. In May the white flowers open. S. thunbergii can also be used — both types should be trimmed once the flowers have faded.

The Low-Growing Hedge — neat and compact

BERBERIS (Barberry)
There is a colourful dwarf form (B. thunbergii atropurpurea 'Nana') which makes a compact, formal hedge about 1½ ft high. Pick a sunny spot to make sure that the reddish leaves will be at their brightest. It is deciduous, and should be trimmed after leaf fall.

BUXUS (Box)
For hundreds of years dwarf Box hedges have been used to divide beds and edge paths in British gardens. B. sempervirens will stand regular clipping to maintain it as a formal Low-growing Hedge.

LAVANDULA (Lavender)
An excellent aromatic hedge which is too well-known to need much description. Once the flowers fade the stalks must be cut, but the trimming of the plants to shape must be delayed until April. Several varieties are available — 'Hidcote' is the deepest blue.

PRUNUS (Crimson Dwarf)
P. cistena is a coppery-leaved dwarf variety which can be grown as a formal hedge about 3 ft high. The young foliage is blood red and the flowers open in spring. Trim once the blooms have faded. If space permits, it can be allowed to reach 4 or 5 ft.

ROSMARINUS (Rosemary)
Like Lavender, this aromatic shrub is used for hedging but it is certainly not as popular. It is not completely hardy and will not thrive in poorly-drained soil. The small flowers appear along the stems in spring — trim the hedge when these blooms have faded.

SANTOLINA (Lavender Cotton)
A hedge which is different — S. chamaecyparissus 'Nana' has silvery evergreen foliage and bears bright yellow flowers between June and August. It grows about 1 ft tall and should be trimmed in April. Remove the dead blooms after flowering.

Clothing Plants

A Clothing Plant is one which can be successfully grown against a wall or open framework and which is primarily designed to provide a decorative effect.

Many plants can be used for this purpose, some of which are natural climbers — see Chapter 4. If you want the minimum amount of trouble and the wall is in good condition, grow a self-clinging climber as no supporting wires or frame will be necessary. Choose Hedera, Hydrangea petiolaris or Parthenocissus.

Other climbers will need some form of support to which they can attach themselves. There is, in addition, a group of shrubs with lax stems which are frequently grown against walls and screens, the stems being attached to the wires or poles by means of ties. Examples are:

Ceanothus (evergreen varieties)	Jasminum nudiflorum
Cotoneaster salicifolius	Kerria japonica 'Pleniflora'
Forsythia suspensa	Rosa (Rambler & Climber varieties)

When growing climbers or shrubs against the wall of the house ensure that you plant them at least 18 in. from the wall. Keep the plant well watered for at least the first season. Support can be provided by either straining wires (see below) or a trellis made of wood or plastic-covered wire netting. Wherever wood is used it must be treated with a wood preservative (not creosote) and left for several weeks before use.

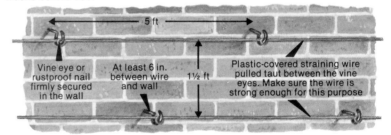

5 ft

Vine eye or rustproof nail firmly secured in the wall

At least 6 in. between wire and wall

1½ ft

Plastic-covered straining wire pulled taut between the vine eyes. Make sure the wire is strong enough for this purpose

Some wall plants, such as Hedera and Polygonum baldschuanicum, are extremely hardy and their need for full sun is limited — this means that they will grow quite happily on a north-facing wall. Others are less hardy or require full sun, and so they need a wall with a south or west aspect. Examples are:

Actinidia	Ceanothus	Solanum
Campsis	Passiflora	Wisteria

Some shrubs can be grown as wall plants even though they are neither true climbers nor plants with lax stems. They are bushy plants or ground-covering shrubs which adopt an upright wall-hugging habit when grown against the house. Examples are:

Chaenomeles	Garrya elliptica
Cotoneaster horizontalis	Pyracantha

Screening Plants

A Screening Plant is one which is grown primarily to protect the garden from an undesirable feature, such as an unpleasant view, noise or high winds.

There is no point in growing a plant with poor covering properties against an unsightly object just because it has pretty flowers — you may draw attention to the thing you are trying to hide.

There are two essential properties of a successful Screening Plant — it must be dense and preferably evergreen and it must be quick-growing. The main job these plants have to do is to hide unpleasant views, such as old sheds, compost heaps, neighbours' gardens, dead trees, etc. The usual way of blocking out an unpleasant view is to plant a line of quick-growing evergreens or semi-evergreens, such as Chamaecyparis lawsoniana, Cupressocyparis leylandii or Privet. Sometimes the problem is an unsightly object and not an unpleasant view, and the procedure then is to grow a Screening Plant against the object itself or on wires stretched across it. Hedera, Vitis and Parthenocissus are excellent Screening Plants for this purpose but the fastest growing one is the Russian Vine (Polygonum baldschuanicum).

On exposed sites a hedge of Screening Plants is grown to provide a windbreak. Sufficient height and width are essential properties, of course, but so is a reasonably open nature. A wall of dense foliage causes turbulence — a less solid growth habit absorbs the wind. The width of the protected zone behind the hedge is six times its height.

A wide band of Screening Plants can significantly reduce the noise level arising from passing traffic, nearby factories, etc. Effective plants are Carpinus, Fagus, Populus, Ilex, Rhododendron, Cupressocyparis leylandii and Thuja plicata. A narrow band of trees will do practically nothing to reduce the noise level.

CHAPTER 10

PLANT TROUBLES

Woody plants are most at risk between planting and the time when they are fully established. Deciduous trees and shrubs planted in the proper way and at the proper time should have no trouble in quickly settling down in your garden, but you will have to water them during dry spells which occur in the first season in their new home.

Evergreens may be more of a problem, and newly-planted conifers can suffer if they are exposed to cold drying winds and to bright morning sunshine after a frosty night – leaf browning is the result.

The established plant is usually capable of living a long and healthy existence provided it is hardy enough for the weather conditions and tolerant of the soil conditions. When things do go wrong it is more likely to be due to a fault in the environment rather than the effect of a specific pest or disease, but the ravages of dutch elm disease show that a tree, like any other living thing, is susceptible to attack by parasites.

You are never likely to see more than a few tree and shrub troubles in your garden, and the purpose of this chapter is to show you what the rest look like and to list the proper control measures.

How to reduce the risk of troubles in your garden

● **Choose wisely.** Make sure that the plants you have picked are not too tender for the climatic conditions in your area, and check that the soil and light requirements can be satisfied.

● **Buy good plants.** Abundant roots and sound stems are essential — see page 100. Don't buy conifers with large, brown patches — reject container-grown plants which easily lift out of the pot.

● **Prepare the ground thoroughly.** A tree or shrub growing in poorly-drained soil is likely to succumb to root-rotting diseases.

● **Plant in the proper place and in the proper way.** This will reduce the risk of problems due to drought, poor root development, waterlogging, wind rock, frost damage and light deficiency. Stake if necessary.

● **Avoid overcrowding.** Do not plant too closely as this can encourage mildew and other diseases.

● **Inspect plants regularly.** Catch problems early, when an occasional caterpillar can be picked off and the first spots of disease can be kept under control by spraying with a fungicide.

● **Provide frost protection if necessary.** Both snow and frost can cause a great deal of damage in a severe winter. Read the section on Winter Protection (page 107).

● **Spray if necessary.** Unlike roses and vegetables, trees and shrubs do not often require spraying. A few may require a preventative spray every year — against peach leaf curl on Flowering Cherries is an example. In general, however, spraying only takes place at the start of a serious problem, such as a sudden and heavy invasion by aphids or caterpillars.

Why trees & shrubs fail to survive

A tree or shrub planted in the manner described in this book should grow and flourish for many years. Failure to survive will almost certainly be due to one of the following causes:

Poor-quality planting material

Poor site preparation

Loose planting of bare-rooted plants

Break-up of the soil ball of container-grown or balled plants

Wind rock especially in exposed sites. Staking of tall specimens in such locations is essential

Waterlogged soil around the roots due to poor drainage

Winter damage and spring scorch — see pages 107 and 121

Dry roots at planting time or during the first season in the garden

One of the fatal pests or diseases — die-back, silver leaf, fireblight, clematis wilt, honey fungus, dutch elm disease, canker or butt rot can kill a susceptible plant

Weedkiller damage is a rare cause of death, but a few general herbicides, such as sodium chlorate, can be fatal if allowed to creep into the soil around the roots

Leaf, Stem & Blossom Troubles

The leaves and shoots of woody plants can be damaged by pests and diseases, but the effects are not usually serious. The small holes made by weevils, beetles and caterpillars do little damage to the plant and most diseases are disfiguring rather than destructive. Leaf-eating caterpillars, such as the magpie moth, are occasionally a nuisance and aphids can be a problem. There are also a few diseases which must be taken seriously — watch for fireblight, silver leaf, clematis wilt and peach leaf curl. Leaf discoloration is usually due to poor growing conditions rather than a specific pest or disease.

LEAF BEETLE

Various species of leaf beetle attack garden trees between May and the end of summer. They are about 1/5 in. long; green, blue or brown in colour and with the peculiar habit of skeletonizing leaves rather than eating holes out of them. Willow, poplar and elm are the usual hosts; damage is rarely severe. Spray with Long-last if necessary.

TORTRIX MOTH

Small brown or green caterpillars which spin leaves together with fine silken threads. Several leaves may be joined together. The caterpillars feed within this protective cover and irregular-shaped holes are formed. May or June is the most likely time of attack. Pick and destroy spun leaves; if necessary spray with Fenitrothion or Long-last.

LEAF-CUTTER BEE

Regular-shaped semicircular holes are cut out of the leaf edges of several varieties of trees and shrubs by these small bees. Roses are the most common host, but lilac, laburnum and privet may also be attacked. The plant is not harmed and so control measures are not necessary.

½ in. beetles

CHAFER BEETLE

The cockchafer (1¼ in. long) and the garden chafer (½ in. long) feed on the leaves of many shrubs and trees in May and June. If the pests are numerous spray the foliage with Long-last. The soil-living grubs of these beetles are serious pests, devouring the roots of vegetables, shrubs and flowers.

TENT CATERPILLAR

These caterpillars produce a characteristic tent of silken webs, within which the insects feed on the foliage. The tents should be picked off and burnt if practical. Alternatively spray with Fenitrothion or Hexyl as soon as tents start to appear.

LACKEY MOTH

BROWNTAIL MOTH

SMALL ERMINE MOTH

VINE WEEVIL

Small U-shaped or irregular notches are cut out of the leaf edges of several varieties of shrubs by these small weevils. Rhododendron is the most common host, but camellia, clematis and azalea may also be attacked. If attack is serious spray plants and the soil with Long-last.

CATERPILLAR

Leaf-eating caterpillars are more serious on trees and shrubs than in the flower garden. Serious defoliation can take place, so early spraying is a wise precaution when caterpillars and their damage are seen. Use a persistent insecticide such as Fenitrothion, Hexyl or Long-last.

BUFF TIP MOTH

Hairy caterpillar, about 2½ in. long, which can defoliate trees such as oak, elm, lime and hazel. Usually occur in large colonies.

EYED HAWK MOTH

Smooth, spectacular caterpillar, about 3 in. long, which attacks willows and poplars.

MAGPIE MOTH

Black and yellow 'looper' caterpillar, about 1½ in. long, which can defoliate some shrubs.

MOTTLED UMBER MOTH

Smooth 'looper' caterpillar, about 1¼ in. long, which attacks a wide variety of trees in spring.

WINTER MOTH

Green 'looper' caterpillar which devours young leaves and may spin them together.

VAPOURER MOTH

Colourful caterpillar, about 1 in. long. Feeds on the leaves from May to August.

NUTRIENT DEFICIENCY

An abnormal change in leaf colour often indicates a shortage of an essential element. Spray the plants with a foliar feed such as Fillip. If the symptoms of iron or magnesium deficiency are severe, water a sequestered compound on the soil around the base of the stems. In spring apply Growmore to the soil and rake in.

NITROGEN SHORTAGE
Red & yellow tints

POTASH SHORTAGE
Leaf edge scorch

MAGNESIUM SHORTAGE
Brown between veins

IRON SHORTAGE
Yellow between veins

POWDERY MILDEW

White, powdery patches appear on the leaves of many shrubs, particularly if they are overcrowded and the soil is dry. Powdery mildew is common on mahonia, clematis, hawthorn, willow and euonymus. Spray with Benlate at the first sign of disease. Repeat one week later. If not sprayed, cut off badly diseased shoots in autumn.

RUST

Yellow or brown raised spots appear on the leaves of many shrubs and trees. Rust is sometimes troublesome on berberis, willow, mahonia, conifers and birch. Pick off and burn the diseased leaves. Spraying is rarely necessary — Dithane 945 can be used at fortnightly intervals. Apply Fillip to restore vigour.

LEAF MINER

Long 'mines' or irregular-shaped blisters are produced by small grubs feeding within the leaves. Holly is particularly susceptible — mined or blistered leaves are also found on privet, honeysuckle, azalea, lilac and birch. Growth is, hardly affected by leaf miner attack so spraying with Hexyl or Long-last is rarely necessary.

ADELGID

Tiny aphid-like insects attack conifers and can seriously affect young trees. If present in large numbers spray with Malathion in April and again 3 weeks later. In summer dense tufts of white 'wool' are produced, coating the underside of the leaves. Conspicuous galls may be produced; pick off and burn them.

DIE-BACK

A serious problem — begins at the tips and progresses slowly downwards. There are several possible causes, including diseases such as canker. If no disease is present, waterlogging is a likely cause. Cut out dead wood, paint with Arbrex. Feed with Fillip. Improve drainage.

WOOLLY APHID

Aphid colonies live on branches, secreting white waxy 'wool' which protects them. Their presence does little direct harm, but the corky galls they cause are a common entry point for canker spores. Brush off 'wool' with an old toothbrush and methylated spirits. Alternatively, spray with Long-last.

LOSS OF VARIEGATION

Many shrubs bear yellow and green patterned leaves ('variegata') or green, yellow and red leaves ('tricolor'). In dense shade the green areas spread and the variegation is diminished. Even in good light there is often a tendency for the shrub to revert to the all-green parent form. Cut out such shoots immediately.

WITCHES BROOM

A dense clump of branching twigs can sometimes be seen on the trunks and main branches of birch, cherry and conifers. The cause is usually a fungus, but it may be a virus or a change in the structure of a growth bud. These 'bird nest' clumps do no harm, but they can be cut off and the wounds painted with Arbrex.

GALLS

These swellings may occur on all types of plants but are met most frequently on shrubs and trees. They are caused by the plant's reaction to the irritation caused by pests or fungi. In some cases they are large and colourful, and may even be decorative. **Purse gall** and **pouch gall** are caused by aphids, **pineapple gall** on conifers is caused by adelgids, **oak apple** and many other tree galls are due to gall wasps, **lime leaf galls** are due to mites and **azalea gall** is caused by a fungus. In nearly all cases there is little or no harm to the plant. Cut off and burn if unsightly.

Oak apple

Lime leaf gall

Azalea gall

Leaf, Stem & Blossom Troubles
continued

LEAF WEEVIL

1/5 in. beetles

Metallic green or brown weevils may appear on birch or other trees in large numbers in June and July. Their feeding causes irregular holes in the foliage, but control measures are rarely necessary as they move away after a few days. If spraying is necessary use Fenitrothion or Long-last.

SILVER LEAF

A serious disease of ornamental cherries which can attack other shrubs such as laburnum, willow and hawthorn. The spores enter through a wound, and the first sign is silvering of the leaves. Die-back of shoots occurs; wood is stained. Cut out dead branches 6 in. below level of infection. Paint with Arbrex. Dig out tree if bracket-like toadstools have appeared on the trunk.

FALSE SILVER LEAF

A common disorder which looks like silver leaf at first glance. Leaves are silvery, but the effect appears all over the tree rather than progressively along a branch. A cut branch reveals that the staining of silver leaf disease is absent. The cause of false silver leaf is starvation or irregular watering. Feed regularly with Fillip and put down an organic mulch in spring.

PEACH LEAF CURL

Large reddish blisters develop on the leaves. Apart from making the tree unsightly this serious disease of ornamental cherries leads to early leaf fall and weakening of the tree. The fungus overwinters in the bark and between bud scales, not on fallen leaves. Spray with Dithane 945 in mid-February, 14 days later and again just before leaf fall.

Why Trees & Shrubs fail to flower

A flowering shrub or tree which fails to bloom is always a disappointment. There are many possible causes — the following checklist should tell you what went wrong in your case.

- TOO MUCH SHADE Many flowering shrubs are sun-lovers and will produce leaves but no flowers if the light intensity is too low. Check the A–Z guide — if full sun is required you will have to cut back surrounding foliage or move the plant.
- IMPATIENCE It is quite normal for some trees and shrubs to take several years after planting before coming into flower. Wisteria, Magnolia and Yucca are just a few examples.
- SHORTAGE OF POTASH Using a high nitrogen/low potash fertilizer will stimulate lush foliage but may inhibit flowering. Use a high potash feed such as Toprose Fertilizer at 4 oz per sq. yard.
- DRYNESS AT THE ROOTS Drought will delay the onset of flowering and can also cause bud and blossom drop. Drought is a common cause of poor berry production. A long period of soil dryness in summer can result in poor flowering in the following year.
- POOR PRUNING Drastic pruning at the wrong time of the year is an all-too-common cause of the production of non-flowering shoots.
- FROST DAMAGE TO FLOWER BUDS The buds and blossoms of a large range of shrubs can be killed by late spring frosts.

SHOT HOLE DISEASE

Laurel and flowering cherry are occasionally attacked by this disorder. Brown spots appear on the foliage; as the leaves expand these brown areas fall out leaving holes scattered over the leaf surface. As only weak trees are attacked, build up their vigour by spraying with Fillip during the summer.

BIRDS

The stripping of flower buds from ornamental trees and shrubs in winter and early spring is a particularly difficult problem, as protective netting is not practical. Forsythia and ornamental cherries are the main victims, and bullfinches the chief offenders. Note that tits devour insects, not buds. Try a bird deterrent spray.

FIREBLIGHT

A devastating disease of shrubs belonging to the rose family. Affected shoots wilt and die. Tell-tale sign is the presence of brown, withered leaves which do not fall. The disease spreads to the stem and the plant is killed. Old cankers ooze in spring. You are obliged by law to notify an outbreak to the Ministry of Agriculture.

BUD BLAST

Infected flower buds of rhododendrons turn brown and are covered with black fungal bristles. They do not rot and remain firmly attached to the bush. Remove and burn diseased buds. Do not confuse with frost-damaged buds, which are soft and easily pulled away. To prevent attacks spray with Long-last in August to kill the disease-carrying leafhopper.

CLAY-COLOURED WEEVIL

Brown weevils, 1/4 in. long, gnaw the bark of woody stems. Shoots of camellia and rhododendron are sometimes killed by this night-feeding pest, and young conifers can be seriously damaged. Control is not easy; hoe the surrounding soil and spray both the tree and ground with Long-last or Fenitrothion. Alternatively, encircle the main stem with a Boltac greaseband.

CHLOROSIS

Many shrubs, such as rhododendron, azalea, camellia, ceanothus and hydrangea develop pale green or yellow leaves if grown in chalky soil. This is lime-induced chlorosis, and is prevented by incorporating peat into the soil and by applying a sequestered compound. Chlorosis of the lower leaves is often due to poor drainage.

LEAF SPOT

Many shrubs are attacked by this type of disease. The usual cause is fungal infection, and the disease may have a specific name — sycamore tar spot, willow anthracnose etc. Spray with Copper or Dithane 945, but control may be difficult. With some shrubs, such as rhododendron and rose, the cause may be poor drainage.

CAPSID BUG

¼ in.
active bugs

The first signs of capsid damage are reddish-brown spots. As the leaf expands these tear to produce ragged brown-edged holes. Damaged foliage is usually puckered and distorted. Spray with Fenitrothion or Long-last.

WINTER DAMAGE

Many trees and shrubs are at risk in a severe winter, especially if they are slightly tender or newly planted. They can be damaged in several ways — waterlogging in an abnormally wet season can lead to root rot; temperatures well below freezing point can cause frost damage (brown blotches on leaves, usually at the tips) and heavy snow can break the branches of evergreens.

DROUGHT

In prolonged dry weather the soil reserves of moisture are seriously reduced. The first sign is wilting of the foliage and in the early stages the effect is reversible if watering takes place. The next stage is browning of the foliage and leaf drop which is extremely serious or fatal, especially with evergreens. Water before symptoms appear, and improve the water-holding capacity of the soil *before* planting.

SPRING SCORCH

Spring scorch is one of the most common yet least understood of all early spring problems. Bright sunny weather after a cold spell surprisingly leads to browning or death of evergreens instead of active growth. The cause is cold-induced drought — sunshine and drying winds stimulate water loss from the leaves, but the roots are not active and cannot replace the loss. So the leaves wilt and dry out. Spray newly-planted evergreens with water in spring; provide protection from frosts and east winds.

CLEMATIS WILT

A destructive disease of clematis, especially young plants of large-flowered varieties. Shoots wilt and then suddenly collapse and die. Cut out affected shoots; new shoots often develop from the base. Spray new growth with Benlate. When planting make sure that 1 – 2 in. of stem is below the surface.

RHODODENDRON BUG

Shiny brown insects with lacy wings feed on the undersurface of rhododendron leaves. Foliage becomes mottled above, rusty brown below. Leaf edges curl downwards. At the first sign of trouble in May or June spray thoroughly with Hexyl or Malathion. Repeat the treatment about a month later.

APHID

Greenfly can attack many shrubs and trees; blackfly tend to be more selective but ornamental cherry, viburnum, honeysuckle and euonymus can all be badly infested. Aphids can be a serious pest — leaves may be discoloured and blistered, shoots distorted and the whole plant covered with sticky honeydew. Spray with Long-last before aphid colonies are large enough to be damaging.

RED SPIDER MITE

If leaves develop an unhealthy bronze colour, look for tiny spider-like mites on the underside. The presence of fine silky webbing is a tell-tale sign. On broad-leaved trees and shrubs the culprits are the **fruit tree red spider mite** and the **bryobia mite**. On conifers the pest is the **conifer spinning mite**. These sap-sucking pests can be crippling in hot, settled weather and spraying is necessary. Apply Malathion or Derris — repeat 3 weeks later.

Bark Troubles

The bark of shrubs and trees can be attacked by a number of pests and diseases. Unlike the leaf troubles described on the previous pages, most of these parasites can seriously damage the plant. Dutch elm disease, honey fungus, butt rot and goat moth are all potential killers.

HONEY FUNGUS

Honey fungus (root rot, armillaria disease) is a common cause of the death of shrubs and trees. A white fan of fungal growth occurs below the bark near ground level. On roots, black 'bootlaces' are found. Toadstools appear in autumn at the base. Burn stems and roots of diseased trees; treat soil with Armillatox.

GOAT MOTH

A wood-boring caterpillar which may live in the tree for years. It is more damaging than the leopard moth which attacks in a similar way. Many caterpillars may be present, forming a network of tunnels in the trunk or branch. The tree is often killed. If detected, cut out and burn the affected branch.

SPLIT BARK

A crack may appear in the bark at any time of the year. The cause can be a severe frost, and it is not uncommon for the base of rhododendron bushes to split in this way. Another cause is poor growing conditions. Cut away any dead wood and paint with Arbrex. Feed and mulch to restore good health.

CORAL SPOT

Raised pink spots appear on the surface of affected branches. Dead wood is the breeding ground for the fungus, and the air-borne spores infect living trees through cuts and wounds. Never leave dead wood lying about. Cut out all dead and diseased branches and always paint pruning cuts with Arbrex to protect the cut surfaces.

CANKER

A general term for a diseased infectious area on the bark. The canker is usually cracked and sunken, and will kill the branch if it is encircled. Many different fungi and bacteria are involved; some attack a range of trees, others are specific (poplar canker, larch canker, etc.). Cut out large cankers back to clean wood; paint with Arbrex.

BARK BEETLE

Several types attack ornamental trees, including the dreaded elm bark beetle which carries the dutch elm disease fungus. Holes are bored into the heart of the tree, or the layer under the bark is mined with tunnels. Most bark beetles attack trees which are in an unhealthy state, so maintain good growing conditions. Remove damaged branches.

DUTCH ELM DISEASE

The first sign of trouble is yellowing of the foliage during the summer months. The leaves turn brown but remain hanging on the tree. The shoots of the dead branches are hooked at the tip. Cut off diseased branches and paint with Arbrex. If the tree is badly infected or dead, dig out and burn the tree. Never leave diseased wood lying about.

BACTERIAL CANKER

Cankers are flat and may not be easily noticed, but the effect on cherry trees is serious. Attacked branches produce few leaves and soon die. Gum oozes from the cankers and leaves develop pale-edged spots. Cut out diseased branches; paint cuts with Arbrex. Spray trees with Copper in August, September and October.

BUTT ROT

Butt rot (*Fomes annosus*) is a fatal disease of conifers. Other trees are rarely attacked. The first signs of infection are yellow and wilted leaves. The tree quickly deteriorates and finally dies. At the base of the trunk bracket-like toadstools may appear. Dig out and burn the tree; do not leave a stump. Do not replant a conifer on the same site.

SCALE

Several types of scale are found on branches, but their lifestyle is generally the same. The adults spend their lives in one place on the stem, protected by a hard shell. Their feeding on the sap causes leaf yellowing and a loss of vigour. Some attack a wide range of woody plants — **brown scale**, **mussel scale** and **oystershell scale** are examples. Others attack only those trees which bear their name — **beech scale**, which produces woolly patches, and **yew scale** are examples. **Willow scale** gives a white-washed effect. If only a few are present, rub off with a cloth and soapy water. For heavier infestations spray with Long-last in May.

Beech scale

Yew scale

Willow scale

CHAPTER 11

TREE & SHRUB GROWER'S DICTIONARY

A

ACID SOIL A soil which contains no free lime and has a pH of less than 6.5.

ADULT FOLIAGE Leaves on a mature branch which differ in shape and size from the *juvenile foliage.*

ALKALINE SOIL A soil which has a pH of more than 7.3. Other terms are chalky soil and limy soil.

ALTERNATE Leaves or buds which arise first on one side of the stem and then on the other. Compare *opposite.*

ANTHER The part of the flower which produces pollen. It is the upper section of the *stamen.*

ARMED Bearing strong thorns.

AURICLE An ear-shaped projection.

AWL-SHAPED A narrow leaf which tapers to a stiff point.

AXIL The angle between the upper surface of the leaf stalk and the stem that carries it.

B

BARE-ROOTED A plant dug up at the nursery and sold with no soil around its roots.

BASAL SHOOT A shoot arising from the neck or crown of the plant.

BEARDED Possessing long or stiff hairs.

BERRY A pulpy fruit bearing several or many seeds.

BISEXUAL A flower bearing both male and female reproductive organs — compare *dioecious* and *monoecious.*

BLEEDING The loss of sap from plant tissues.

BLOOM A fine powdery or waxy coating.

BOLE An alternative name for the trunk of a tree.

BOSS The ring of stamens when it is prominent and decorative.

BRACT A modified leaf at the base of a flower.

BREAKING BUD A bud which has started to open.

BUD A flower bud is the unopened bloom. A growth bud or *eye* is a condensed shoot.

C

CALCAREOUS Chalky or limy soil.

CALCIFUGE A plant which will not thrive in alkaline soil.

CALLUS The scar tissue which forms over a pruning cut or at the base of a cutting.

CALYX The whorl of *sepals* which protect the unopened flower bud.

CAMBIUM A thin layer of living cells between the bark and the wood.

CANKER A diseased and discoloured area on the stem.

CATKIN A chain of tiny male or female flowers which lack coloured petals.

CHLOROSIS An abnormal yellowing or blanching of the leaves due to lack of chlorophyll.

COMPOST Two meanings — either decomposed vegetable or animal matter for incorporation in the soil or a potting/cutting mixture made from peat ('soilless compost') or sterilized soil ('loam compost') plus other materials such as sand, lime and fertilizer.

COMPOUND A type of leaf which is composed of several leaflets.

COROLLA The whorl of petals within the *calyx* of the flower.

CROCK A piece of broken flower pot used at the bottom of a container to improve drainage.

CROSS The offspring arising from cross-pollination.

CULTIVAR Short for 'cultivated variety' — it is a variety which originated in cultivation and not in the wild. Strictly speaking, all modern varieties are cultivars, but the more familiar term *'variety'* is used in this book.

CUTTING A piece of stem cut from a plant and used for propagation.

D

DEAD-HEADING The removal of faded flowers.

DECIDUOUS A plant which loses its leaves at the end of the growing season.

DIOECIOUS A plant which bears either male or female flowers. Compare *monoecious.*

DORMANT PERIOD The time when the plant has naturally stopped growing due to low temperature and short day-length.

DOUBLE A flower with more than a single whorl of petals.

DOWNY Covered with soft hairs.

E

ENTIRE An undivided and unserrated leaf.

EVERGREEN A plant which retains its leaves in a living state during the winter.

EYE Two unrelated meanings — a dormant growth bud or the centre of a single or semi-double bloom where the colour is distinctly different from the rest of the flower.

F

FASTIGIATE A plant with erect branches set closely together.

FERTILIZATION The application of pollen to the *stigma* to induce the production of seed. An essential step in hybridisation.

FIBROUS A root system which contains many thin roots rather than a single tap root.

FILAMENT The supporting column of the *anther*. It is the lower part of the *stamen*.

FLORET The small individual bloom borne by a large, flower-like *inflorescence*.

FOLIAR FEED A fertilizer capable of being sprayed on and absorbed by the leaves.

FOOTSTALK The pedicel or flower stalk.

FROST POCKET An area where cold air is trapped during winter and in which tender plants are in much greater danger.

FRUIT The seed together with the structure which bears or contains it.

FUNGICIDE A chemical used to control diseases caused by fungi.

FUNGUS A primitive form of plant life which is the most common cause of infectious disease — mildew and rust are examples.

G

GENUS A group of closely-related plants containing one or more species.

GLABROUS Smooth, hairless.

GLAUCOUS Covered with a *bloom*.

GRAFTING The process of joining a stem or bud of one plant on to the stem of another.

H

HARD PRUNING A system of pruning where much of the old growth is removed.

HARDENING-OFF The process of gradually acclimatising a plant raised under warm conditions to the environment it will have to withstand outdoors.

HARDY A plant which will withstand overwintering without any protection.

HEAD The framework of stems borne at the top of the stem of a standard.

HEELING-IN The temporary planting of a new tree or shrub pending suitable weather conditions for permanent planting.

HIRSUTE Covered with coarse or stiff hairs.

HONEYDEW Sticky, sugary secretion deposited on the leaves and stems by such insects as aphid and whitefly.

HYBRID Plants with parents which are genetically distinct. The parent plants may be different *cultivars*, *varieties* or *species*.

I

INFLORESCENCE The part of the plant bearing the flowers; the flower-head.

INORGANIC A chemical or fertilizer which is not obtained from a source which is or has been alive.

INSECTICIDE A chemical used to control insect pests.

INTERNODE The part of the stem between one *node* and another.

INVOLUCRE A whorl of *bracts* surrounding a flower or cluster of flowers.

J

JUVENILE FOLIAGE Young leaves which differ in shape and size from the *adult foliage*.

K

KEY A winged seed, technically referred to as a samara.

L

LANCEOLATE Spear-shaped.

LANKY Spindly growth — a stem with a gaunt and sparse appearance.

LATERAL BRANCH A side branch which arises from a main stem.

LEACHING The drawing away of chemicals from the soil, caused by rain or watering.

LEADER The dominant central shoot.

LEAFLET One of the parts of a compound leaf.

LOBE Rounded segment which protrudes from the leaf margin.

M

MONOECIOUS A plant which bears both male and female flowers. Compare *dioecious*.

MULCH A layer of bulky organic material placed around the stems — see page 107.

MUTATION A sudden change in the genetic make-up of a plant, leading to a new feature. This new feature can be inherited.

N

NATIVE A *species* which grows wild in this country and was not introduced by man.

NECTAR Sweet substance secreted by some flowers to attract insects.

NEUTRAL Neither acid nor alkaline — pH 6.5-7.3.

NEW WOOD Stem growth which has been produced during the current season.

NODE The point on the stem at which a leaf or bud is attached.

NUT A one-seeded hard fruit which does not split when ripe.

O

OLD WOOD Stem growth which was produced before the current season.

OPPOSITE Leaves or buds which are borne in pairs along the stem. Compare *alternate*.

ORGANIC A chemical or fertilizer which is obtained from a source which is or has been alive.

OVULE The part of the female organ of the flower which turns into a seed after fertilization.

P

PANICLE A flower cluster bearing its many blooms on small branched stalks.

PEDICEL The flower stalk.

PERGOLA An arched structure used to support climbing plants.

PETAL One of the divisions of the corolla — generally the showy part of the flower.

PETIOLE The leaf stalk.

pH A measure of acidity and alkalinity. Below pH 6.5 is acid, above pH 7.3 is alkaline.

PINNATE A leaf with a series of leaflets borne on either side of a central stalk.

PISTIL The female organ of a flower, consisting of the *stigma, style* and *ovule.*

PITH The spongy material at the centre of the stem.

POLLARD A tree which has had its branches repeatedly cut back to the trunk.

POLLEN The yellow dust produced by the *anthers.* It is the male element which fertilizes the *ovule.*

POLLINATION The application of *pollen* to the *stigma* of the flower.

PROPAGATION The multiplication of plants.

PROSTRATE Growing flat on the soil surface.

PRUNING The removal of parts of the plant in order to improve its performance.

R

REVERSION Two meanings — either a *sport* which goes back to the colour or growth habit of its parent or a cultivated variety which is outgrown by suckers arising from the rootstock.

ROOTSTOCK The host plant on to which a cultivated variety is budded.

RUGOSE Rough and wrinkled.

RUNNER A shoot which grows along the soil surface, rooting at intervals.

S

SCABROUS Rough to the touch.

SCION The technical term for the bud which is grafted on to the rootstock.

SEMI-EVERGREEN A plant which keeps its leaves in a mild winter but loses some or all of its foliage in a hard one.

SEPAL One of the divisions of the *calyx.*

SERRATE Saw-toothed.

SESSILE Stalkless.

SIDE SHOOT Same as *lateral branch.*

SIMPLE A leaf that is not *compound.*

SINGLE A flower with a single ring of *petals.*

SNAG A section of stem left above a bud when pruning.

SPECIES Plants which are genetically similar and which reproduce exactly when self-fertilized.

SPIKE An *inflorescence* bearing stalkless flowers along a central stalk.

SPIT The depth of the spade blade — usually about 9 inches.

SPORT A plant which shows a marked and inheritable change from its parent; a *mutation.*

SPUR Two meanings — a tube-like projection from a flower or a short leaf-bearing shoot which does not increase in size.

STAMEN The male organ of a flower, consisting of the *anther* and *filament.*

STANDARD A tree or trained shrub with a single straight stem which is clear of branches for 5-6 ft from the ground. This stem length is 4-5 ft on a *half standard* and 3-4 ft on a *short standard.*

STELLATE Star-shaped.

STIGMA The part of the female organ of the flower which catches the *pollen.*

STIPULE The small outgrowth at the base of the leaf stalk.

STOLON A shoot at or below the soil surface which produces a new plant at its tip.

STRIKE The successful outcome of taking cuttings — cuttings 'strike' whereas grafts *'take'.*

STYLE The part of the female organ of the flower which connects the *stigma* to the *ovule.*

SUCKER A shoot growing from the rootstock.

SYNONYM An alternative plant name.

SYSTEMIC A pesticide which goes inside the plant and travels in the sap stream.

T

TAKE The successful outcome of budding — grafts 'take' whereas cuttings *'strike'.*

TENDRIL A modified stem or leaf which can wind around a support.

THICKET Dense growth of upright stems.

TOPIARY The cutting and training of shrubs or trees into decorative shapes.

TRANSPLANTING Movement of a plant from one site to another.

TRUSS A cluster of fruit or flowers.

U

UNDERPLANTING Growing low-growing plants below taller shrubs or trees.

V

VARIEGATED Leaves which are spotted, blotched or edged with a different colour to the basic one.

VARIETY Strictly speaking, a naturally occurring variation of a species (see *cultivar*).

W

WHORL Several leaves, branches or petals which are arranged in a ring.

Societies

ARBORICULTURAL ASSOCIATION
Ampfield House, Ampfield
Hampshire SO5 9PA

BRITISH BONSAI ASSOCIATION
23 Nimrod St, Streatham
London SW16 6SZ

HEATHER SOCIETY
7 Rossley Close, Highcliffe
Dorset BH23 4RR

MEN OF THE TREES
Turners Hill Rd, Crawley Down
Sussex RH10 4HL

NATIONAL TRUST FOR SCOTLAND
Greenbank House, Clarkston
Glasgow G76 8PB

THE NATIONAL TRUST
42 Queen Anne's Gate
London SW1H 9AS

ROYAL FORESTRY SOCIETY
102 High St, Tring
Hertfordshire HP23 4AH

TREE COUNCIL
35 Belgrave Sq
London SW1X 8QN

CHAPTER 12

PLANT INDEX